BRITAIN IN OLD PHOTOGRAPHS

AROUND HARROGATE

CATHERINE ROTHWELL

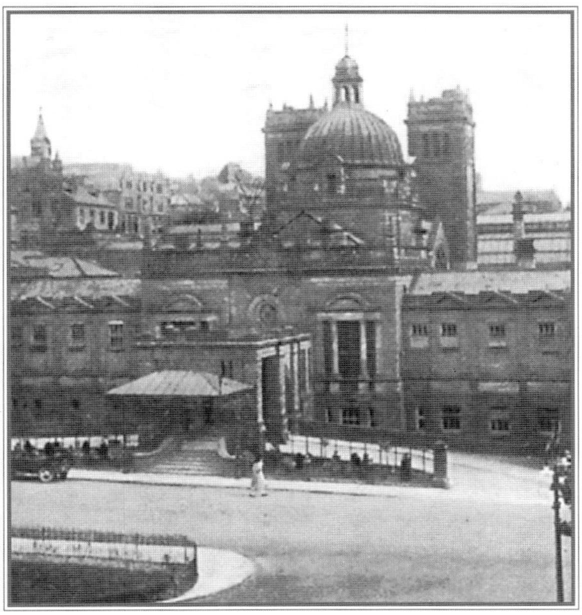

SUTTON PUBLISHING LIMITED

Sutton Publishing Limited
Phoenix Mill · Thrupp · Stroud
Gloucestershire · GL5 2BU

First published 1997

Cover photographs: *front*: the driving team of Wrays of Harrogate, *c.* 1942; *back*: the Café Imperial, Harrogate.

British Library Cataloguing in Publication Data
A catalogue record for this book is available from the British Library.

ISBN 0-7509-1549-8

Typeset in 10/12 Perpetua.
Typesetting and origination by
Sutton Publishing Limited.
Printed in Great Britain by
Ebenezer Baylis, Worcester.

Dedicated to the Church of St Mary the Virgin, Hanbury, Worcestershire. All royalties from this book will go towards the Restoration Fund of this parish church which has associations with the BBC Radio programme The Archers.

CONTENTS

HARROGATE

is one of the finest Spas and Health and Pleasure Resorts in Europe.

As a SPA it claims supremacy over all the Spas of the World by virtue of having no less than EIGHTY-EIGHT DIFFERENT MINERAL WATERS, and a most elaborate and completely-equipped Bathing Establishment, with a Staff of Medically Trained and Medically Certificated male and female nurses. It is really a compendium of the World's Spas.

As a HEALTH RESORT it is famed for its remarkably pure and bracing air, its fine shops and residences, its open spaces, parks, high-class amusements and entertainments, and last, but not least, its proximity to some of Great Britain's most Famous and Historic Abbeys, Castles and Country Mansions.

As a MOTORING DISTRICT it is unequalled; the wide roads, the open moors, and the exquisite beauty spots in the district provide a fresh run for almost every day for weeks.

As a TOWN nothing is wanting in Harrogate to minister to the needs of those who love the gaieties of life; or, on the contrary, if a quiet, restful time be needed, then the open moors creeping up to the outskirts of the town, will provide the mental rest and physical well-being needed by the seeker after health and peace.

Free Cure and Holiday Brochures with List of Accommodation, &c., from
JOHN E. WILSHERE, *Director of Publicity,*
"W.L." Dept. - - - Harrogate.

John E. Wilshere, Director of Publicity, issued this countrywide advertisement for Harrogate in 1930.

INTRODUCTION

Situated in part of the former Forest of Knaresborough, Harrogate is referred to as 'the heart of Yorkshire'. Its glory continues to lie in its open spaces – 'the country brought to town'. Bowden's 'Hotel, Hydropathic Establishments and Boarding House Directory' of 1895 devotes a whole page to Harrogate: 'The Queen of Inland Watering Places. . . . It is situated upon lofty table land, 20 miles from York . . . and 70 miles from the German Ocean and Irish Channel. Placed in the centre of the island at an altitude of four to six hundred feet above sea level, it possesses an atmosphere remarkable, alike for purity, dryness and all the invigorating salubrity of true highland air. Harrogate is a place of many waters, possessing Springs which in number and variety are unique. In no other health resort in Europe (if not the world) are found medicinal springs approaching in number and variety those of this favoured place: 80 Springs of Mineral Waters; peerless climatic advantages; annual death rate 13.8 per thousand; handsome Pump Rooms; Bathing Establishments; Turkish and Montpelier Baths; Spa Concert Rooms and Pleasure Gardens etc.'

Representing, as it does, Harrogate at its zenith under Town Clerk Mr W. Henry Wyles, this glowing testimonial deserves to be quoted in full, for today's visitor to the elegant, spacious town, while appreciating the amenities, may have little knowledge of such a past.

'Harrogate is also the centre of a district remarkably rich in antiquities, natural and rural beauties including the ancient city of York, castles of Knaresboro, Ripley etc., the abbeys of Bolton, Fountains, Jervaulx, the valleys of the Wharfe and Nidd, Brimham Rocks, Ilkley . . .', the report continues.

I have been in and out of Yorkshire now for sixty years, exploring the Dales, caravanning, motoring, walking, coming by train, always interested in the history and enthralled by the drama of scenery set in such heroic mould. Hills march away in all directions amid infinite light and space. Limestone caves, tumbling waterfalls, ancient pack horse routes; in sheer size and scope it takes the breath away. Recently, in search of old Yorkshire recipes, I culled a further wealth of historical interest: the Otley Statutes or hirings held just before Martinmas in the market place; labourers and farmers sealing the terms of a year's work, with a God's Penny. While first-class men could get £25–30 per annum in the 1870s with food and board found, young girls received only £8–10. When a crowd of 30,000 gathered at Leeds to hear statesman and Prime Minister W.E. Gladstone, 'the finest orator', one Yorkshireman afterwards walked 14 miles home in the darkness to his village not far from Harrogate, a village which drew the Guisley Brass Band of Musick to its annual Feast. After Club Walks there was much mischief, such as upsetting Jack Sheppard's spice stall or 'ducking the chimney sweep in the trough'.

The oldest of the Harrogate springs was the Tewit Well, so called because of the many lapwings or 'tewits' in the area of the Stray. It was discovered by William Slingsby in 1571, a man who had travelled widely and was familiar with the health-giving properties of springs he had tasted on the Continent. St John's Well, on the Stray Road leading to Wetherby Lane (it was close to St John's Chapel, the precursor of Christ Church) next found favour. When early Harrogate society began to gather, 'the former spring, marked by a depression at the trees near the Queen Hotel, was patronised by visitors to the Granby Arms and the Green Dragon. The Granby Arms was known as the House of Lords and the

Green Dragon as the House of Commons. Visitors used to interchange civilities on an admission charge of one shilling and four shillings for gentlemen who danced.'

As time went on this spring disappeared, but it is interesting to note that in the 1930s sulphur water was so near to the surface that a sinking of the ground could have produced it again. In fact, on Harlow Moor after heavy rain sulphur overruns the surface. High and Low Harrogate were unknown until the mid-sixteenth century when William, uncle of Sir William Slingsby of Bilton Hall, made his discovery, likening the water to 'the two most famous acidic fountains at the famous Spaw in Germany'. There is evidence, however, that there was awareness of the curative powers at the time of King John.

Within six years of Queen Victoria's Golden Jubilee the Swan Hotel was offering Turkish baths as marvellous rejuvenation and body cleansers. The Cairn Hydro and the Harlow Manor Hydro soon followed suit. Stables for many horses were in Market Square and the hotels made provision for horses and carriages. Bath chair ranks became a familiar sight, hiring charges in 1890 being 1*s* 3*d* per hour.

Fashionable Harrogate, dressed to the nines and promenading by day in Crescent Gardens, by evening would doubtless transport itself to the rich interior of the Kursaal with its horseshoe-shaped balcony. The *Young Ladies' Journal of Fashion* illustrated the elaborate dress worn for theatre attendances: silks, velvets, satins and chinchilla-trimmed capes. D. Nicholson and Company, Silk Mercers patronised by Queen Victoria, were prepared to send 1,000 patterns of newest silks and dress materials post free.

The Victoria Park Company aimed at joining the ancient hamlets of Low and High Harrogate to form a modern town. The making of Victoria Avenue, the completion of the Belvidere in 1861, now Harrogate College of Art, the Congregational Church, the fine Regency terrace on West Park, all noble buildings enhanced by grass verges, wide roads and pavements – these were to prove an inspiration to future generations.

By the 1930s balconies, verandas, conservatories and large grounds offered every advantage for views and fresh air. Demand was such that for years even such large premises as the Cairn could be filled during the season. The owner of the Crown Hotel, John Thackwray, had built tiled and marble premises with a pump room conveying water from six springs, which later became known as Montpellier Baths and Gardens. By 1939, however, the Spa Rooms were demolished and in March 1969 the Royal Baths, except the Turkish Baths, were closed, as the previous year the Hospital Board decided not to renew its contract for patients' treatments. So disappeared 'Mr W. Hardy's Electric Baths', one of many kinds of therapy. During filming in Harrogate of the life of Agatha Christie, the famous detective story writer, the mild electric shock bath became part of the exciting theme.

Yesterday's Harrogate had its glittering balls and theatre; today's has its conferences, flower show, Festival of Music and Harrogate Festival. Truly, Harrogate, or as the Danes described it, 'the heroes' road' (Haro gata), remains a town for all seasons.

1974 saw the formation of Greater Harrogate, which embraced Knaresborough, Boroughbridge and Ripon within its boundaries. (This is the area that is covered in this book.) The decision to build a huge new Conference Centre linked with seven Exhibition Centres has caused history to repeat itself, for this has placed Harrogate once more firmly in the national and international arena. Opened in 1982, the huge auditorium of this imaginatively designed concourse seats 2,000 people. Germany recently selected Harrogate as an excellent tourist centre, praising the well organised back-up facilities which have made possible a new role. The town can be proud of its smooth transformation.

Through the magic of about 200 photographs I hope to portray former glory, to revisit scenes that were lodestones for the tourists of last century and whose interest remains. The impression persists: a town of liveliness and imaginative uplift. Tradition continues in service of another kind conferred efficiently.

SECTION ONE

HARROGATE

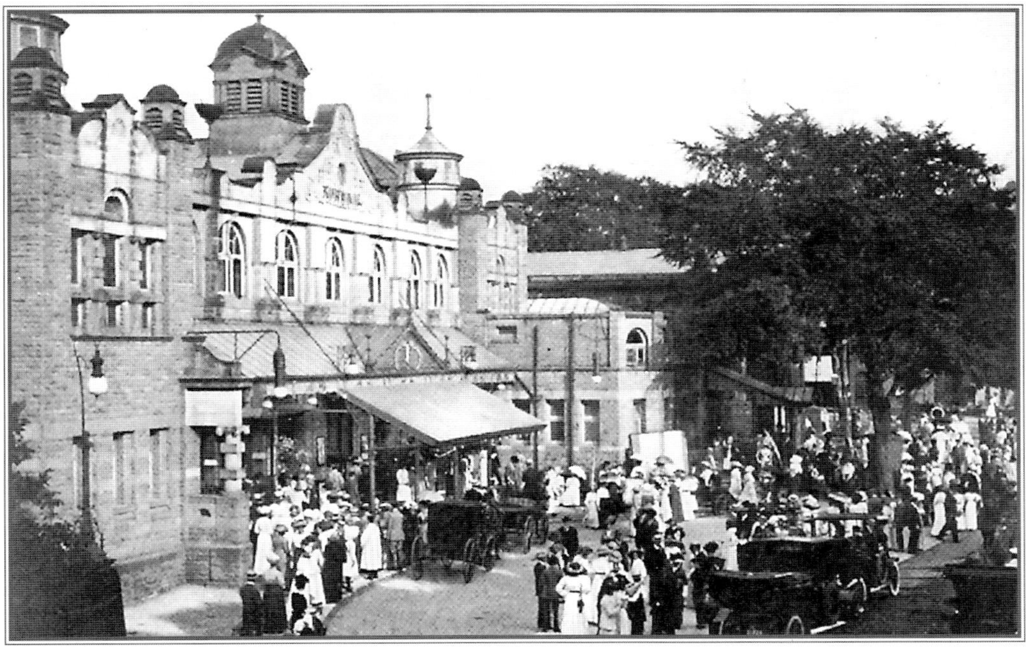

A fashionable crowd of theatre patrons gathers outside the Kursaal for an evening performance, summer 1903. Floodlighting in the 1930s made the Kursaal even more eye-catching.

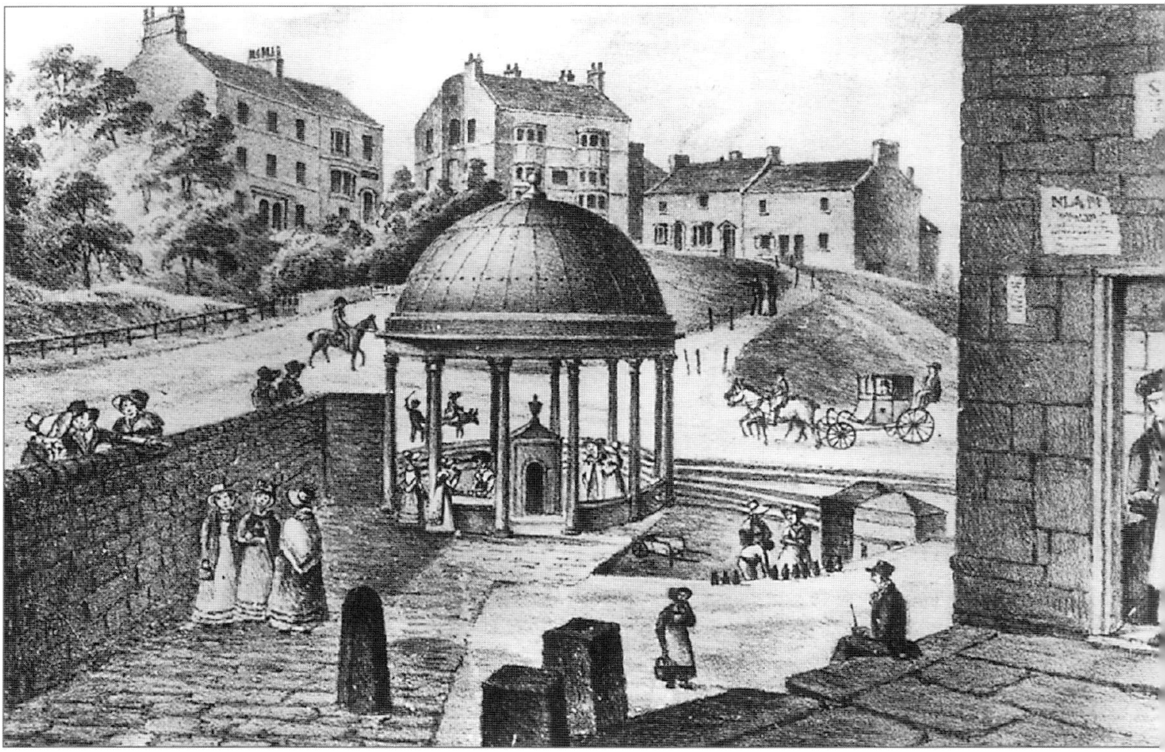

The Spa Well, Low Harrogate, 1829, a lithograph by J. Stubbs showing Well Hill and the temple built by public subscription in 1808 when the population was only 800. By 1812 it had risen to 1,500. Word of the Spa Well or 'The English Spaw', as it was labelled by Dr Timothy Bright, had travelled far and set in motion coachloads of invalids and the curious in hopes of entertainment and, above all, complete cures. Dr Deane was the first medical man to give his opinions, but when other doctors joined in its praises, the general public took further note. William Slingsby, uncle of Sir William Slingsby, had from his home at Bilton Park declared the virtues of the 'Tewit Well' some twenty years earlier. Apparently flocks of birds were attracted to the minerals that crystallised on the well's outskirts, mainly the crested lapwings known locally as 'tewits'.

In the course of time many famous people also heard of the town's progress, one of whom was the Lord Chancellor, Alexander Wedderburn, who bought land, a shrewd investment. He built Wedderburn House in 1786 and erected the stone pump room over St John's Well. He was also interested in the first Harrogate theatre.

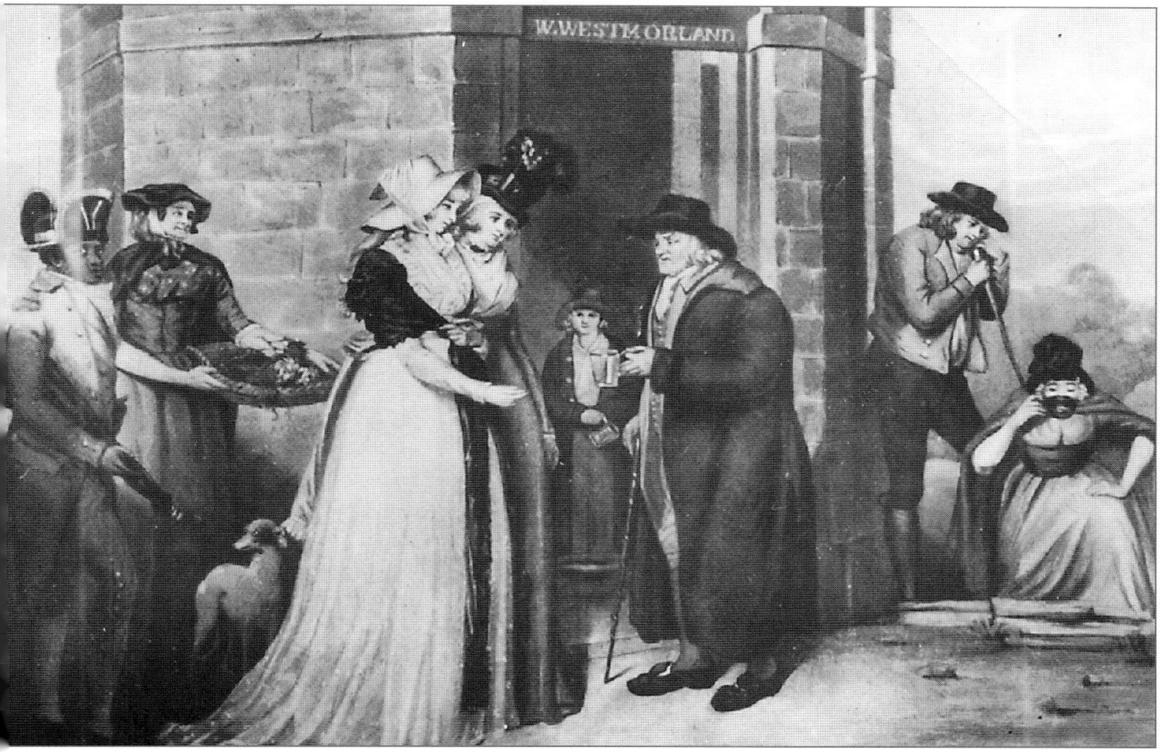

The John Well (St John's Well) or 'Chalybeate Well at Harrogate', 1796, by John Raphael Smith. This was the second curative well to be discovered, and as its waters were so much more palatable and less offensive to the nose it became known as the Sweet Spa – soon outstripping the Tewit Well in popularity.

Of High and Low Harrogate, unknown hamlets before these discoveries, High Harrogate would appear to be the older of the two communities. Here the main paths intersected where the first mineral wells were investigated and here also was the now vanished fifteenth-century chantry chapel. For two centuries the nearest churches were at Knaresborough or Pannal, and whatever the weather devout visitors and villagers trudged to one or the other.

It was High Harrogate which in 1663 opened the first public bathing place, 'Doctor Neale's Baths', next to the Sweet Spa. By the end of the seventeenth century twenty warm water bathing houses were being greatly appreciated. At the time of the Civil Wars, for a safer, quiet life, Harrogate residents sided with Commonwealth Rule, apart from a few who were imprisoned in York. John Sergeant of Harrogate was hanged for his part in an abortive Royalist disruption.

Early accommodation in the town was offered by enterprising farmers but some visitors went to Knaresborough, a long-established community, as it was then more important. In 1749 St John's Chapel, Harrogate, was built mainly by dint of visitors' generosity.

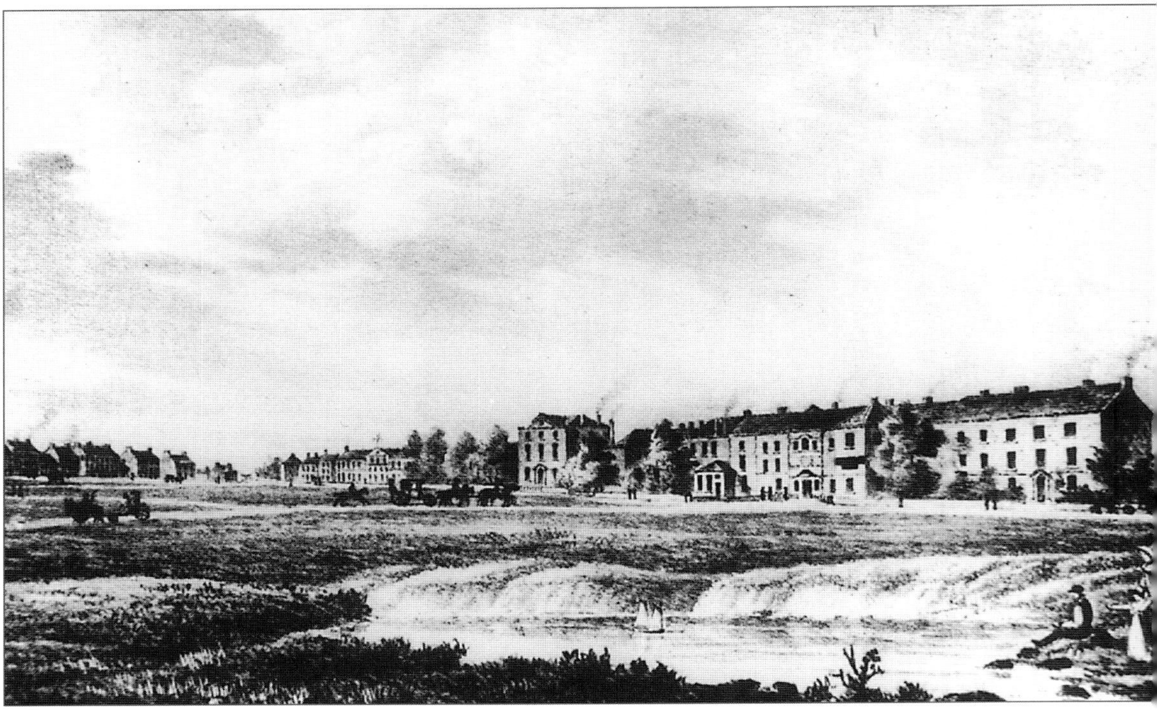

An engraving of High Harrogate, 1829, by J. Stubbs. On the right, just behind the pond, is the Granby Hotel, originally called The Sinking Ship. For 200 years the Granby was held in the highest esteem. Dukes, earls, duchesses, members of parliament and statesmen such as Clive of India were all welcomed there as guests by mine host Mrs Wilks, and later Jonathan Benn. The Duchess of St Albans and her daughter always stayed there and it was this daughter, Angela Burdett Coutts of banking fame, who presented the splendid market clock to the town. The hotel dates from the seventeenth century and it was here that, at the time of the Turnpike Trusts, Blind Jack of Knaresborough played his violin. The distinction of being the first hotel in the town was claimed by the Queen, erected as early as 1687. Its position between two wells, the Tewit and St John's, also known as the Sweet Well, was just what early visitors desired.

J. Stubbs made further engravings in 1829 including the Dragon Hotel in High Harrogate, known in early days as the Green Dragon. W.P. Frith, the Royal Academician, lived there in about 1830, his father being the innkeeper. In 1870 this building became Harrogate College, but was demolished in 1883 to make way for Mornington Crescent.

In spite of their considerable wealth, successful Manchester, Birmingham and Leeds businessmen eager to take the waters were not welcome at the Granby. Such mill owners stayed at the Queen, which became nicknamed the 'Manchester Warehouse'. Most of these hotels were coaching inns in the days of the 'Roaring Dillies', or diligences as these coaches were known. Names like Rocket, Dart, Tantivy and Tally Ho expressed their speed, and time schedules which were rigidly kept. Some of the coachmen became as famous as the landlords of the day. (North Yorkshire County Library)

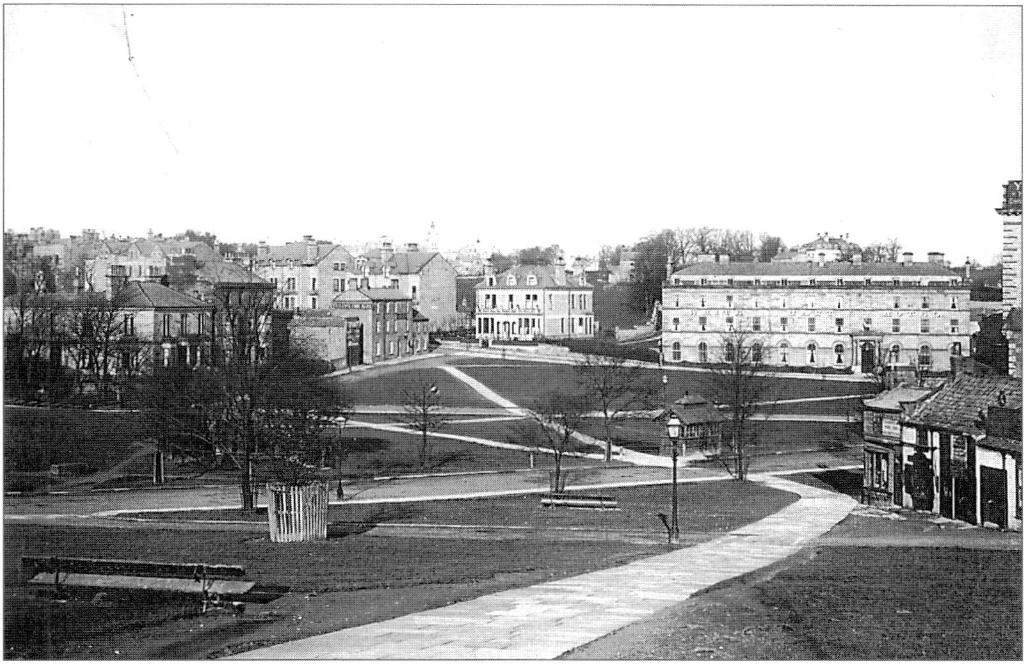

Low Harrogate, 1890. On the right is the long line of the White Hart Inn with its life-size statue of a deer above the portico. Next, at the bottom of Cold Bath Road, is the Victoria Inn, now demolished. After the Battle of Waterloo Harrogate expressed its joy by staging a Grand Ball at the White Hart.

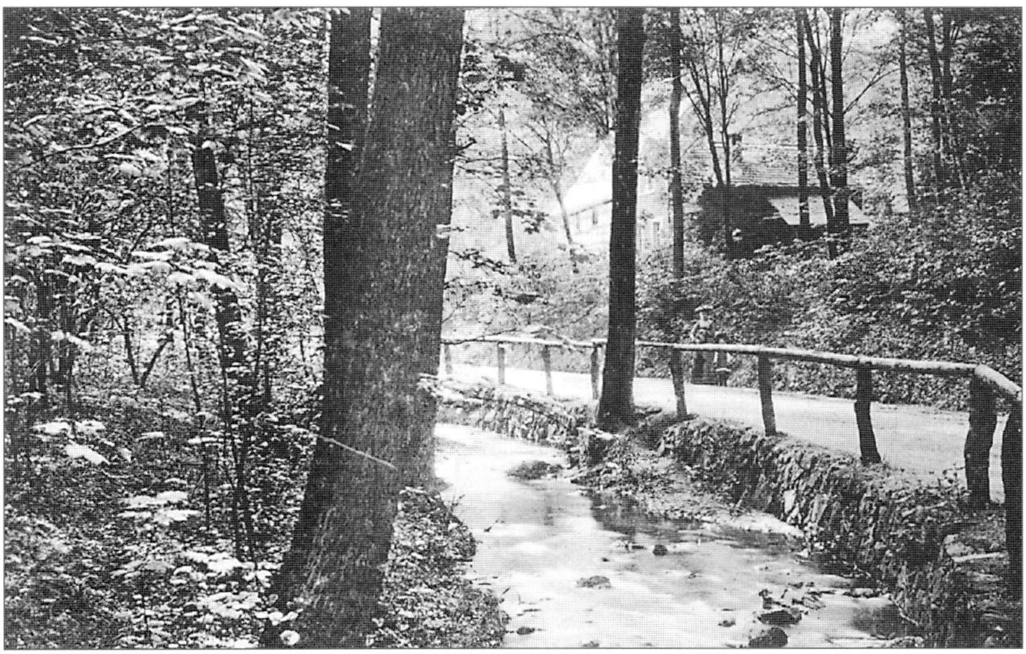

Harlow Car Woods, 1908, leading to Harlow Car Gardens, which together covered 60 acres. Gardens were laid out alongside the streams. The Harlow Car Springs, 2 miles from the town, one chalybeate and four alkaline sulphur, had been acquired by the Corporation by the 1930s, and their waters transmitted to the Royal Baths for the 'Harlow Treatment' of patients.

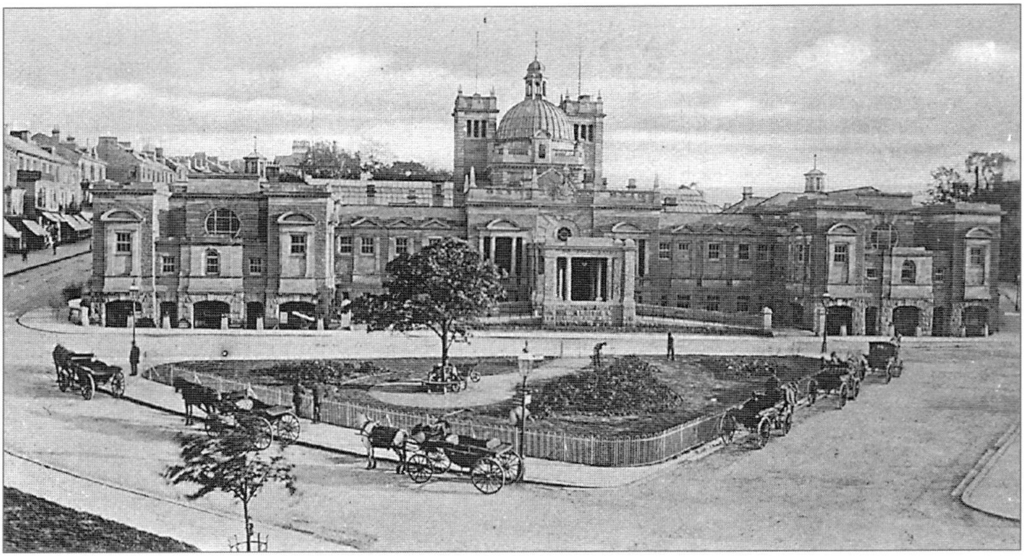

Royal Baths Assembly Rooms, *c.* 1899, designed by two London architects, F.T. Baggaley and F. Bristowe, where everyone gathered in Queen Victoria's day. In 1835 the classically styled Cheltenham Pump Rooms had been completed, a triumph for Harrogate. From the decorated, barrelled ceiling hung a huge crystal chandelier and there was a musicians' gallery. The first assembly room was called the Promenade and is now the Mercer Gallery.

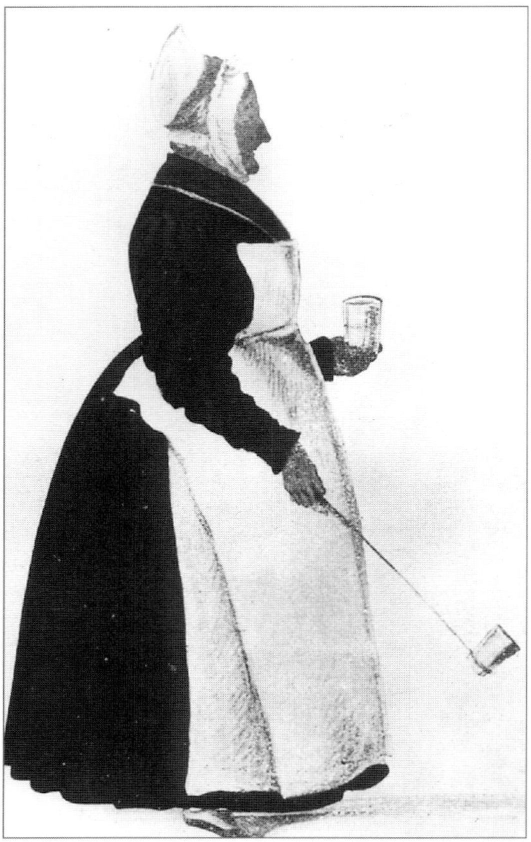

Betty Lupton became known as the 'Queen of Harrogate' in the early nineteenth century because she presided for so long at the Sulphur Well. In 1796 Mr W. Westmorland was the presiding genius but there were a number of ladies like Betty who toiled in the background pouring water into drinking vessels. Although the sulphur well was unpleasant, accused by some of 'smelling of bad eggs', it became famed for its medicinal qualities. Betty also became famed so that when she did eventually retire, aged over eighty, she was awarded a pension, which in those days was a most unusual gesture.

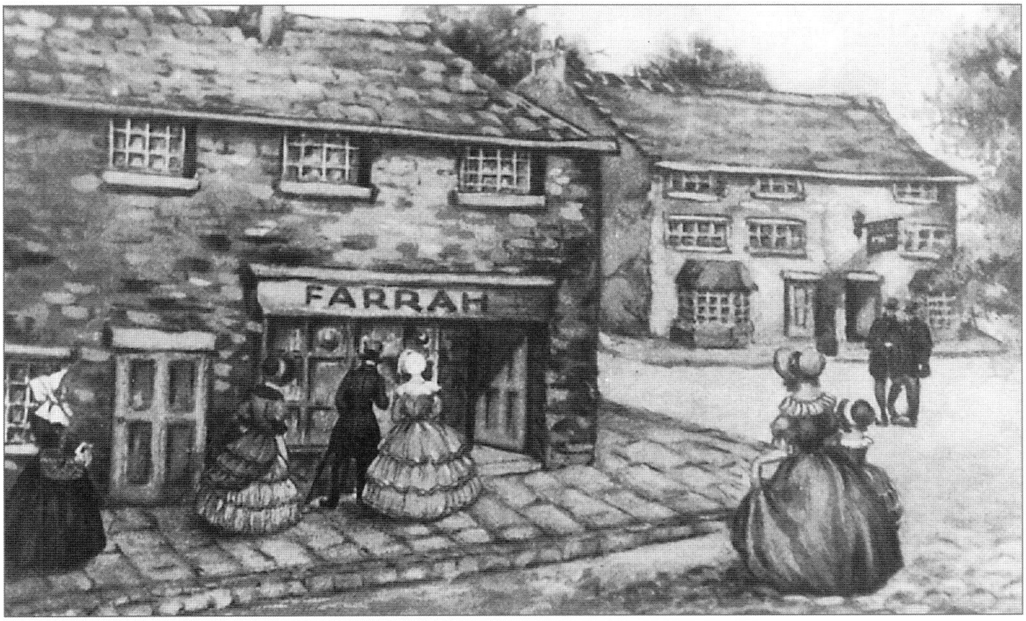

John Farrah's original Harrogate toffee shop and grocery on Royal Parade 1840. In a county traditionally famous for recipes, Harrogate and Doncaster specialised in toffee while York offered a range of fudges. At the British Empire Exhibition at Wembley in the 1920s Farrah's Toffee was among products 'flying the flag' for Harrogate.

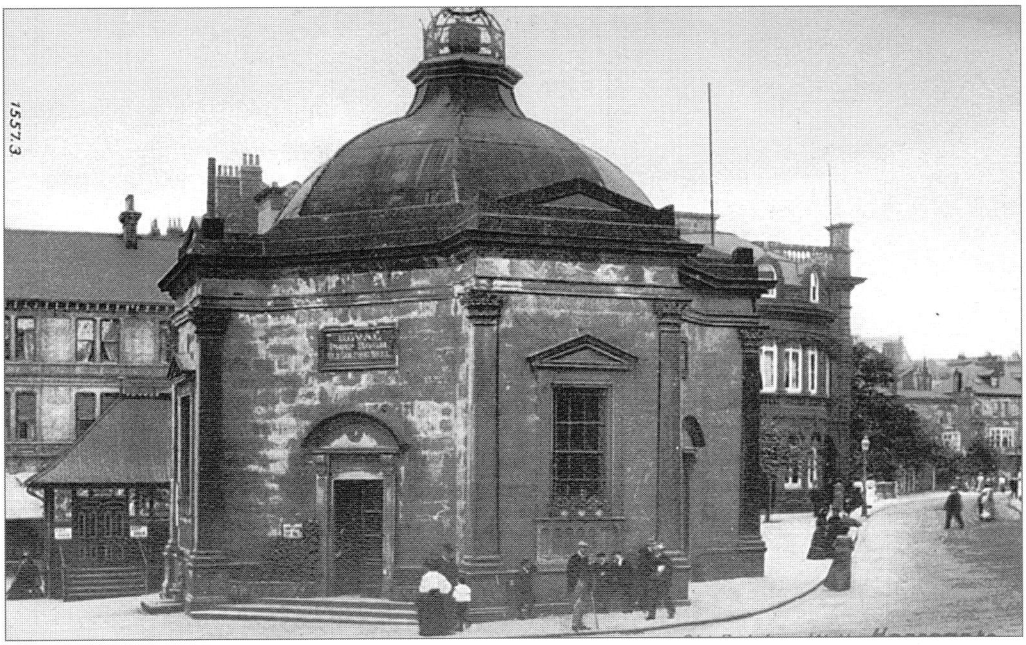

Royal Pump Room, the Old Sulphur Well, 1900. In 1804 this octagonal building designed by Isaac Shutt was erected over the Spring (referred to in early days as 'the stinking spaw'). In one morning alone more than a thousand glasses of the sulphur water were drunk. The original well head is still in the basement but the Pump Room became a Museum of Local History.

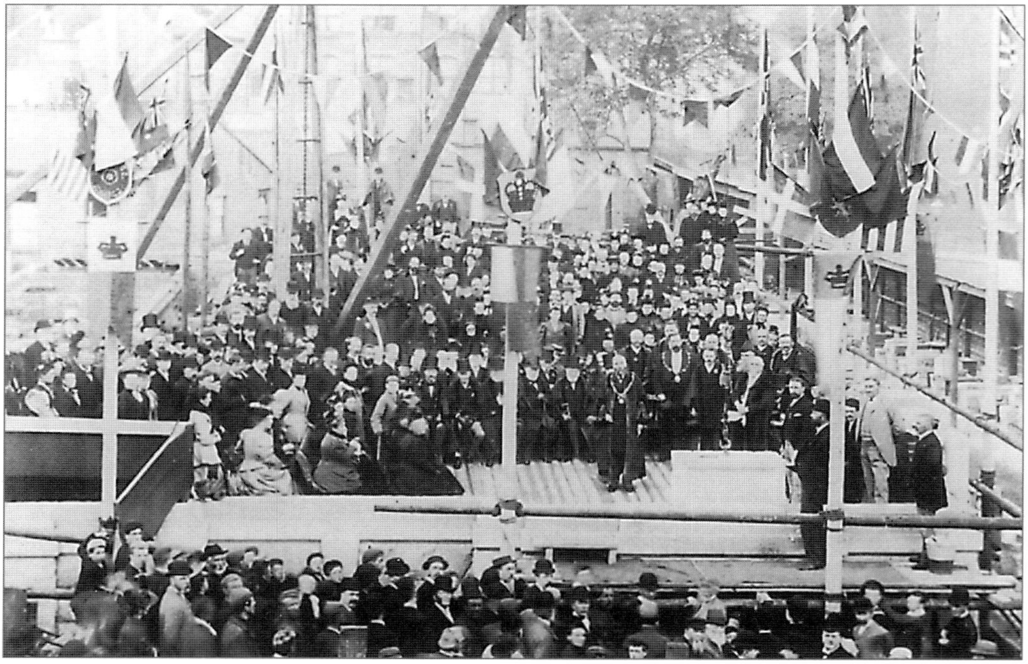

A great occasion, 10 July 1894, when the foundation stone was laid for the Royal Baths and Winter Gardens, which were completed in 1897. The Duke of Cambridge officially opened them on 23 July. By this time over 60,000 people were coming annually because of the success of Harrogate waters 'externally and internally'. (North Yorkshire County Library)

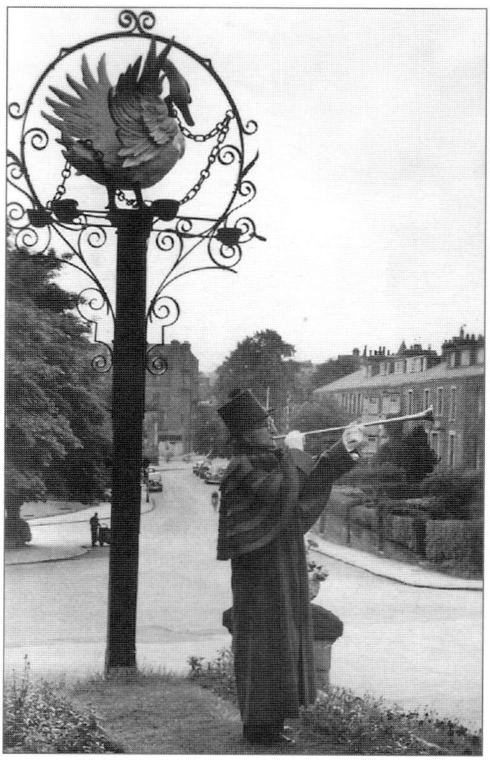

Outside the Old Swan Hotel stands the Harrogate hornblower, *c.* 1900. Note the beautiful inn sign. In the 1820s the Diligence stage coach left the Swan Inn at 9 a.m. every day for the Rose and Crown at Leeds, returning at 3 p.m. from the Golden Lion. The Swan achieved fame under its owner Jonathan Shutt as it was he who thwarted a dastardly attempt in 1835 to divert the waters of the Old Sulphur Well. The culprit was Joseph Thackwray of the Crown. All the important innkeepers, Mr Dearlove of the Queen, Mr Frith of the Dragon and so on, were alerted and a meeting was called which eventually led to the case being heard at York Assizes. Mr Thackwray must have had a good lawyer for he was acquitted on a small point of law. However, twenty-one Improvement Commissioners were elected in 1841 to prevent any similar threats to Harrogate's *raison d'être*. Isaac Thomas Shutt, son of Jonathan Shutt, won the competition to design a Pump Room to enclose the old Sulphur Well, and by 1842 this was complete.

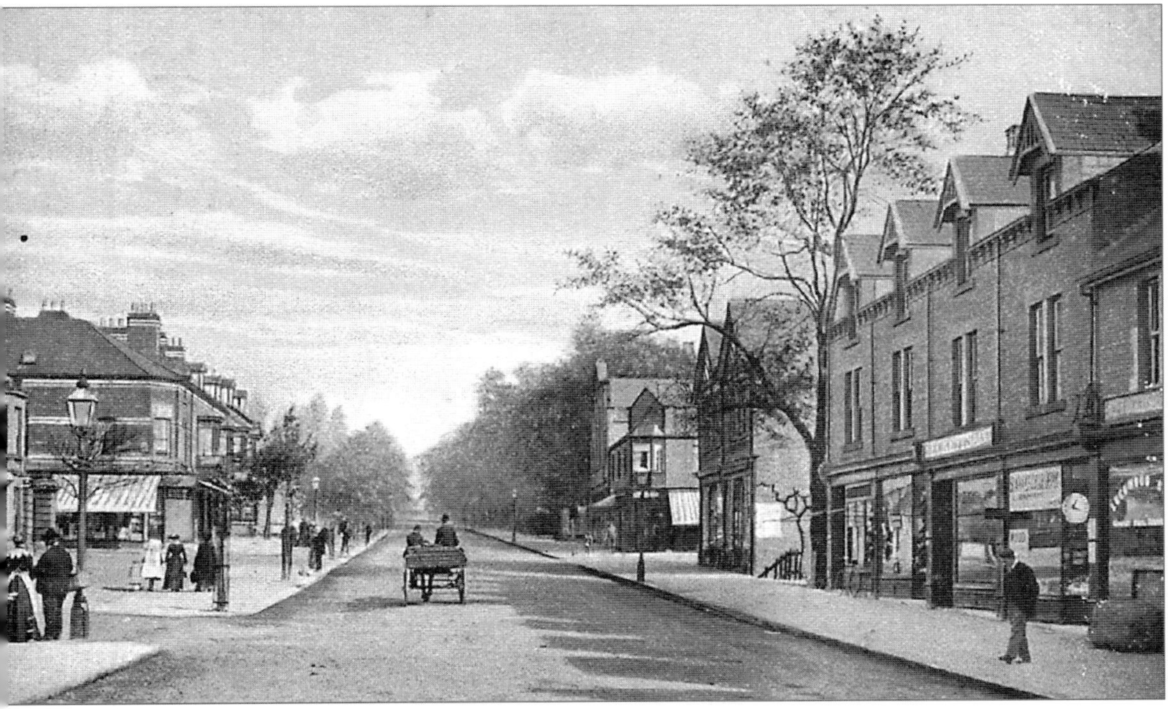

Starbeck High Street, 1911. An additional station to serve Harrogate was opened at Starbeck. Well away from the society life of Harrogate, a workhouse for paupers was opened close to Starbeck in 1810. Before this date poor and destitute people were sent to Pannal.

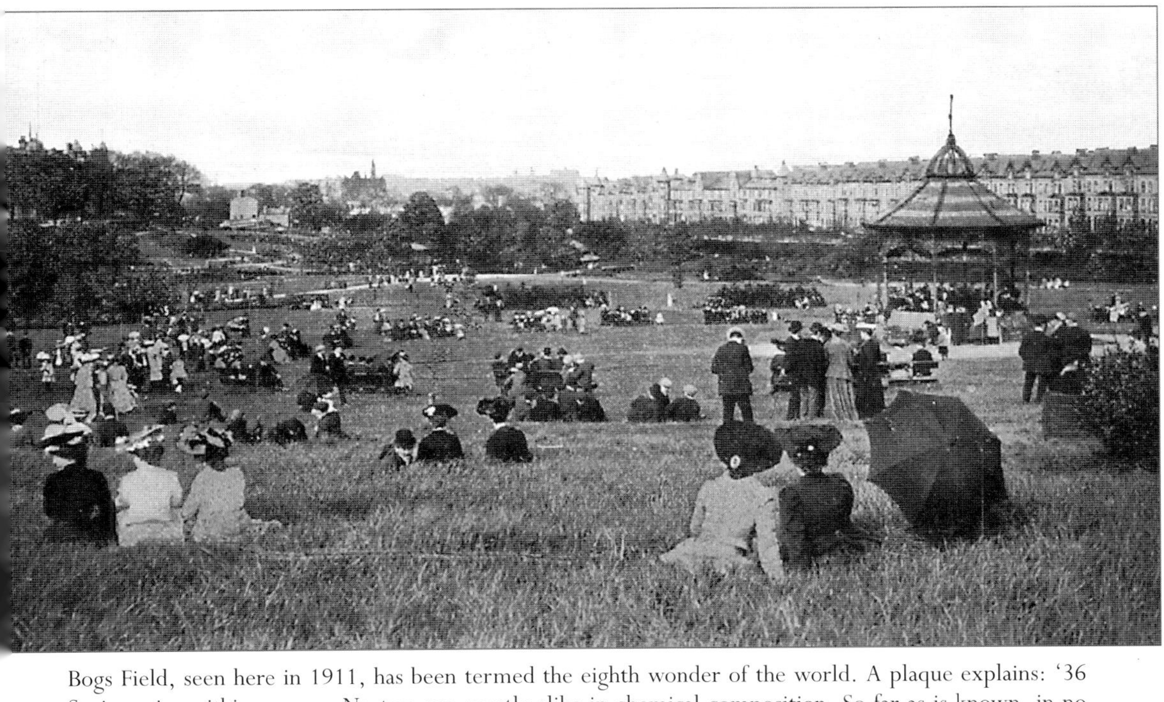

Bogs Field, seen here in 1911, has been termed the eighth wonder of the world. A plaque explains: '36 Springs rise within an acre. No two are exactly alike in chemical composition. So far as is known, in no similar area in the world can such a diversity of Springs be found.'.

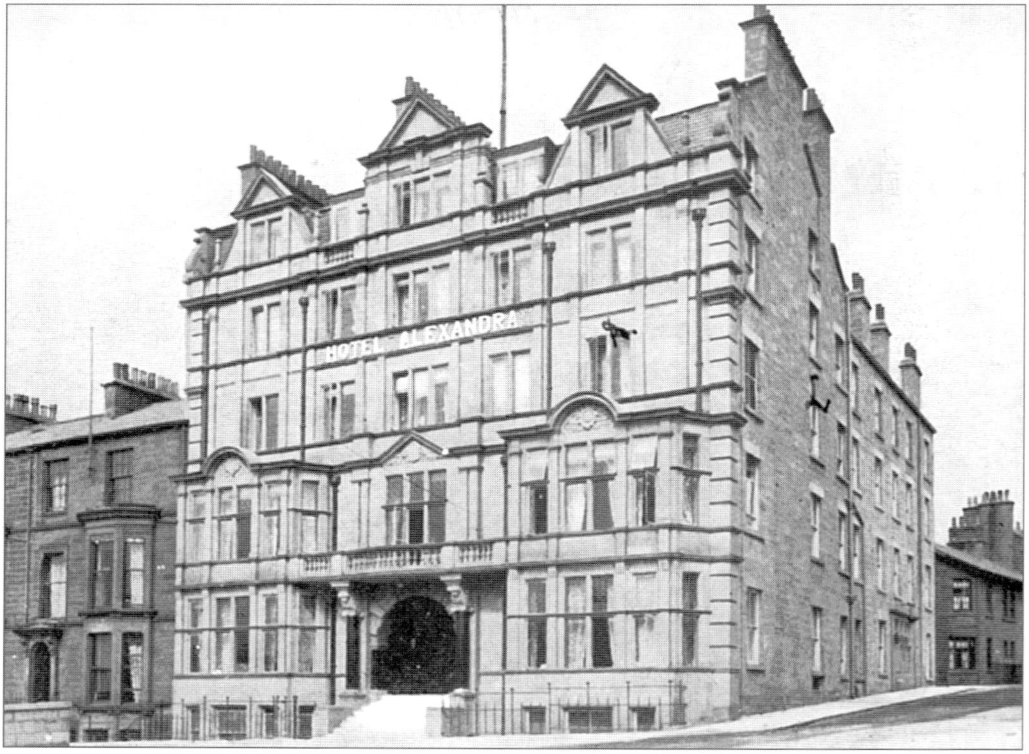

Hotel Alexandra, 1915. A Harrogate man, Pickersgill Palliser, found time to be schoolmaster, postmaster, printer and bookseller. He issued a 'List of Visitors' staying at the hotels, which he published weekly during the season. More and more information was demanded and Palliser's modest list eventually became the *Harrogate Advertiser*.

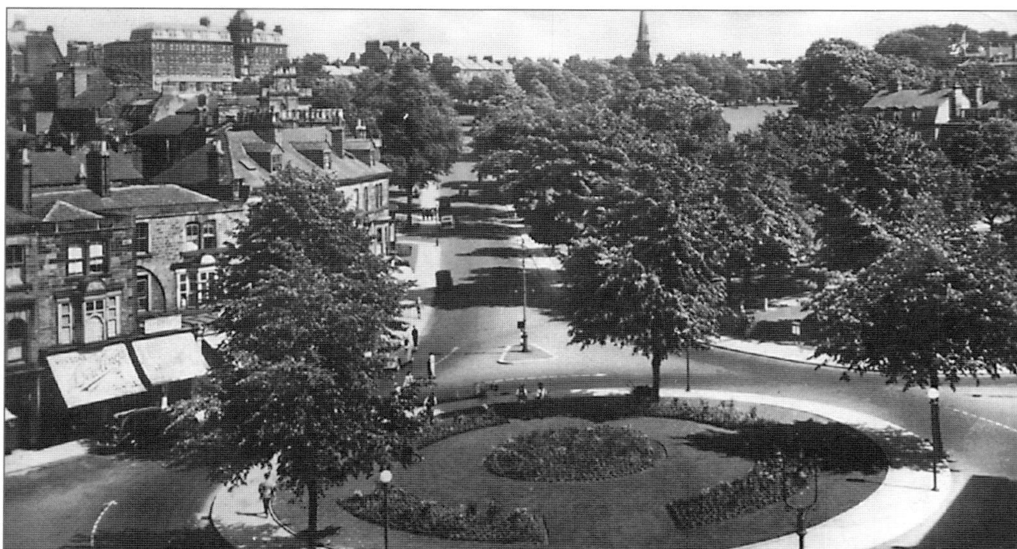

Montpellier Parade, 1967. Exclusive shops were made inviting by grassed and wooded areas, with glorious displays of flowers changing with the seasons. All the grandeur of Victorian and Edwardian Harrogate was mirrored in this spacious approach to Prospect Place.

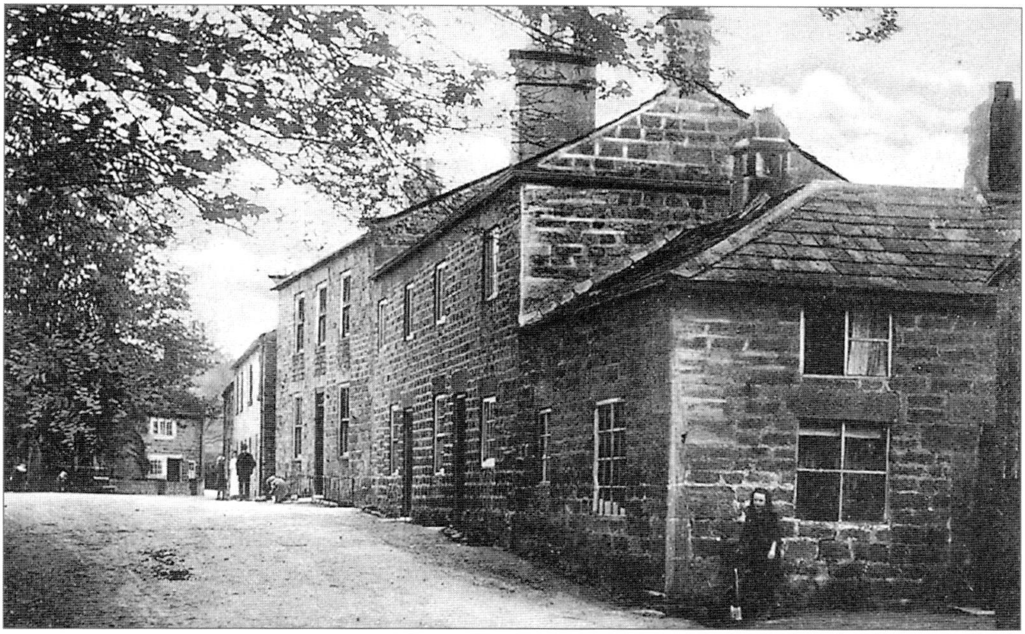

The village street, Pannal, 1912. A favourite Sunday walk for Harrogate visitors was to the pretty village above Crimple Valley. They came to see the church and the interesting monument about Joseph Thackrey (*sic*) 'who by the grace of God brought sulphur wells to fame 1740'. (See page 14.)

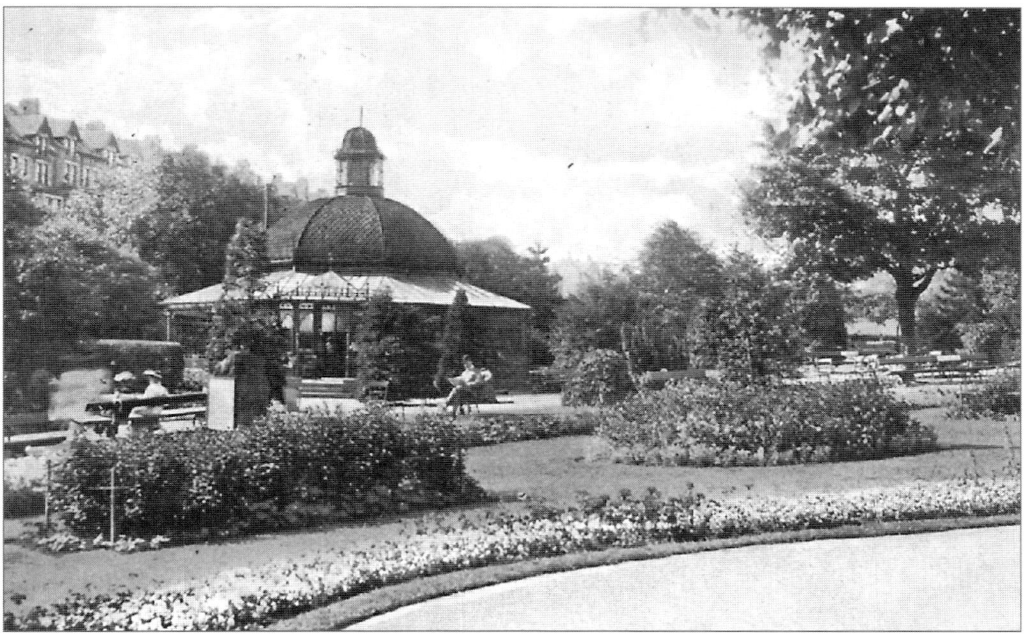

The Magnesia Well, seen here in 1906, was situated in Valley Gardens and supplied potable and palatable mineral water which was also available at the counter in the Royal Pump Room. The list of diseases mitigated by drinking the Harrogate waters ran to nineteen, and even included consumption (later termed tuberculosis), bronchitis and malaria.

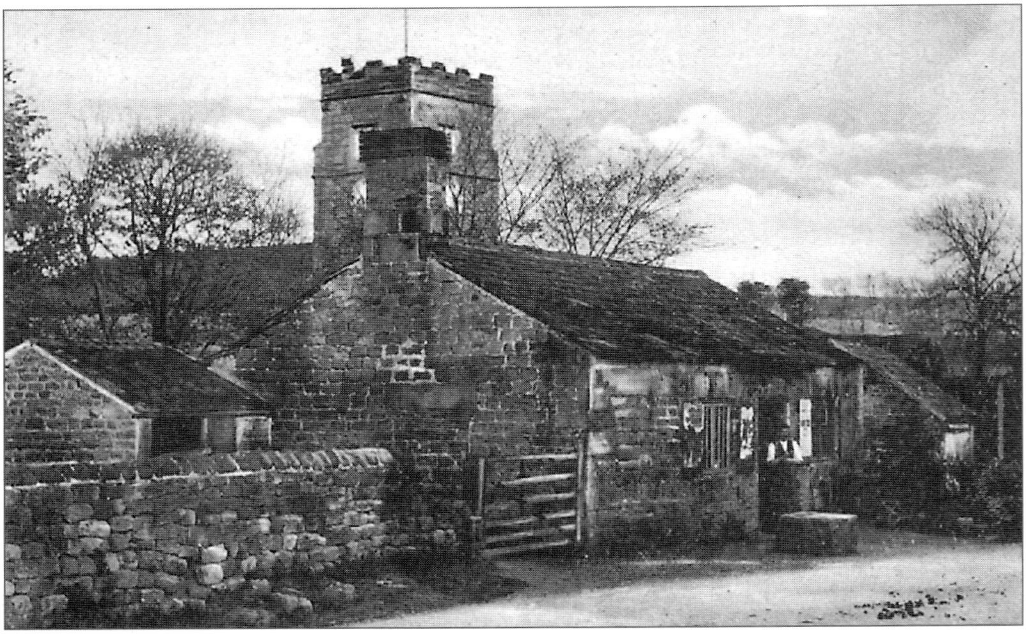

The village blacksmith, Pannal, 1904. This picture is especially interesting as it emanated from the enterprising Lydia Ward's shop. It is one of a series of picture postcards of the village which she had printed. Before Christmas she would canvass the villagers for orders so they could be used as greetings cards.

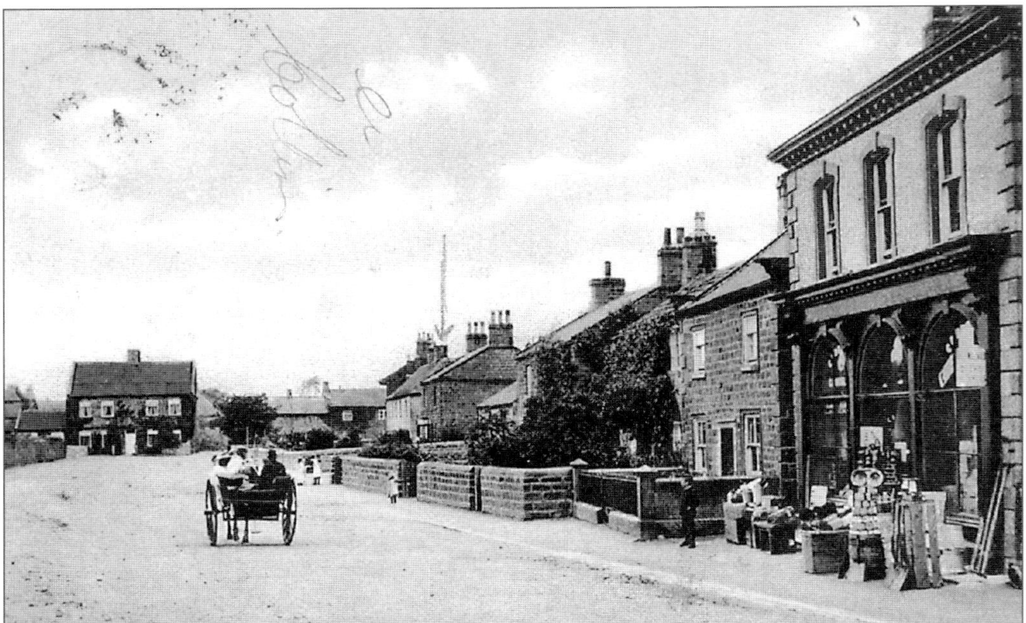

Spofforth village, 1908, with on the right, an example of the hardware shop which sold everything from paraffin to brooms and even gunpowder if the owner had a licence. On view are shovels, clothes maidens, buckets and business-like spades, indispensable in an agricultural area. Ancient Spofforth Castle was once the stronghold of the old Kingdom of Northumbria.

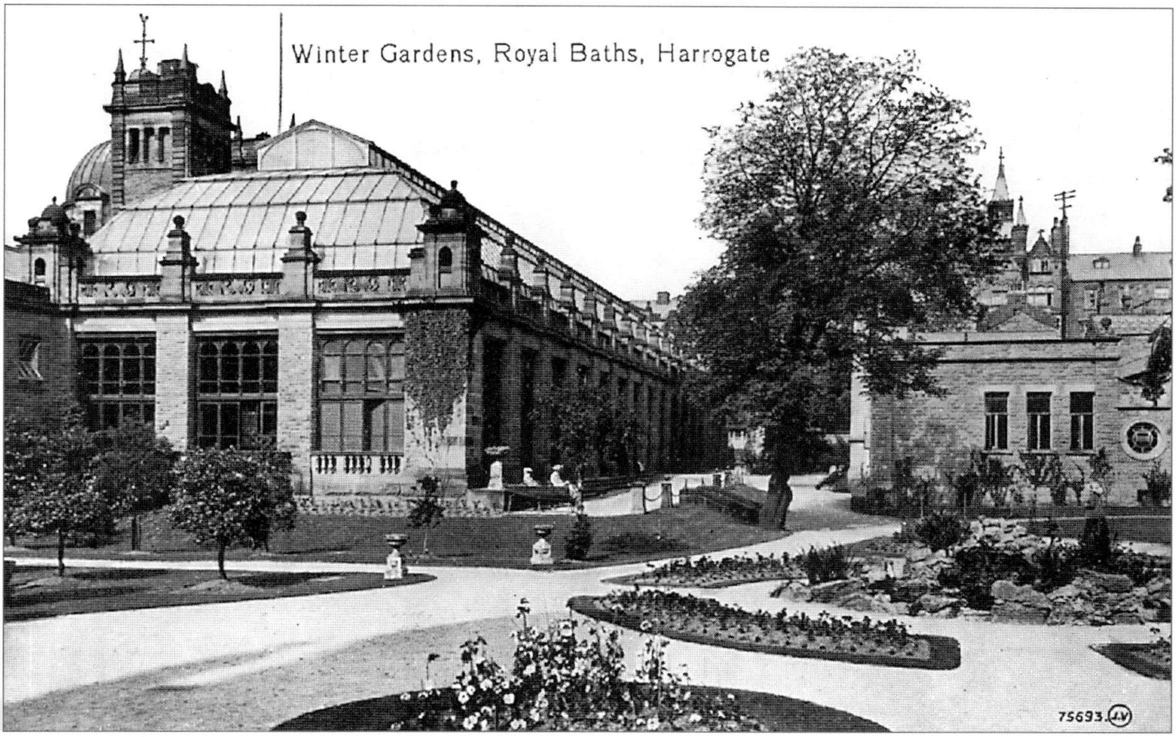

Winter Gardens, Royal Baths, 1906. It was in the eighteenth and nineteenth centuries that Harrogate was developed. As more and more springs with iron or sulphur deposits were discovered it became a leading spa, offering cures for a range of ailments: rheumatism, gout, nervous dyspepsia, neurasthenia and skin complaints. The Countess of Buckingham declared her asthma cured and in 1632 a shoemaker of York was reported cured of the scurvy after bathing in the waters at Harrogate. As early as 1571 William Slingsby drank from a spring at Knaresborough and recognised the similarity with Continental springs. Timothy Bright went further, declaring such springs to have healing properties. Sulphur baths and hot sulphur and mud poultices were among a wide range of treatments.

Demands for 'the cure' continued well into the twentieth century. After 1950 the cure was even obtainable under the National Health scheme. The Royal Baths, opened in 1897, were one of the largest establishments in the world offering such treatments. In 1969, demand having fallen away, the baths were closed but the assembly rooms are still used for conferences. In the town there was much consternation but Leeds Regional Hospital Board had firmly announced in February 1964 that no more National Health patients would be sent for treatment at the Royal Baths after March 1968. The treatment centre finally closed in 1969, the council having tried but failed to continue. The beautiful Spa Rooms had been demolished in 1939.

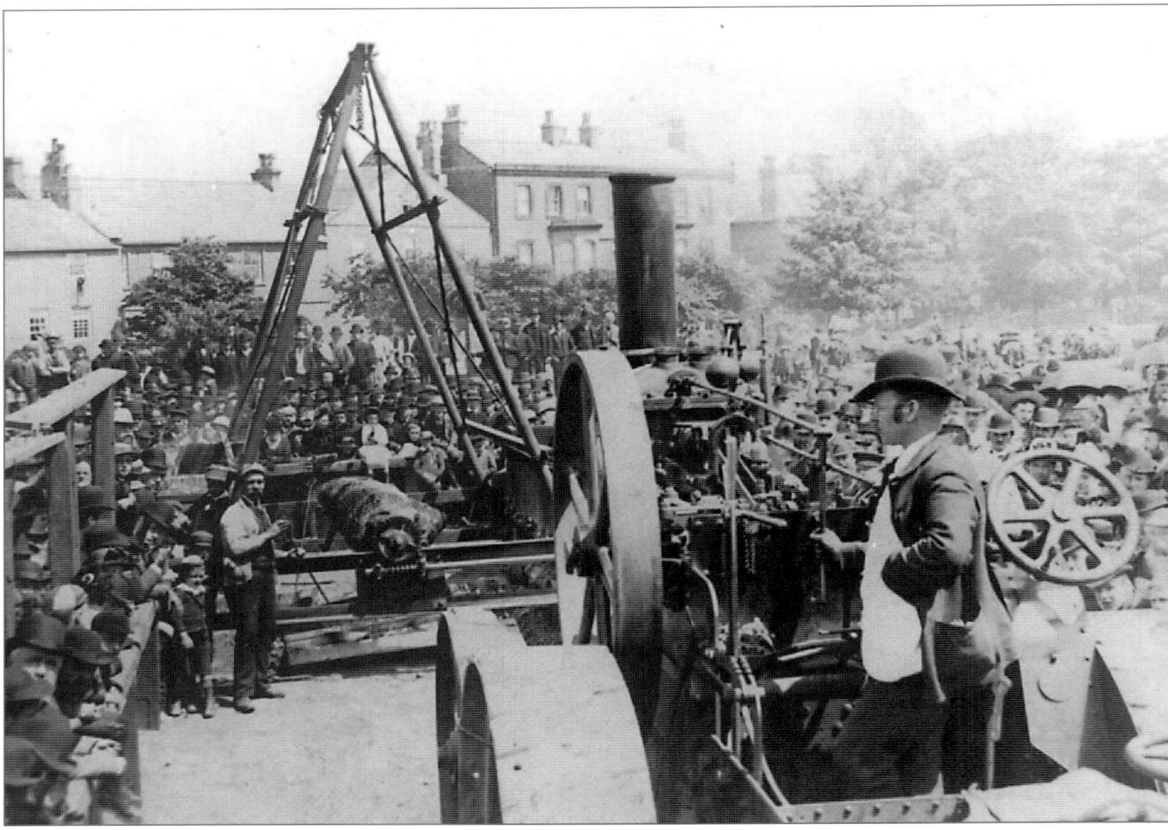

Ox-Roasting on the Stray, High Harrogate, in celebration of Queen Victoria's Jubilee, June 1887. The treat was paid for by Samson Fox who was Harrogate's Lord Mayor from 1889 to 1892.

By 1887 the Queen had reigned over an increasingly prosperous Empire-building Britain. From cities to hamlets her subjects knew this was something to be proud of. Even in the tiniest localities, in readiness for the great Jubilee Day, children were taught to sing hymns specially composed for the occasion. Committees were set up in every town to organise events, especially the inevitable long processions of rejoicing, with bands and banners, in which everyone played a part. According to how much money the municipality or local council could raise, permanent expression varied from elaborate monuments like that of Harrogate to wrought-iron lamps or clocks erected in the heart of the community. Decorations were splendid and imaginative: giant kites, crowns, triumphal arches, placards and lots of large photographs of 'our glorious Queen'. The lasting memory for the public was of the waiting in long lines, with plate and fork ready, to file past the huge spit and the white-coated chefs, to receive slices of roasted ox with bread. These were consumed on the spot, in the open air, on the greensward.

As for Samson Fox of Grove House, wealthy iron master from Leeds, he planted an oak tree in 1902 to commemorate his ox-roasting and also to mark the coming of peace at the end of the South African War.

(North Yorkshire County Library)

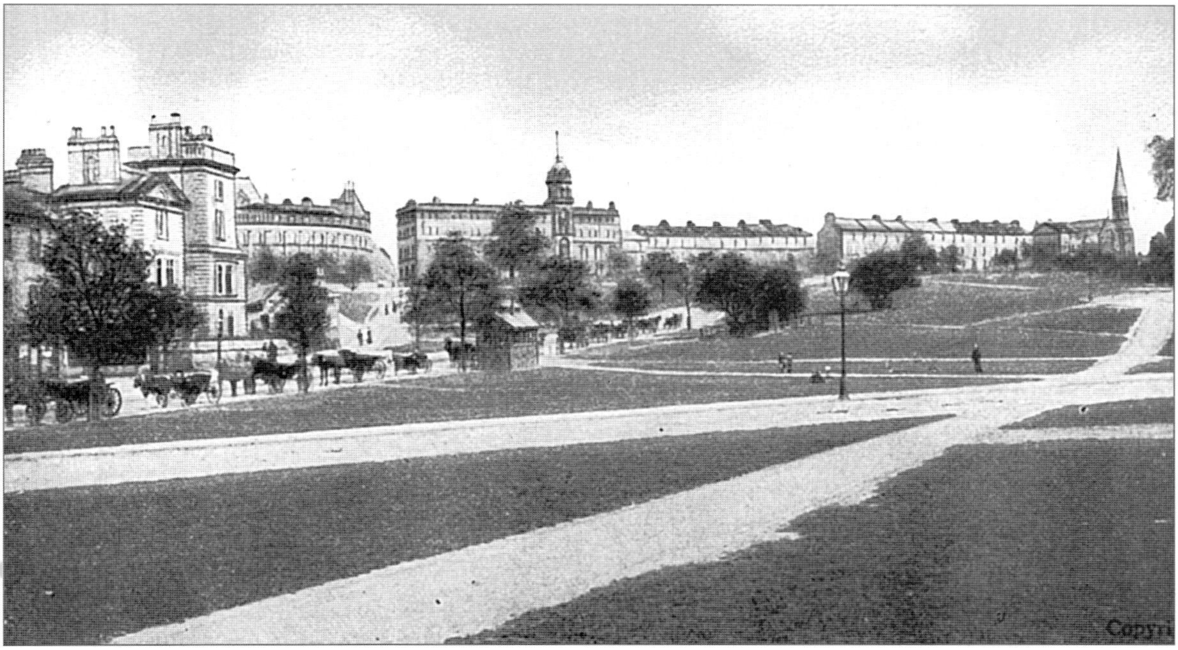

The Stray, an ancient term relating to the movement of cattle and sheep, early 1900s. On the far right (West Park Stray) is the Gothic style Trinity Weslyan church built in the early 1860s. The fine terrace of houses next to the church was erected about sixty years earlier.

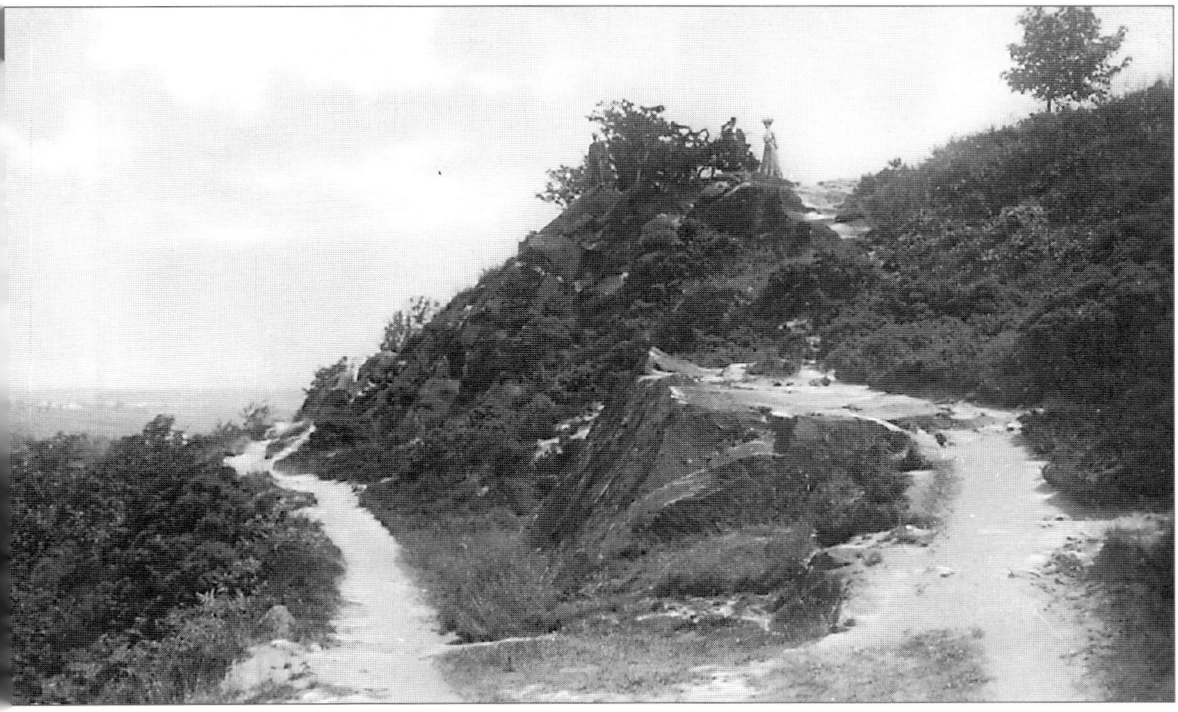

Birk Crag, 150 ft high and within walking distance of the town, through Valley Gardens, Irongate Bridge Road and past the reservoirs, 1908. On clear days visitors were rewarded with views of Great and Little Whernside.

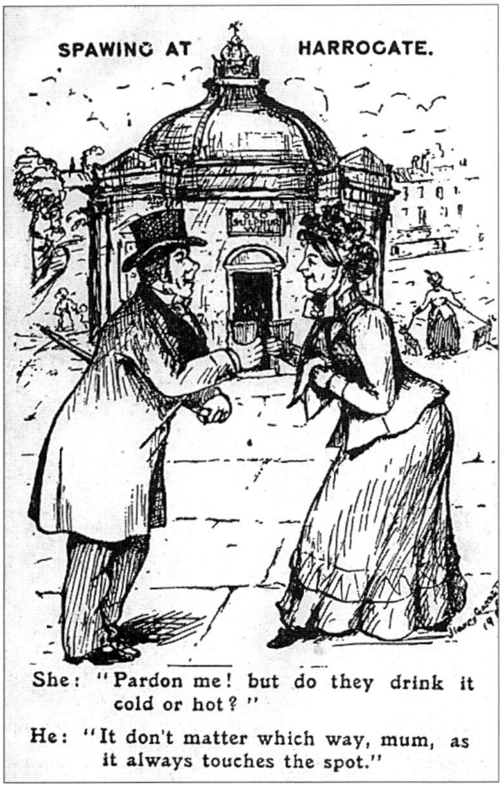

'Spawing at Harrogate', 1906. Harry Garrett produced a series of amusing cards showing visitors 'taking the waters' and their reaction to the unusual taste. 'Pardon me, but do they drink it cold or hot?' says this lady. The gentleman's reply is, 'It don't matter which way, mum, as it always touches the spot.' Another card captioned 'It touches the spot' shows a lady and gentleman leaning on each other, apparently touching their stomachs in pain. As with the sea water craze, however, visitors persisted, some starting early in the morning and drinking up to two quarts a day. Lizzy, a visitor in 1904, wrote from Crescent Gardens, 'Up at seven, took 16 ounces of strong sulphur water.'

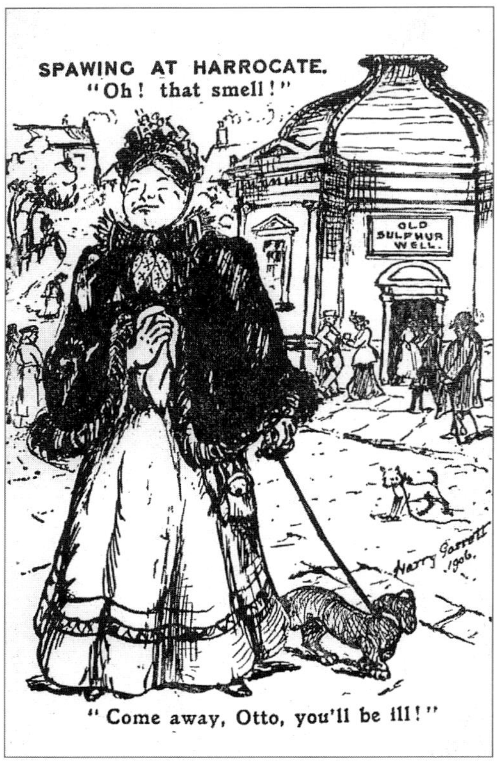

Spawing at Harrogate, 1906. 'Oh, that smell! Come away Otto, you'll be ill,' murmurs this lady to her dog in another Harry Garrett comic postcard. Postcards sent home recorded visitors' reactions. One in 1903 calls the water of this celebrated mineral spring 'very invigorating but not very tasty'. In 1842 Betty Lupton, who had presided over the Sulphur Well since the eighteenth century, celebrated her eightieth birthday but did not retire. 'Old Betty, the Queen of Harrogate', became a legend. Celia Fiennes, who travelled all over England on horseback in 1697, drank 'a quart a day for two days' but admitted she had to hold her breath and could not force her horse near the Harrogate well, 'he so disliked the sulphurous vapours'.

As for external treatment, this could involve warm mud or peat. Tobias Smollett had a gruelling time, in May 1766, his hot sulphur bath resulting in a haemorrhage. This is revealed in his novel *Humphry Clinker*, which gives an illuminating account of Harrogate society.

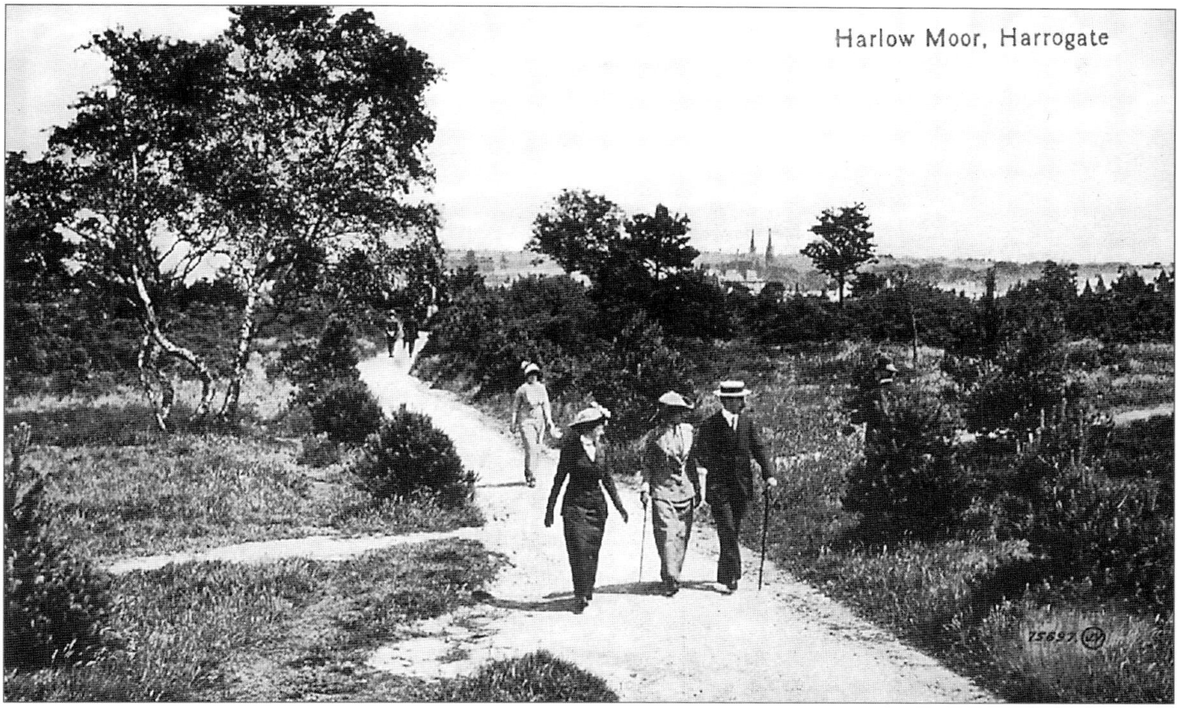

Harlow Moor, Harrogate, 2 miles from town, 1909. Fir trees, gorse and heather covered the moor, from which extensive views are obtainable. The Observatory, a 90 ft high tower 600 ft above sea level, commanded views of '17 castles, 24 abbeys, 20 market towns and 17 battlefields' (admission 3*d*). Broad paths like the one in this photograph made it possible to push invalids in bath chairs which were available for hire in Harrogate. The elegant clothes worn by ladies of that era are instanced in the walkers on Harlow Moor. Within the 65 acre area of Harlow Moor and Bogs Field lie the 6 acres of King's Plantation, a great pine wood formed in 1796. On the side of Harlow Moor near to Bogs Field a memorial called a 'Calvary' was raised to the men of Harrogate who died in the First World War. Amid this woodland were set the pillars from the demolished Royal Spa Concert Rooms, erected by John Williams of Cheltenham. The rooms were demolished in 1939, about the same time as when the old Harrogate Market was burned down.

The Harlow Manor Hydro had been built by John Milling in the 1870s as a private house, but in view of the great possibilities, it opened to the public as a hydro. Turkish, Russian and other medicinal baths were offered to hotel patrons as well as hot and cold plunges. The Harlow treatment was available at the Royal Baths as the Corporation had acquired the right to transmit the water from Harlow Car Springs. Harlow Moor was bought by the Corporation in 1898. The water, with its wonderful action in cases of skin complaints, had previously not been available in Harrogate itself.

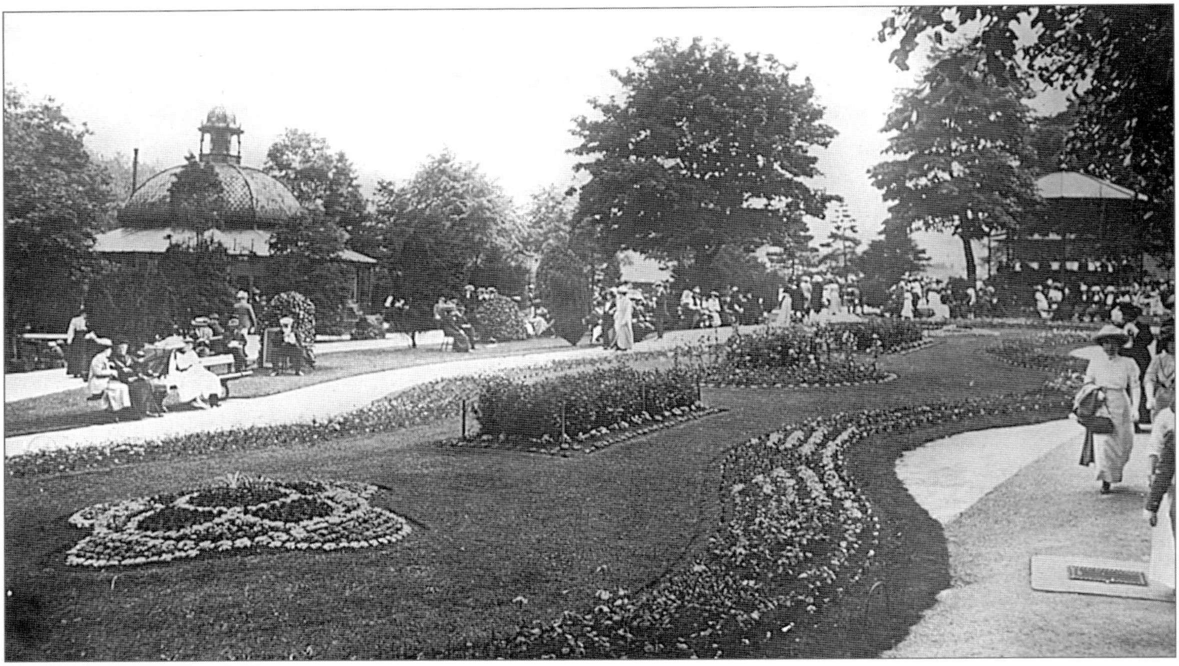

Valley Gardens and Magnesia Well. This well was housed in a small 'Gothick pump room' which was erected in 1858 but twice burned down, in 1924 and 1983. It may be restored yet again for use as a café. Otto Schwartz and his German band played in the area of Prospect Place and Valley Gardens in the 1900s.

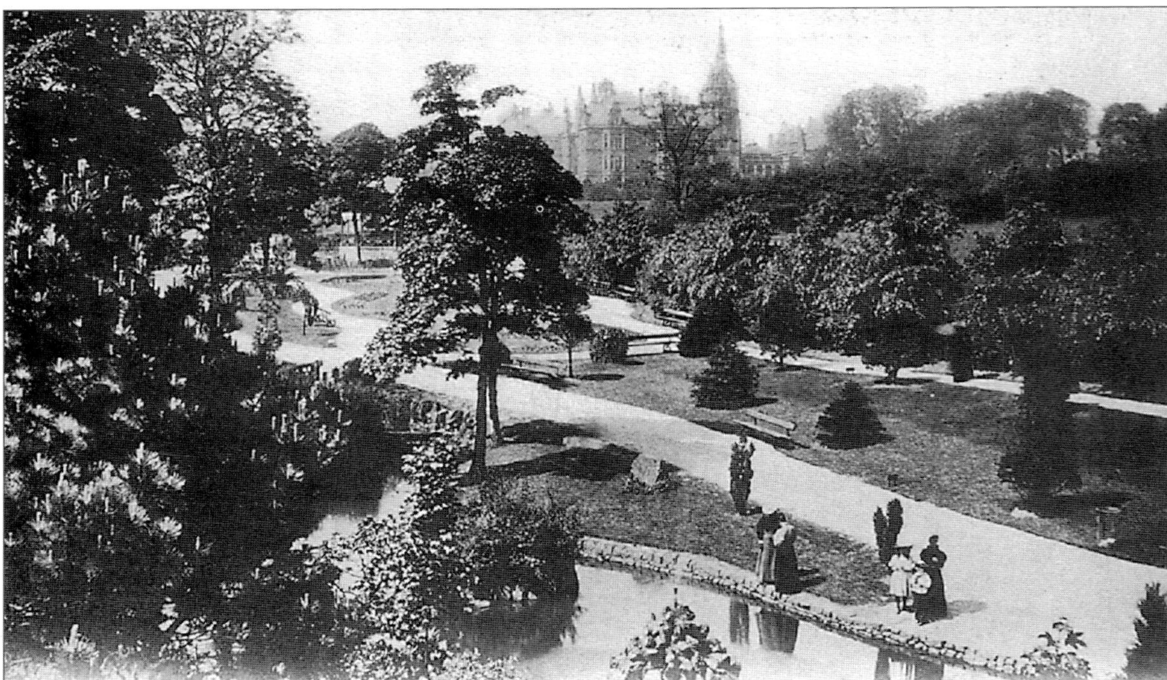

Bogs Valley Gardens, south of Valley Gardens, *c.* 1900. Here thirty-six of the eighty-eight wells were sited, some only a few feet apart, yet all different. Magnesia water from the Bogs Field was the only one used for drinking, the rest being carried to curative baths.

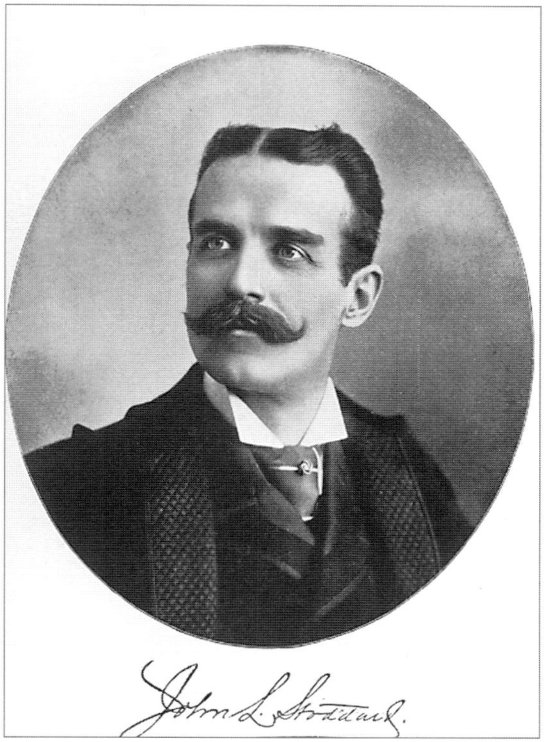

John L. Stoddard, an American who travelled the world collecting photographs, also appears to have had a stake in early tourism. His photographs of women in long skirts crossing the Mer de Glace in Switzerland or climbing the huge blocks of the pyramids in Egypt with masculine help are outstanding. Famed all over Europe, he later came to towns like Harrogate with a view to arranging visits, an extension of the old classic Grand Tour. Harrogate's fame spread abroad and obviously reached the USA. Not only the rank and file but also well-known and famous people were eager to visit. On one day in the year 1911 there were three queens staying in the town: Queen Alexandra, Empress Marie of Russia and Queen Amélie of Portugal.

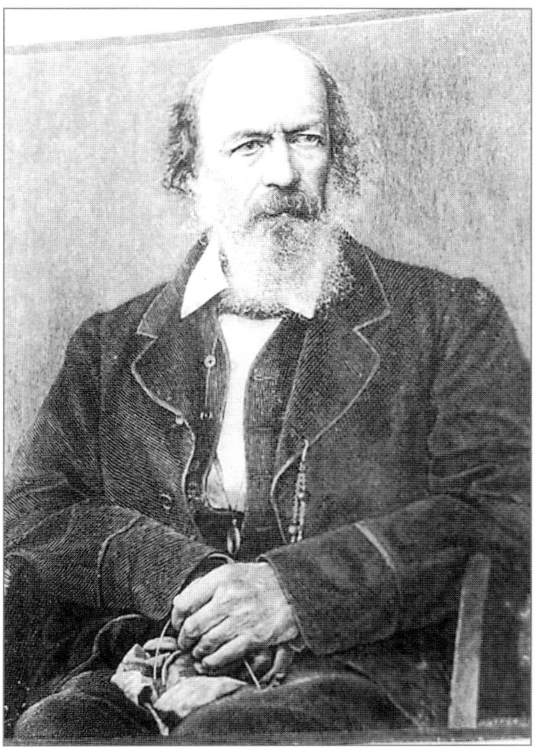

Alfred, Lord Tennyson, seen here in about 1860, was among the distinguished visitors to the town who hoped to benefit by 'the Cure', but he felt that the damp weather he experienced during his family's stay militated against any benefits gained. In the year that the three queens stayed every visitor received a free copy of a view of Station Square, one of a series issued with Shurey's Publications. A czarina of Russia was a visitor, as was Lord Byron who stayed at the Crown. On a lecture tour in 1858 Charles Dickens was quite disgruntled, calling Harrogate 'the queerest place with the strangest people in it'. The arrival of the railway made it an international spa. By the 1840s High Harrogate had fifty-one hotels and lodging houses, Low Harrogate seventy-nine and Central Harrogate twenty-one. In the year of Lord Byron's stay, 1810, there were 5,858 visitors.

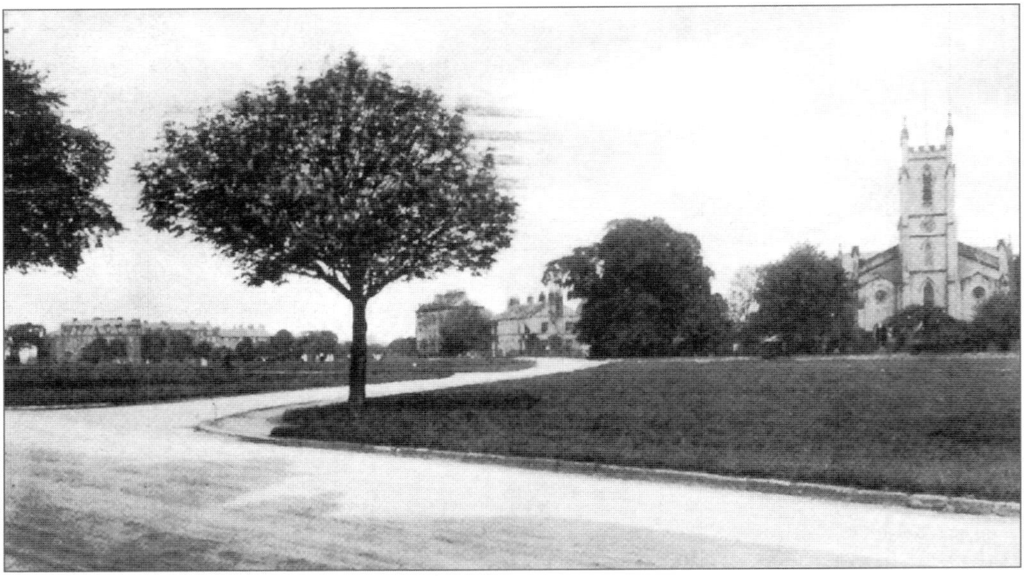

The Stray and Christ Church, 1925. One of many fine buildings, Christ Church, situated at High Harrogate, replaced St John's Chapel in 1831. As so many people were coming to Harrogate great changes would be needed so the 1841 Improvement Act was passed. By 1935 250,000 treatments a year were being administered. Park Parade near Christ Church, once known as Paradise Row, was one of the oldest streets.

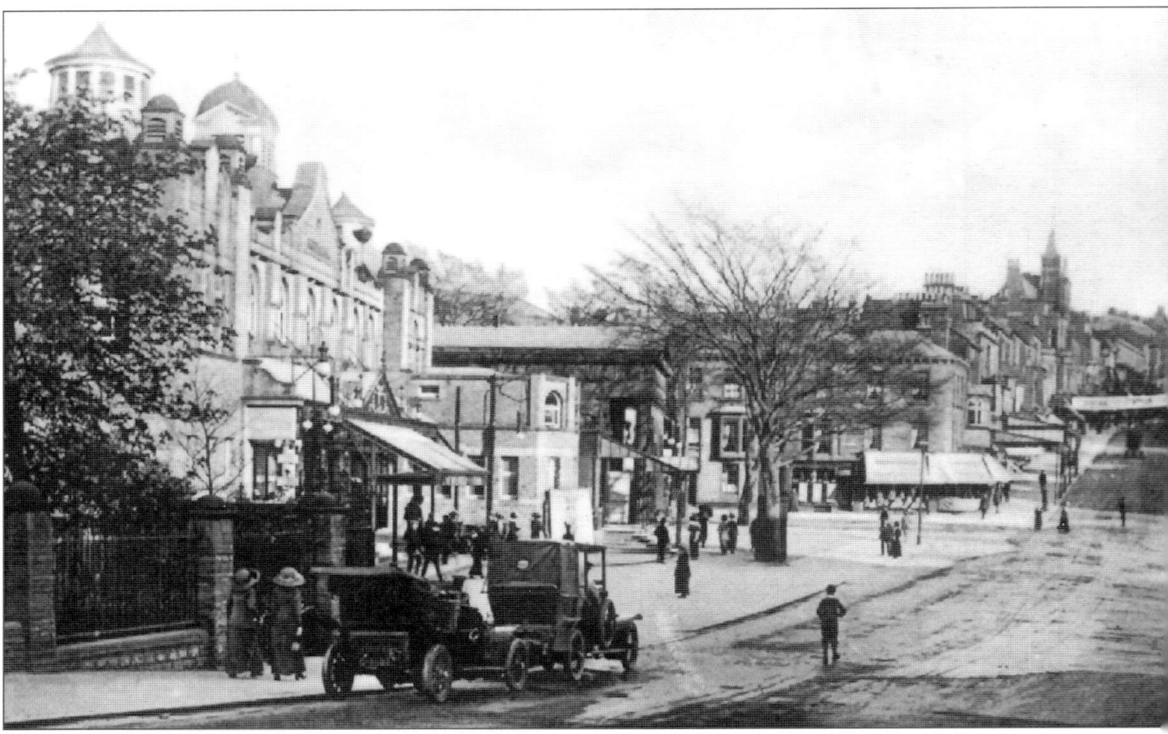

Kursaal and Parliament Street, with vintage vehicles and the latest fashions of theatre goers to be seen, 1924. Writing this postcard from Harrogate at the time of the 1924 Exhibition, 'Ada' reported the town 'full of visitors'.

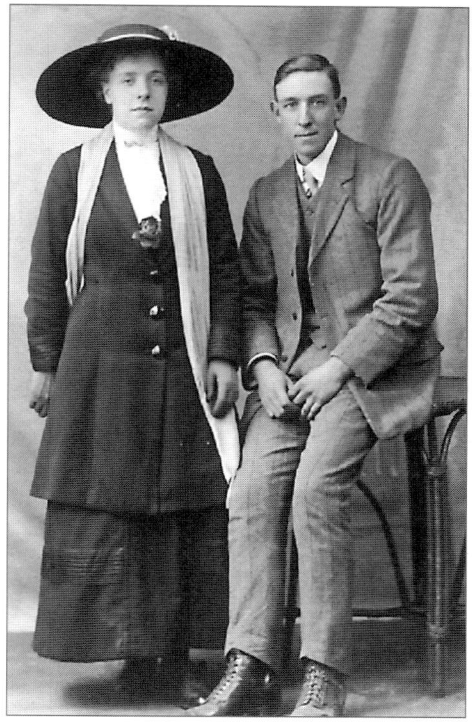

These two young people, Harold and Cissie Briggs, visited Harrogate in 1912 then travelled on to Scarborough where they were photographed in the studio of E.J. Seaman. They also had a 'while you wait' photograph taken on South Sands among crowds of day trippers. By using a small, rapid developer tank an almost instant likeness on thin metal could be produced to capture the memories of the Yorkshire seaside: Derrick's Black Minstrel Show, cockle and shrimp stalls and bathing vans. From the Bell Inn, Bland's Cliff, wagonettes and motor charabancs ran across the moor to Whitby. Harold, a booking clerk at Waterfoot railway station in Rossendale, was granted travel concessions so both he and Cissie became regular trippers. On 20 July 1848 a branch of the York and North Midland Railway came to Brunswick station on the Stray, Harrogate, and this trebled the number of visitors.

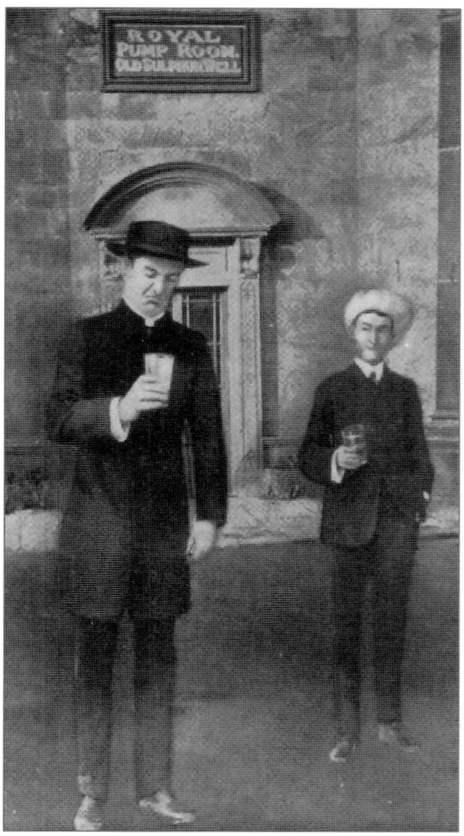

A series of cards entitled 'Drinking the Waters at Harrogate' was printed in 1905. This one, number 3, shows a wry and dubious clergyman having his glass outside the Royal Pump Room, Old Sulphur Well. Sending it to her boyfriend, D.J. writes: 'I would just like to see you taking it for fun . . . it would put you through your drills but you need not make a face like this.' Situated on the Stray opposite the Prince of Wales Hotel, the Tewit Well of pure chalybeate water, discovered by William Slingsby, was the oldest of all the Harrogate wells. The next in age was St John's Well where John Hardisty had been the well keeper. Near the Wetherby Road, this was discovered in 1631 by Dr Michael Stanhope and mentioned in his book *Cures Without Care*. A brass band played at this well and the thoughtful Improvement Commissioners provided an outside tap for poor people.

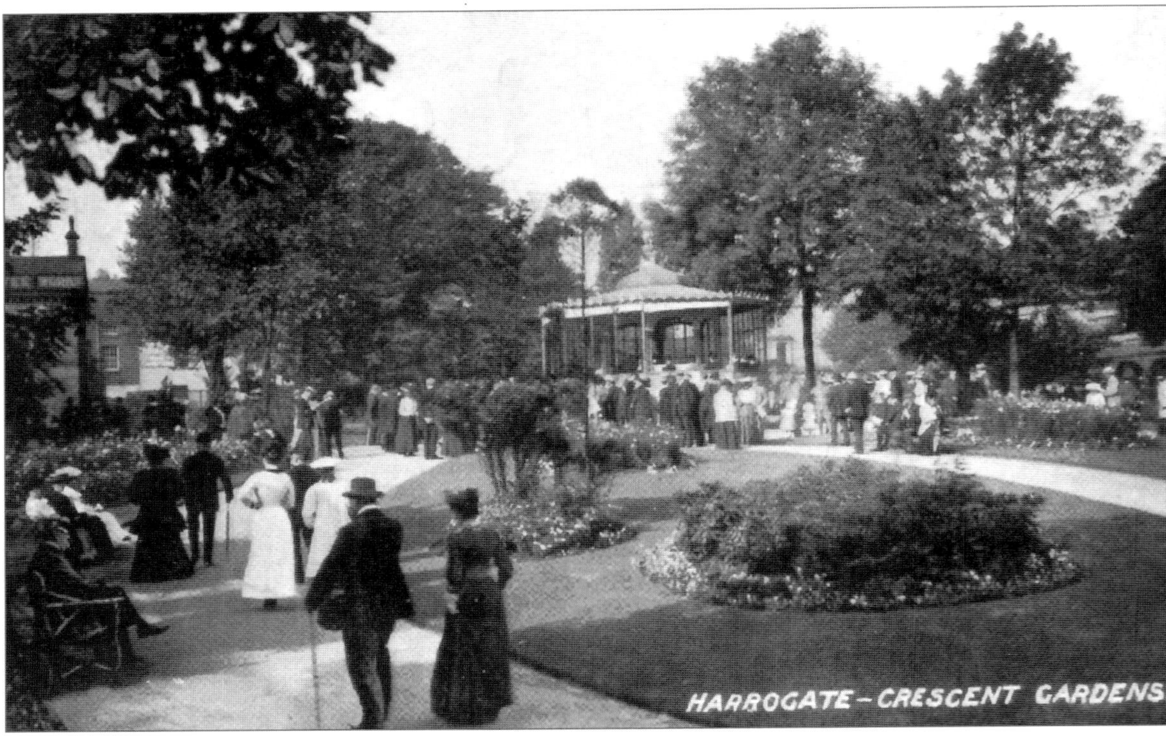

Crescent Gardens, *c.* 1901. The elegant town dubbed itself 'the Mecca of the ailing, the playground of the robust', but the fashionable side of town life is brought out in many photographs of times past such as this. In this summer scene a well-dressed crowd is gathered round the bandstand with its delicate poles and canopy. On the right is a building labelled Coffee Works. Rustic seats and the layout of blossoming, orderly flower beds make the pleasant gardens complete, although the majority of people seem to be enjoying strolling and chatting in order to show off their up-to-the-minute outfits.

In 1832 on the site of Crescent Gardens John Williams, connected with Cheltenham, another famous spa town, built the Victoria Baths. New Victoria Baths were opened forty years later at a time following the in-filling of Central Harrogate, the land that lay between the original hamlets of Low and High Harrogate, much of which had for a long time been purely agricultural.

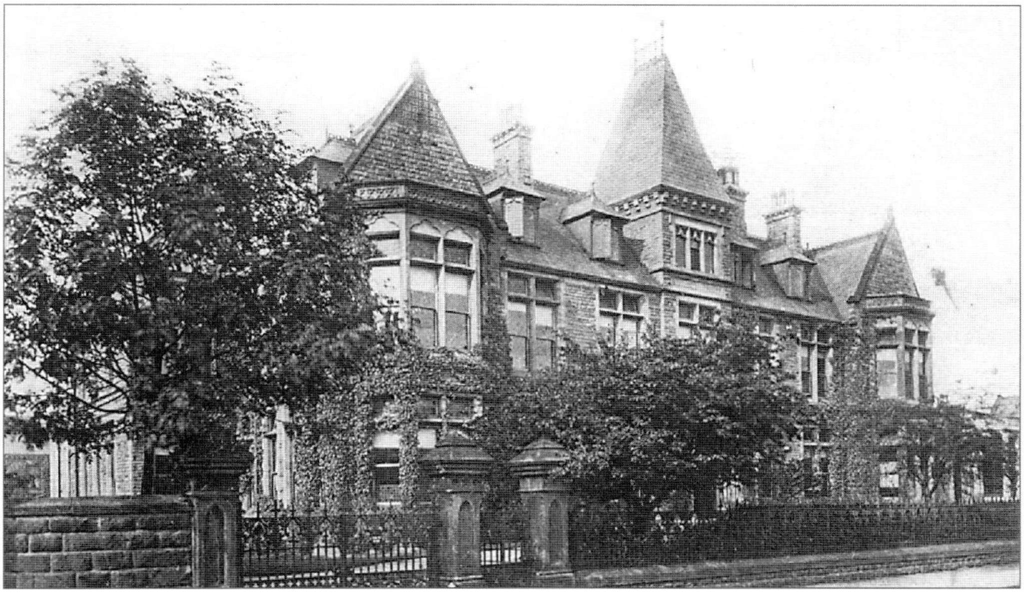

Harrogate Infirmary, *c.* 1903. This was opened on 18 July 1889 by the Duke of Clarence. Triumphal arches were erected in the town to welcome him, notaby one near the station. In 1824 Lord Harewood had founded the Bath Hospital for which £36,000 was raised by public subscription. Beneficial spa waters were pumped to this building for the cure of poor patients, of whom 2,181 were admitted between 1826 and 1837.

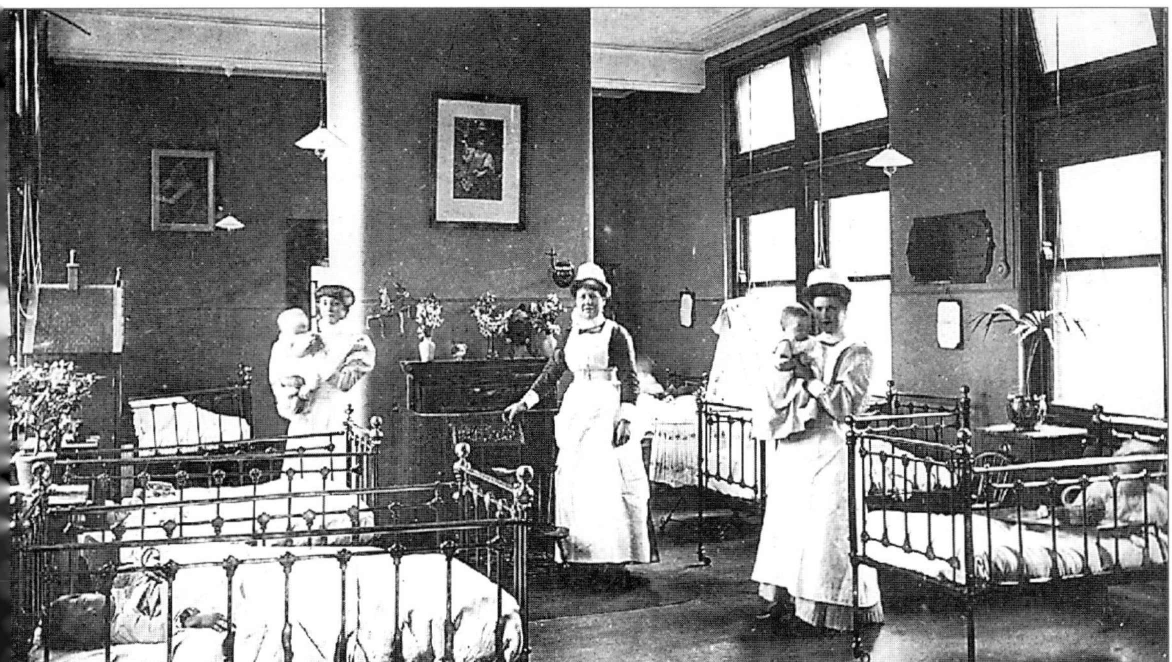

Interior of Harrogate Infirmary, the Children's Ward, 1903. Lord Harewood's avowed wish was that skilled hospital treatment, sometimes involving the benefits of the Harrogate cures, should be available for people and their children who might otherwise not be able to afford it.

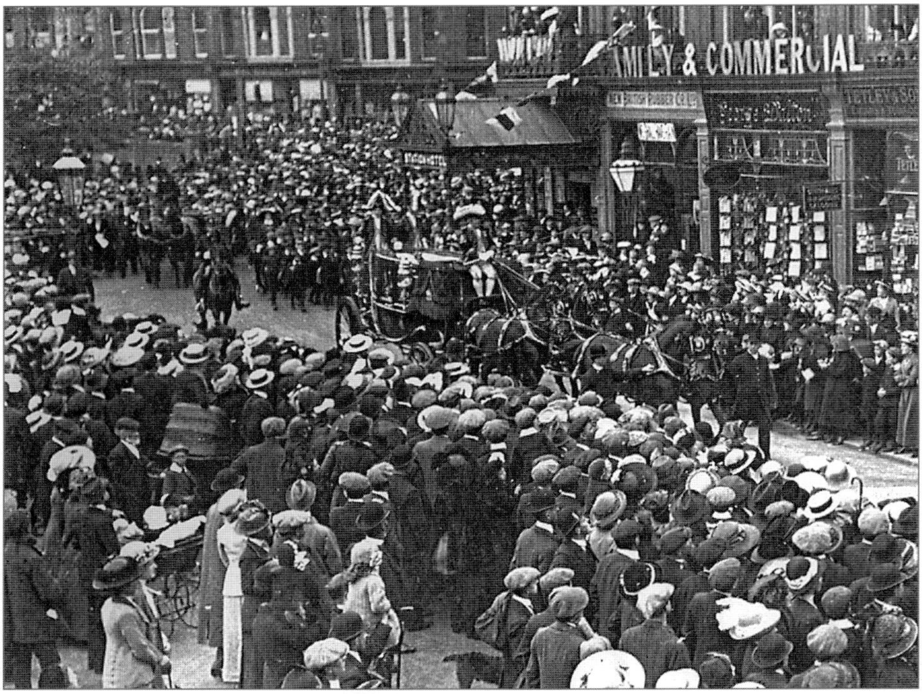

Harrogate gave itself up to civic splendour when the Lord Mayor of London, Sir David Burnett, came to open the Annexe to the Royal Pump Room on 7 June 1913. With liveried footmen in attendance, he can be seen in his coach drawn by four horses passing the Station Hotel, the premises of the New British Rubber Company and Tetley and Sons.

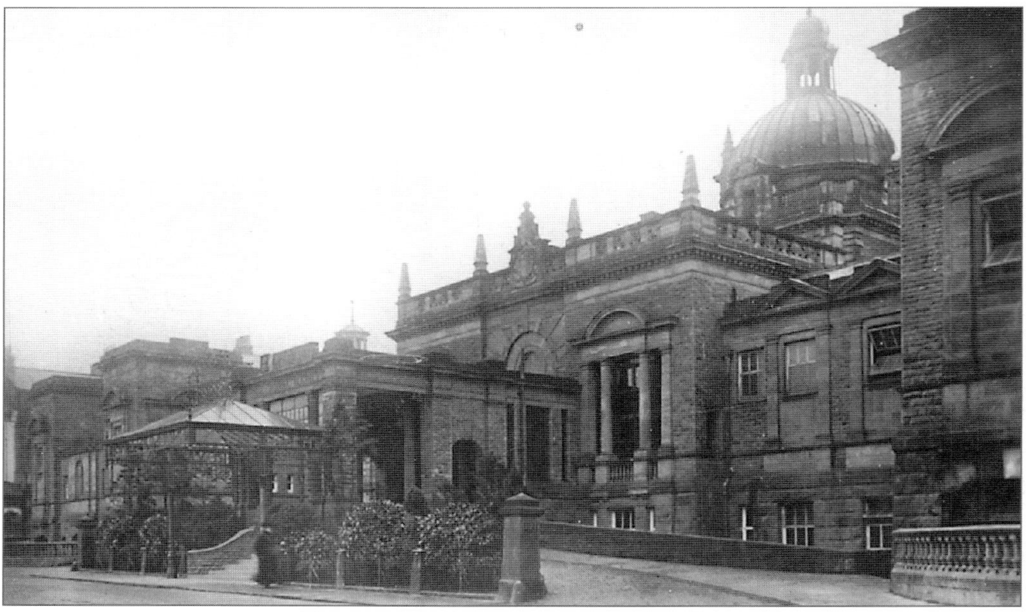

The Royal Baths, 1916, showing the glass and iron extension opened by the Lord Mayor of London. Four hundred guests including medical men, the Mayors and Mayoresses of important Yorkshire towns and other dignitaries were invited to attend the ceremony and banquet. They drove through a town festooned with decorations.

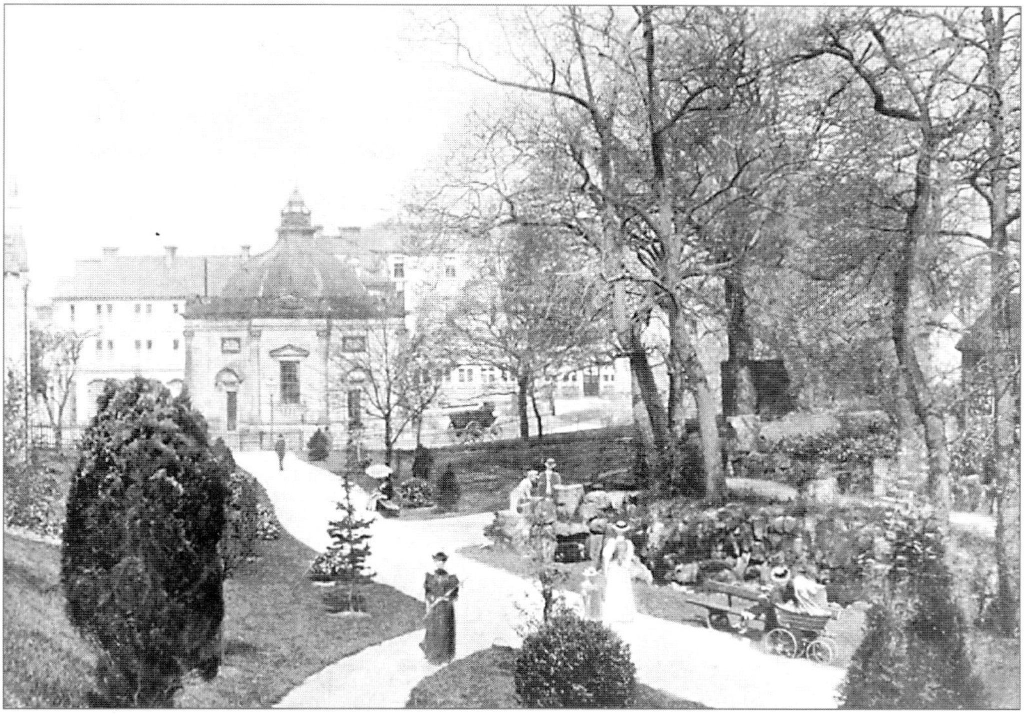

In 1902 *Pictorial England and Wales* printed photographs of all the important tourist places. The one of Bogs Valley Gardens represented Harrogate which was described in glowing terms: 'This celebrated British Spa has had a reputation for medical waters since 1571 . . . chalybeate, saline and sulphur springs abound in the town.'

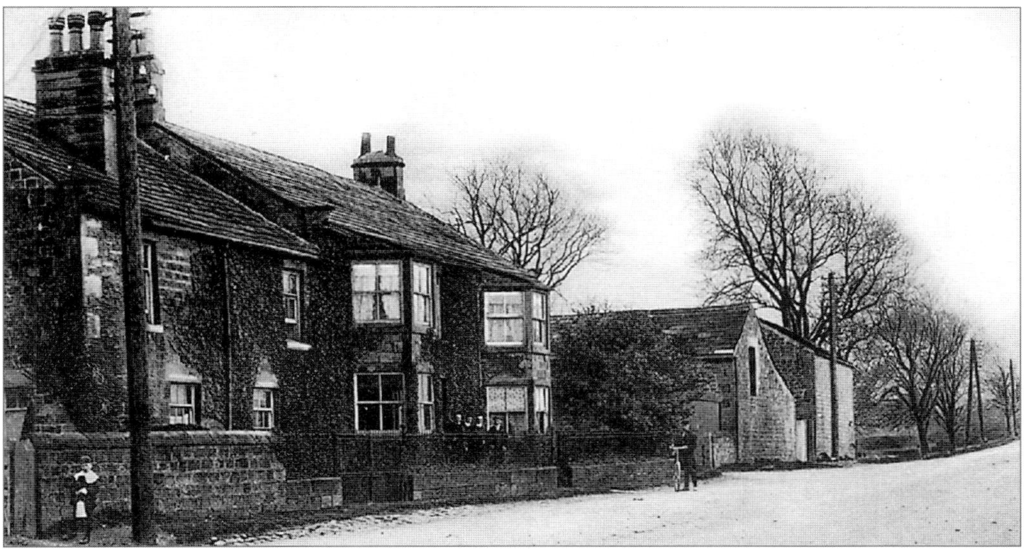

Spacey Houses near Harrogate, 1906. This was a favourite public house, Spacey being the family name of the publican. Not far away was Pannal Ash where five huge ash trees were cut down in 1810. Their trunks, measuring 6 feet in diameter, had been a prominent landmark and so were greatly missed. The busiest turnpike road ran from Harewood Bridge through Spacey Houses and Harrogate to Killinghall Bridge.

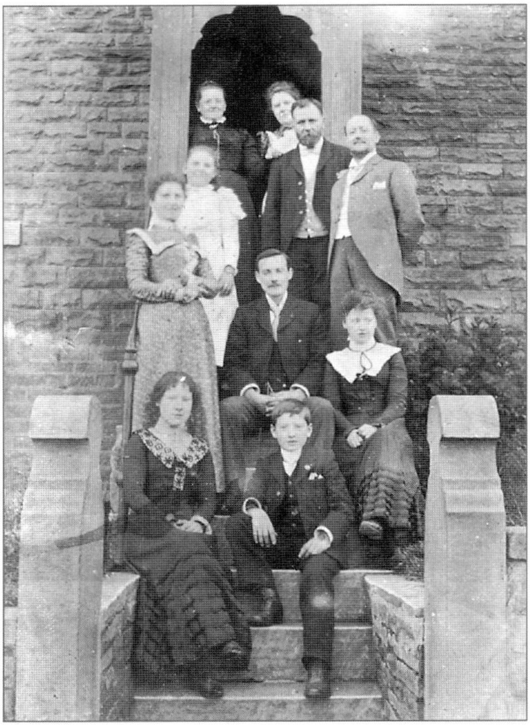

A Harrogate family gathering, *c.* 1889. As the town approached its zenith everybody wanted to experience the round of pleasure and health-giving qualities. There was provision for all. The Granby, where duchesses and eminent statesmen stayed, offered luxurious, expensive accommodation, as did the Crown, the George, the Queen, the Prospect and the White Hart. The lodging houses around Park View, Belmont Road and Cold Bath Road (once known as Robin Hood Lane) catered more for the rank and file visitors. These were conveniently situated for the Royal Baths, exclusive shops, the gardens and lovely countryside. That authority on English architecture, Sir Nikolaus Pevsner, classed the White Hart Hotel as the finest building in the Spa in his monumental work 'The Buildings of England' of 1951–74.

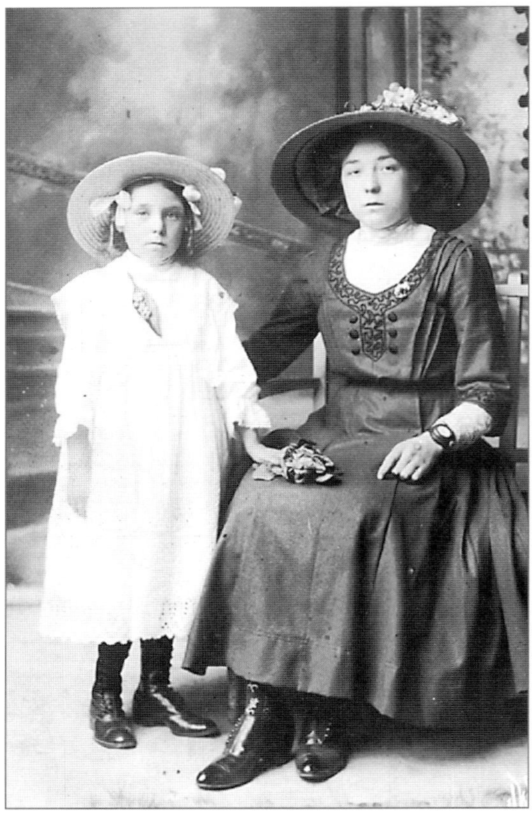

Sisters Mary and Lillian Lord in Sunday best clothes with button-boots and new Whitsuntide hats are photographed in a Harrogate studio, 1923. It was customary to buy new outfits for the whole family to greet the sun. Mary, the little girl, has a white dress, almost certainly intended for taking part in the Whitsuntide procession from her church back home. In the background can be seen the usual trappings of 'bobbed' chemille curtains. The Lords, who came from Lancashire, were great trippers up and down England when annual holidays came round. Before the Second World War they graduated to trips to the Continent.

Enterprising photographers like Lonsdale Yates set up studios alongside their existing businesses in Harrogate. Lonsdale sold 'pure ices' and had a hot peas stall pulled by a donkey. In 1890 on the side of his four-wheeled contraption he lettered 'Yates's Tit Bits Studio'. Photography for the masses was still in its infancy but the Camera Club with studio, enlarging room and library had many members.

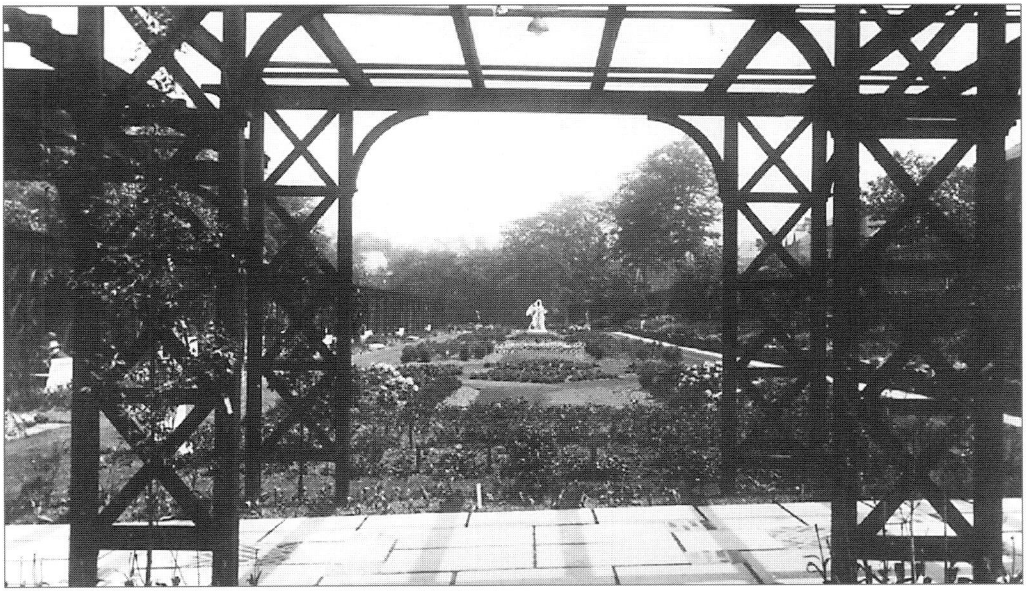

Royal Hall Gardens, 1929. Harrogate's most attractive features are its open spaces and gardens. In 1793 Bachelors' Garden School was built by brothers Francis and Richard Taylor in a garden, and the land they left for its support was laid out as gardens.

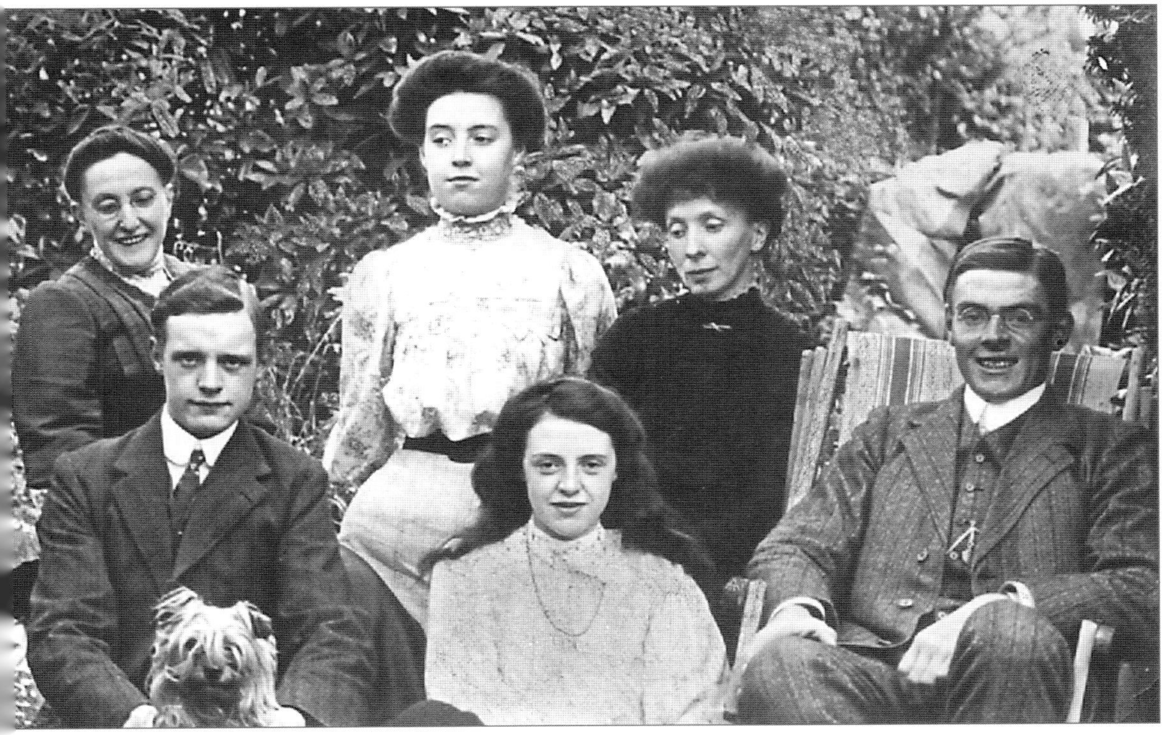

A Manchester family (mother and two daughters, centre) were photographed at Harrogate from where they had toured the Yorkshire Dales, 1919. In glorious weather they visited Pykingcroft Farm, Killinghall, 2 miles away. This village is mentioned in Domesday Book as Chenihalle or Kennel Hall, the district having been part of a forest where hunting dogs were kept.

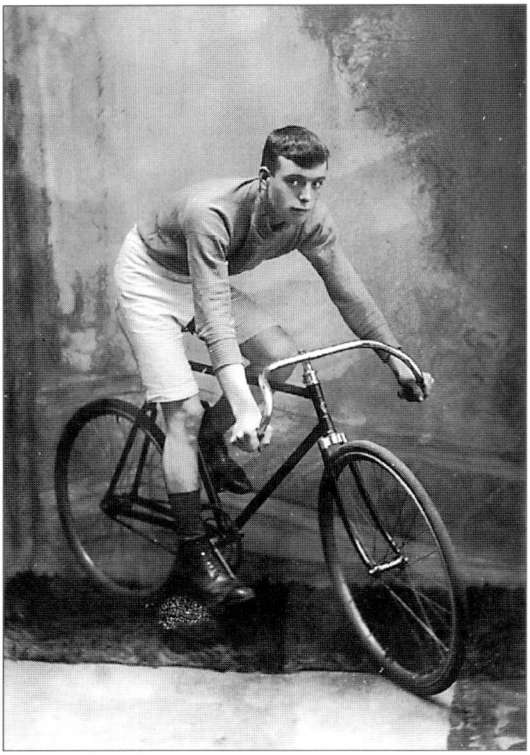

Member of Harrogate Cycling Club, a studio portrait from the days of the cycle club craze, 1911. It was customary to be photographed with, for example, bicycle, tennis racquet, hockey stick or musical instrument according to one's interest. On special occasions photographers encouraged the wearing of Sunday best and sometimes working clothes, so it was not surprising to see miners with their lamps against a studio backdrop. There were recognised places such as inns, 'cyclists' rests', temperance huts and public houses that catered for them on long 'spins' up hill and down dale in Yorkshire. Cycling in Harrogate is commemorated by a plaque at the Hotel St George garden: 'The first cycling club in the world was formed here on August 5th 1878 when a group of cyclists founded the Bicycle Touring Club which became the Cyclists' Touring Club in 1883.' The George Inn, which became St George, had an excellent site on the Ripon turnpike road.

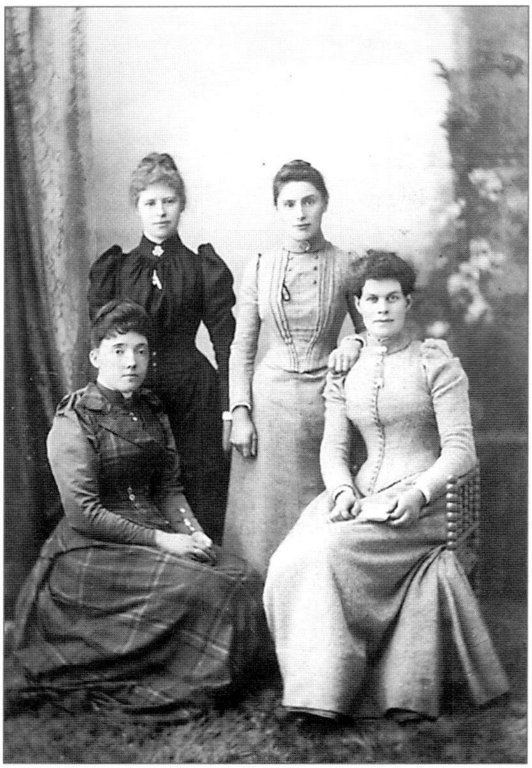

Nellie Bates, standing on the right with her three friends from Oswestry, was enjoying visits to Harrogate almost a hundred years ago. Nellie collected country recipes some of which, still preserved in her family, are to appear shortly in a book on traditional Yorkshire recipes. They included port wine made from elderflowers, beetroot wine recommended for anaemic girls, cleat wine, herb beer and fennel water which was believed to have antiseptic qualities. North Yorkshire families were famed for home-cooked meats produced at christening teas and funeral breakfasts. A North Yorkshire brawn recipe is as follows: ½ lb shin beef; 1 cow heel; ½ lb ham or oxtail. Cover with water and cook for 4 hours along with 4 peppercorns, 2 bay leaves, 4 cloves and a bunch of herbs, the last 4 ingredients tied up in muslin. Add a finely chopped onion as well. Slow simmering is the secret. Allow to cool, remove meat from bones and place in a mould. Strain the stock over the meat and leave to set on a cold, marble larder shelf. If you are happy eating beef, slices of this brawn are delicious, especially in summer with crisp salad.

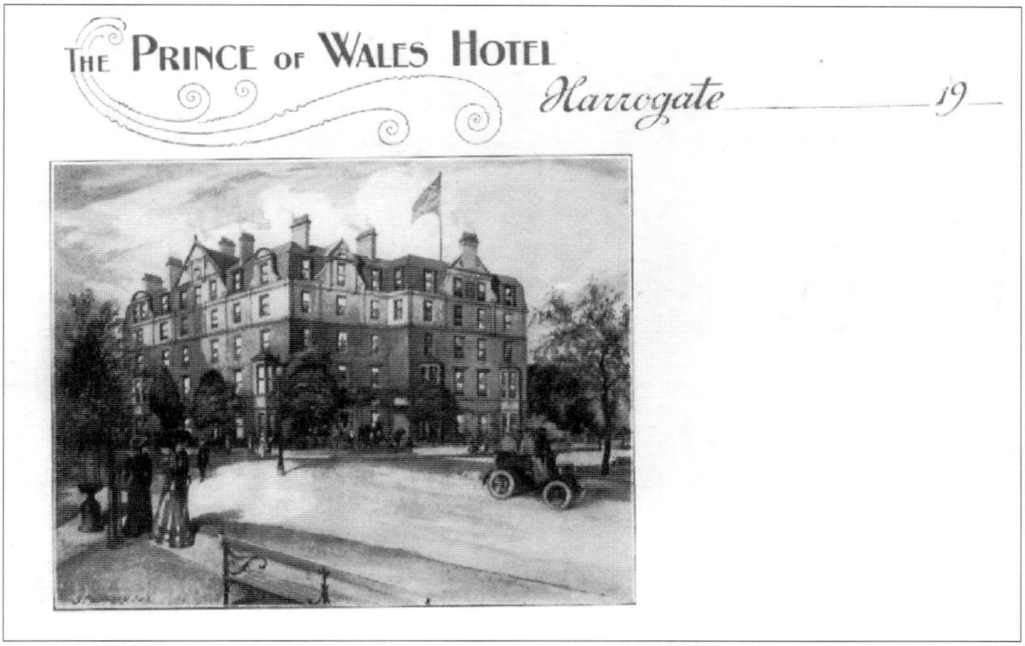

The Prince of Wales Hotel courtesy card of the early 1900s. Built at the main turnpike crossroads (Leeds to Ripon, Otley to Knaresborough), it was known in early days as Hattersley's but has now been made into luxury flats. The old boundary of the turnpike roads, a tall gritstone pillar, has been preserved.

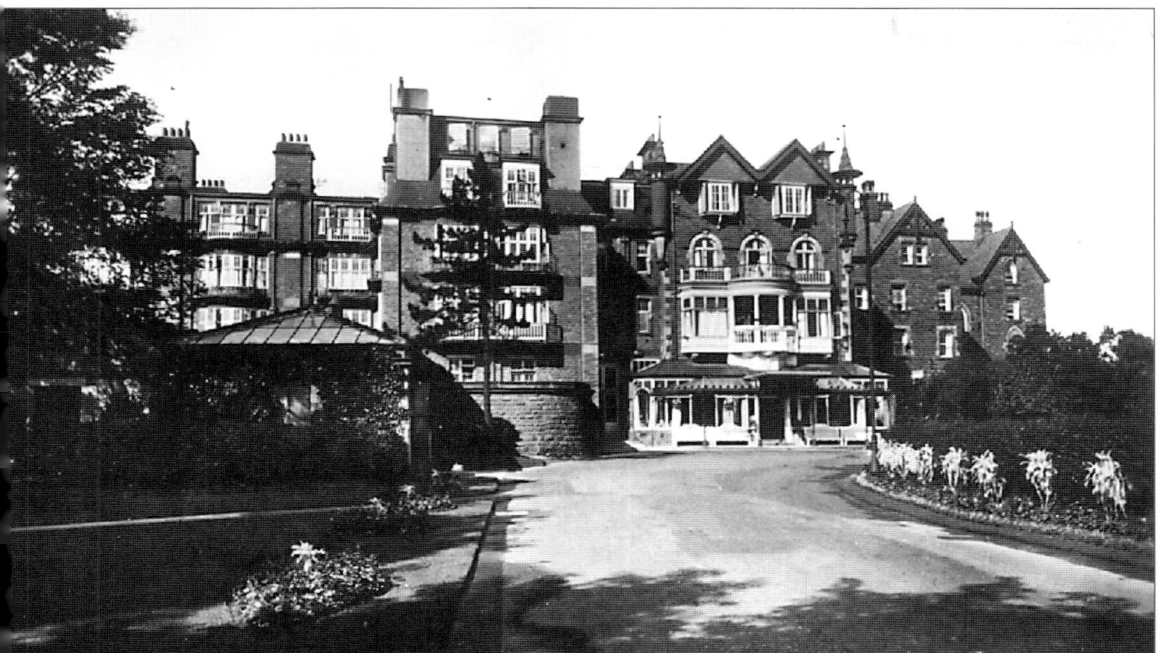

The Cairn on Ripon Road, 1930s. As at the Harrogate Hydro (formerly the Swan) and the Harlow Manor Hydro, treatment facilities and hotel accommodation were available in the same building. This was appreciated by invalids in bath chairs. Built in 1890, the Swan was originally called the Cairn Hydropathic.

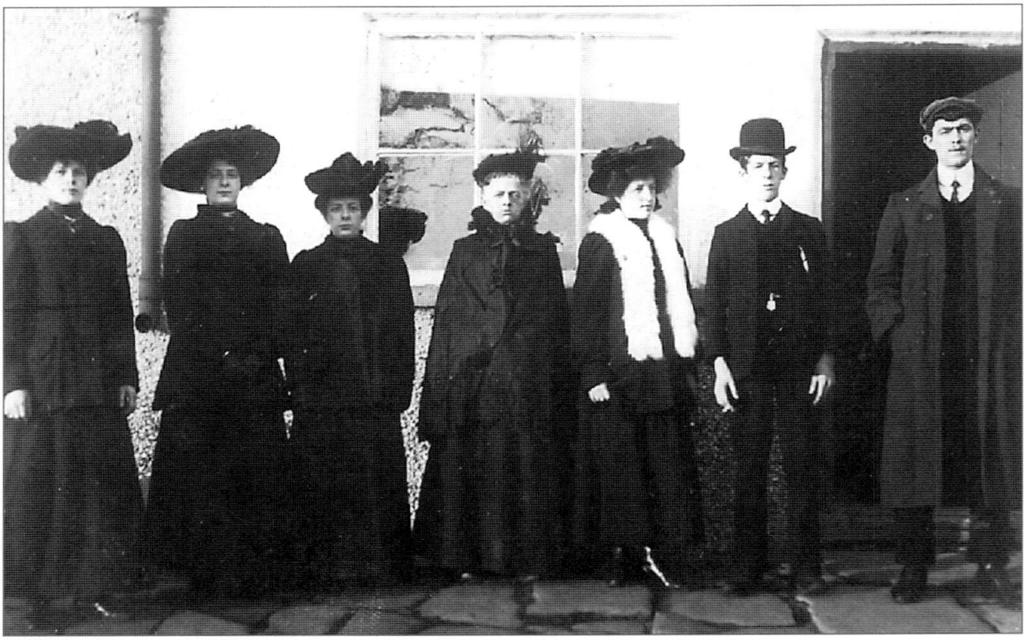

Visitors to Harrogate took advantage of the increased services made by the Hydropathic Company and the recently incorporated Borough. Storage tanks and reservoirs conserving water from thirty different mineral springs in the splendidly laid out Valley Gardens, complete with walks and bandstand, were all ready in time for Queen Victoria's Golden Jubilee in 1887.

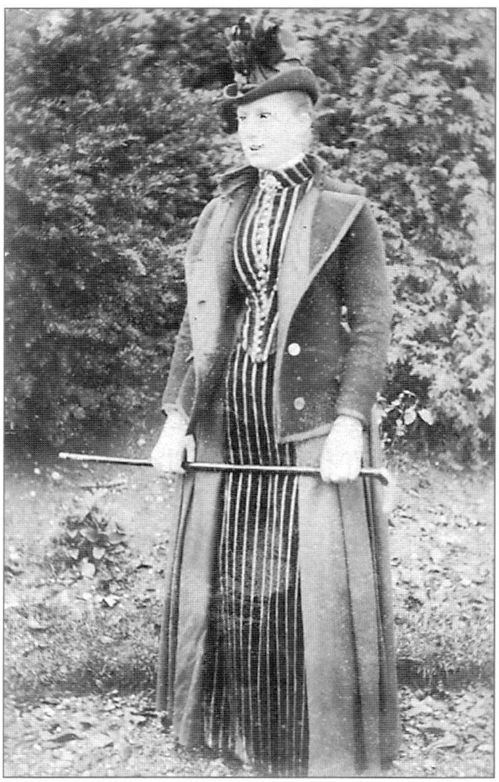

In the 1880s, at the time of this photograph, riding and hunting were popular with yeomen farmers, gentry and visitors, North Yorkshire's broad acres being ideally suited. The York and Ainsty (north), the Bramham Moor Hounds and the Bilton and Airedale Beagles with their water hounds met 'in easy distance of Harrogate and enjoyed unhindered coursing'. From the 1860s the Annual Meet of the Hounds was held in Low Harrogate where participants assembled in front of the Crown Hotel watched by a crowd. The men wore shiny 'chimney pot' hats and the ladies crinoline gowns, some favouring Scottish plaid shawls made popular by Queen Victoria. Such details are gleaned from old photographs of the town in those days.

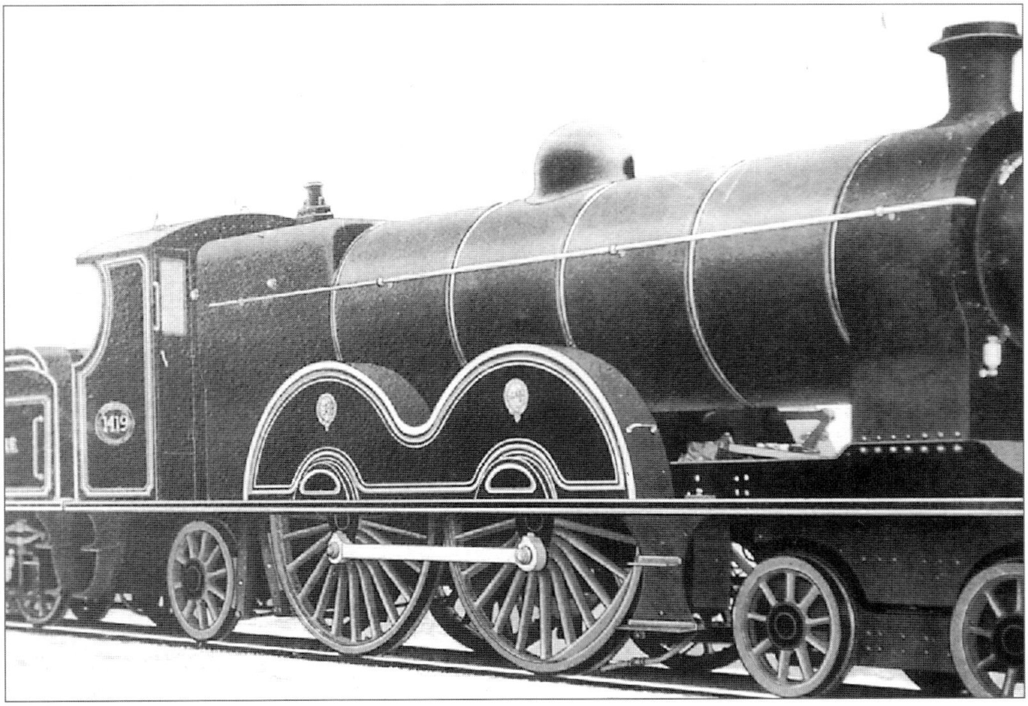

Lancashire and Yorkshire steam locomotive No. 1419, photographed in 1889. Designed by John Aspinall, this was the prototype of a successful class intended for work in hilly country such as North Yorkshire. In 1923 the Harrogate to London Pullman was introduced. On West Park Stray a large boulder commemorates the site of Brunswick station.

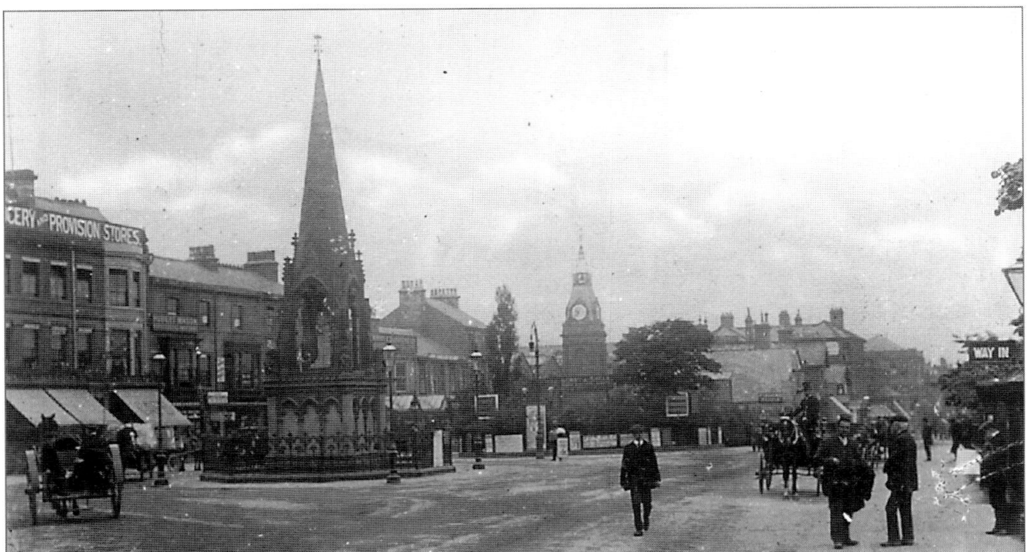

Station Square, where the writer of this postcard stayed the night at the Station Hotel, 1924. The 1904 *Railway Clearing House Handbook* shows that at Harrogate North Eastern, which served Leeds and Ripon, other companies converged: Lancashire & Yorkshire, Great Northern, Midland. From York, lines fanned out across the Pennines, to the coast, to Harrogate and to London. The Market Clock is to the right of Queen Victoria's memorial.

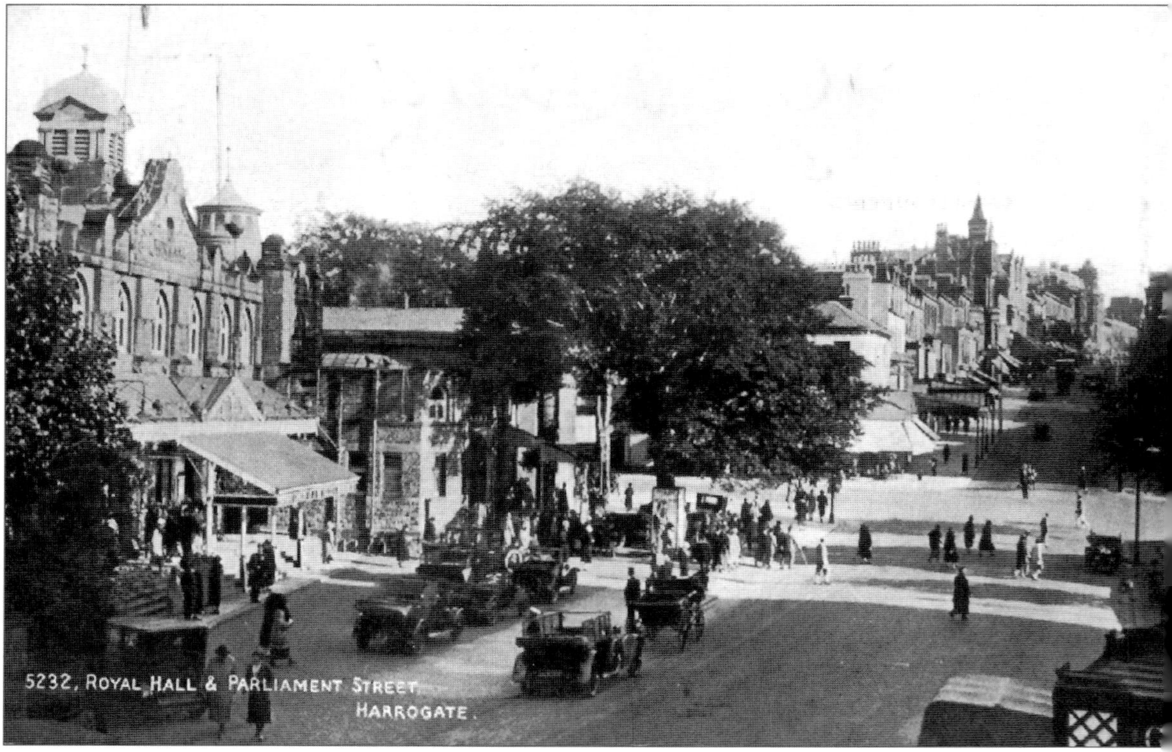

Royal Hall and Parliament Square, *c.* 1920. The name Kursaal, dating from 1903, still to be seen in the stonework of the frontage, was changed to Royal as during the First World War anything Germanic became abhorrent. Built in Renaissance style in yellow stone and standing in 6 acres of ground, the Hall was further enhanced by a belt of trees. Situated in a valley, the building was sheltered from all winds. Along with R.J. Beale, Frank Matcham, theatre architect who built 'the prettiest theatre in the kingdom' (The Grand at Blackpool), designed the Kursaal. In addition to the great theatre at the Royal Hall were reading rooms, smoking rooms and a café. Tennis courts and bowling greens were laid out in the grounds. Entertainment in Harrogate was lavish, from the Royal Spa Concert Rooms to the Grand Opera House in Oxford Street – where first-class operatic and dramatic companies appeared nightly.

A chain of large, successful theatres in Yorkshire included the Theatre Royal, Leeds, where Charlie Chaplin appeared in 1898, the Sheffield Empire which could accommodate 3,000 people, and the Empire Theatre, Bradford, founded by Sir Edward Moss, where Lottie Lennox, Vesta Tilley and Little Tich appeared, as they did at Harrogate. Other great artistes to appear in Harrogate were Sarah Bernhardt, Ellen Terry, Kreisler, Paderewski and Pavlova, the last-mentioned a ballerina famed worldwide for her portrayal of the dying swan.

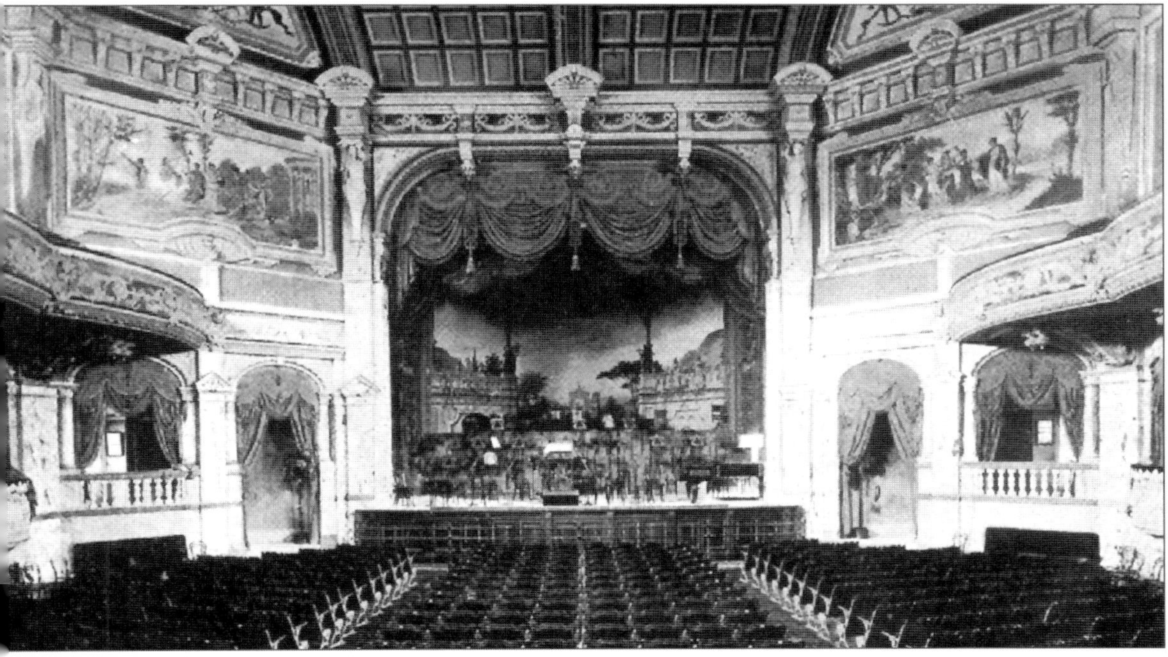

Interior of the Kursaal, 1906. Ornate ceiling, large coloured murals, velvet curtains, heavy gold swags, cosy boxes and a grand proscenium were all expressions of what was expected from lavish, Edwardian theatre productions. Audiences of up to 1,300 enjoyed dressing up for these glittering occasions.

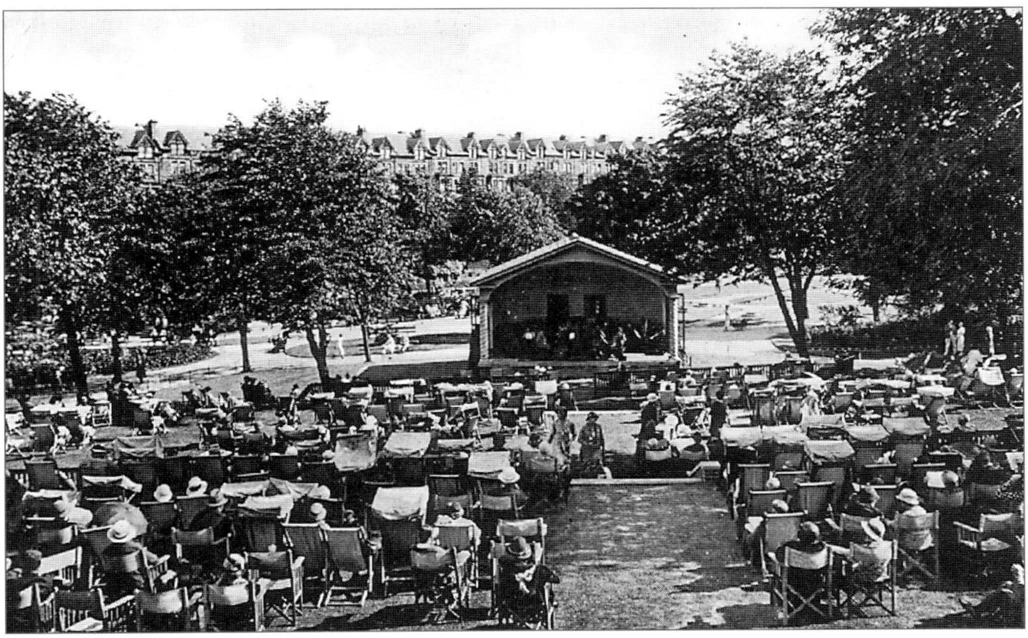

The bandstand, Valley Gardens, summer 1941. Entered from Valley Road or Cornwall Road, these superb gardens were enlarged to their present size in 1901. In 1945 officers and nurses of the US Army 216th General Hospital Division erected a commemorative stone in Valley Gardens. In serving their country during the Second World War they 'spent happy days in Harrogate'.

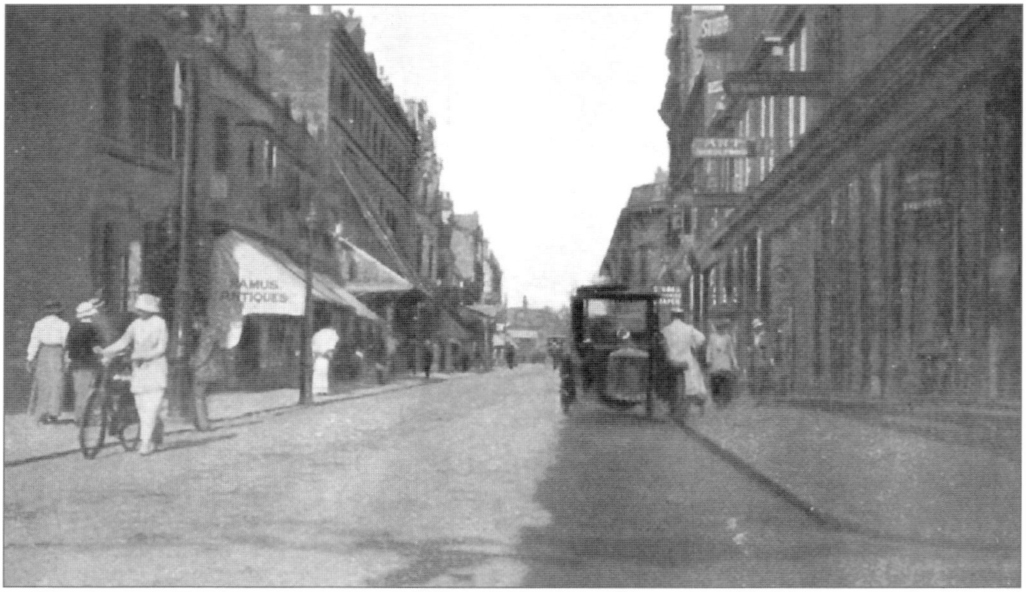

James Street, *c.* 1912, when Ramus Antiques (left) and Stubbs Drapers (right), who had an Art Needlework department at no. 35, were beginning to serve customers arriving by car. Tom Coleman, fancy goods dealer, had premises at 24 Lowther Arcade and 28 Market Hall. This is one of a series of Harrogate street views issued by him.

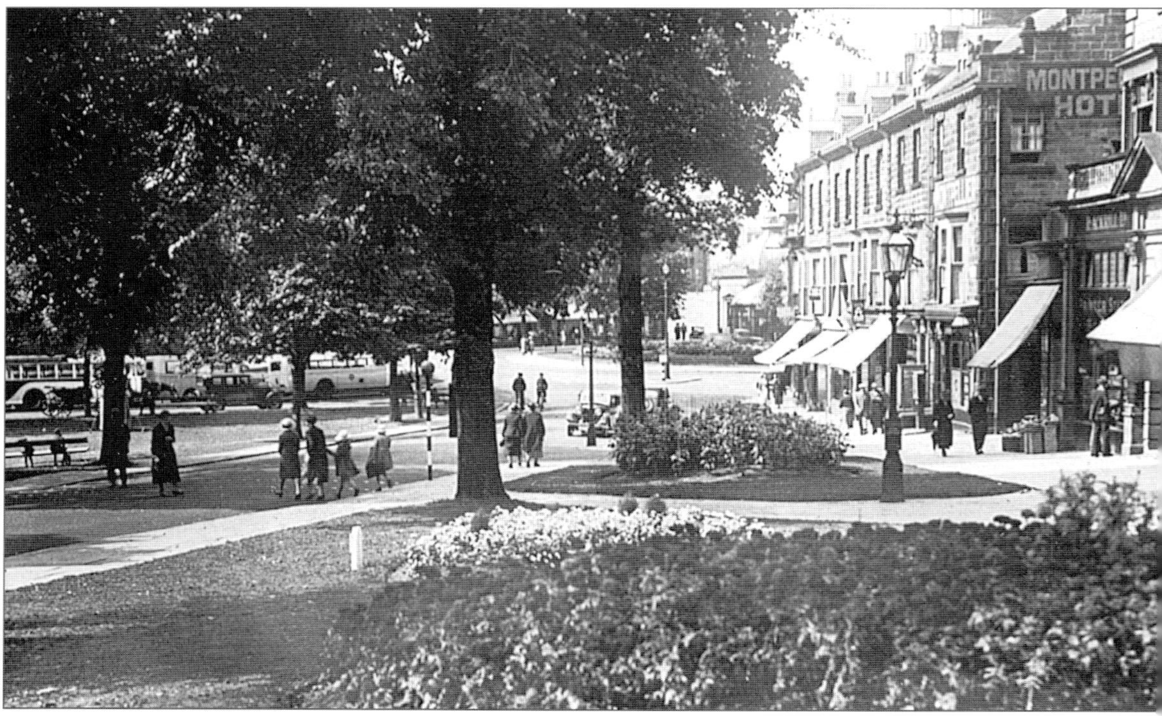

Montpellier Parade in full leaf and bloom, August 1946. On the right is the Montpellier Hotel. The Thackwray family, quite a power in the land, originally owned Montpellier Gardens and Montpellier Square. Joseph Thackwray, a great-uncle of the Joseph Thackwray of 1834, who built the Montpellier or Crown Baths, had built the Crown Hotel in 1740.

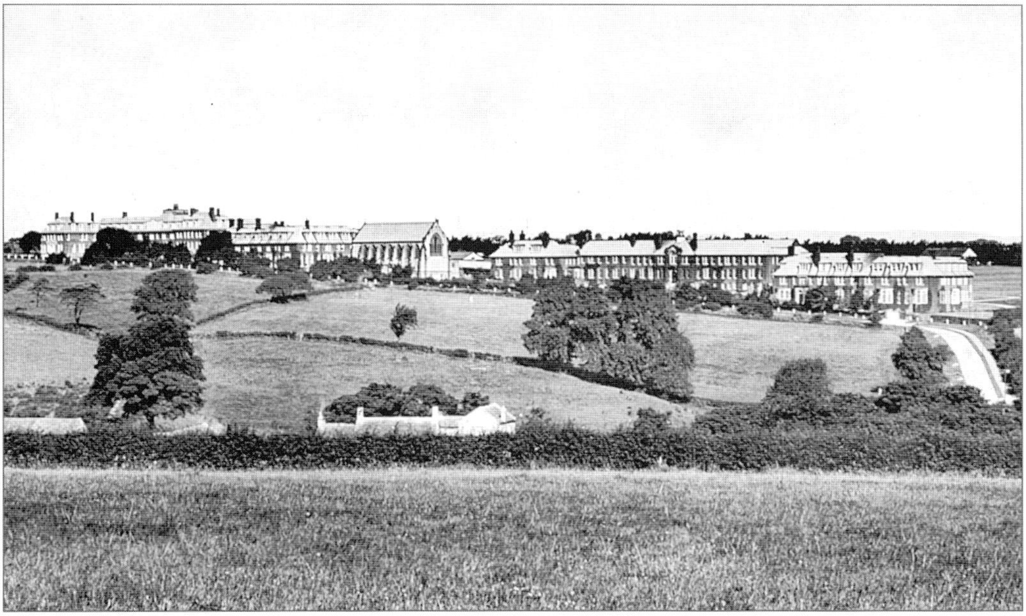

Queen Ethelberga's public school for girls, photographed in about 1926, was opened by the Duchess of Albany in 1912. With the purity of Harrogate's water and unpolluted moorland air extolled by doctors, the town's reputation as a centre of excellence for healthy life promoted the establishment of private boarding and day schools. The building has since been demolished and Queen Ethelberga's School moved to Thorpe Underwood Hall.

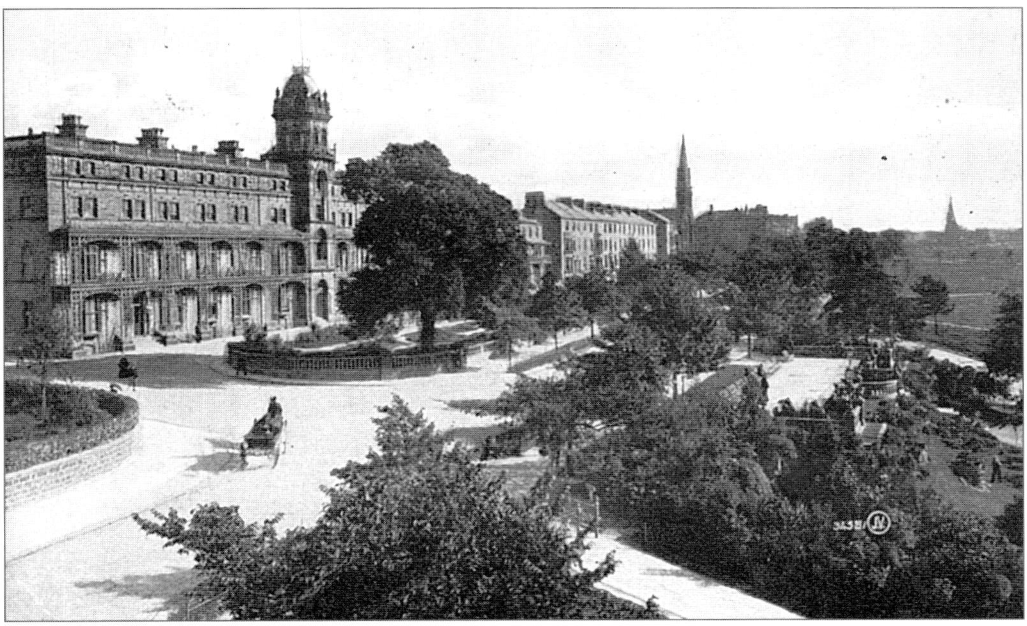

Looking south from Prospect Square, *c.* 1890, before the 'Pierhead' and gardens had been made and before motor vehicles arrived. The Prospect Hotel was built in 1859 and later enlarged. Burgess's Livery Stables of White Hart Mews provided the victorias and wagonettes. They also had a riding school at Victoria Park.

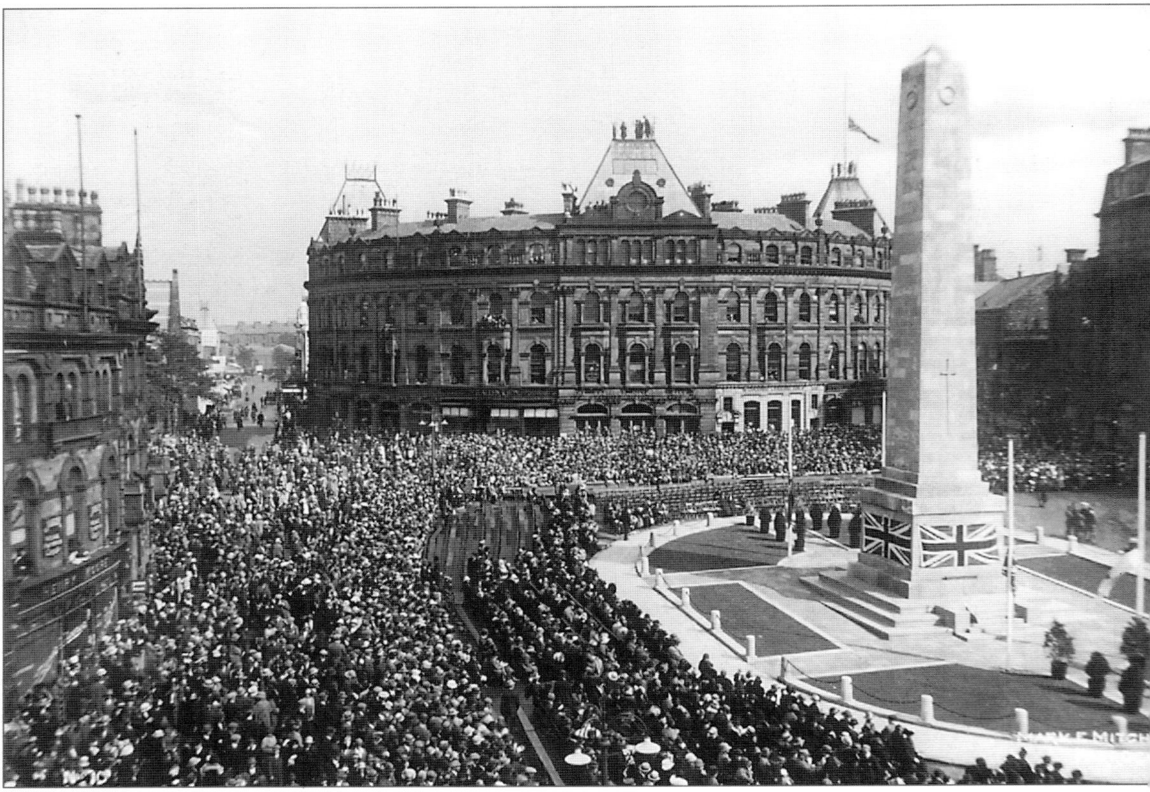

Unveiling of the War Memorial in the presence of Princess Mary and Viscount Lascelles, 1 September 1923. The rows of soldiers who stood in silent tribute received a water baptism as it was a very wet occasion. On two sides of this imposing obelisk of white Portland stone were placed two bronze panels bearing the names of 841 men and women who gave their lives in the First World War. The site of the Memorial in Prospect Square was ideal, with St Peter's Church in close proximity and the classical sweep of Cambridge Crescent in the background. It was also a prestigious business area with Lloyd's Bank, Betty's Café Tea Rooms and other well-known shops.

The guests of honour, Princess Mary and Viscount Lascelles, who first lived at Goldsborough Hall and later at Harewood House, took an interest in the town. Princess Mary's mother, Queen Mary, enjoyed antiques hunting in Harrogate. In 1928 she saw a set of fire screens, made by a Yorkshireman Wilfred Dowson, which had been awarded first prize at Harrogate Festival. She bought them for use at Buckingham Palace. (North Yorkshire County Library)

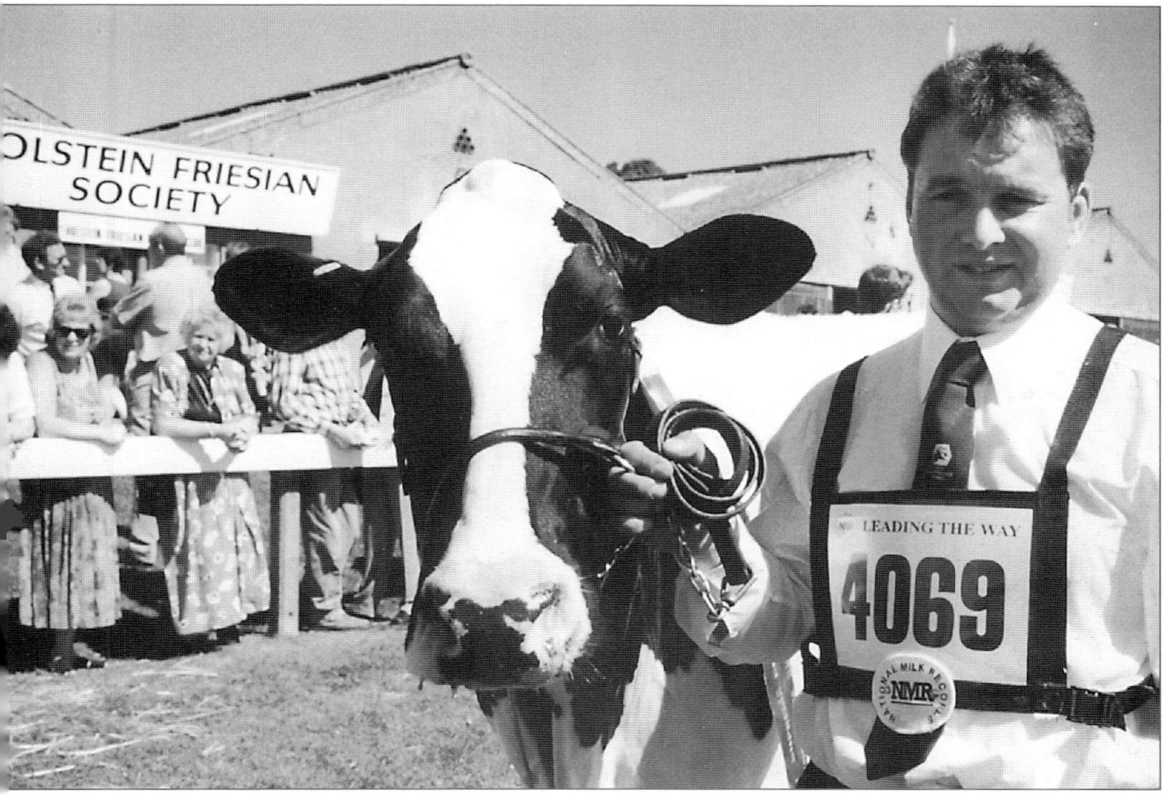

The Great Yorkshire Show, 1970s. This photograph highlights the importance of black and white Friesian herds. Their enormous milk yields led to the adoption of this breed throughout the country. No. 4069 was the winner of the National Milk Records Award. This annual three-day event staged at Harrogate in the second week of June is one of the United Kingdom's most prestigious agricultural shows. It has become a huge crowd-drawing event, classed as a marvellous day out for the family as there is so much variety in what it has to offer: animals, flowers, crafts, dancing, show-jumping.

With its capacity to handle crowds, transport system, conference centres and spacious surroundings, Harrogate proved to be the natural centre for many large events. Early spring heralds the one-week Harrogate International Youth Music Festival. Indoor and outdoor performances throughout the District of Harrogate reveal the talent of young musicians from around the world, to sing, play and dance. In mid-summer national and international performers come to Harrogate to present the North of England's premier Annual Arts Festival of music, theatre and outdoor entertainment. Another popular event is the three-day Harrogate Cricket Festival held in June at the County Ground. Harrogate is also host to the important Northern Antiques Fair held in the Royal Baths Assembly Rooms, the historic building which celebrates its centenary in 1997. Everything is for sale and all items must follow the strict rule of being at least 100 years old.

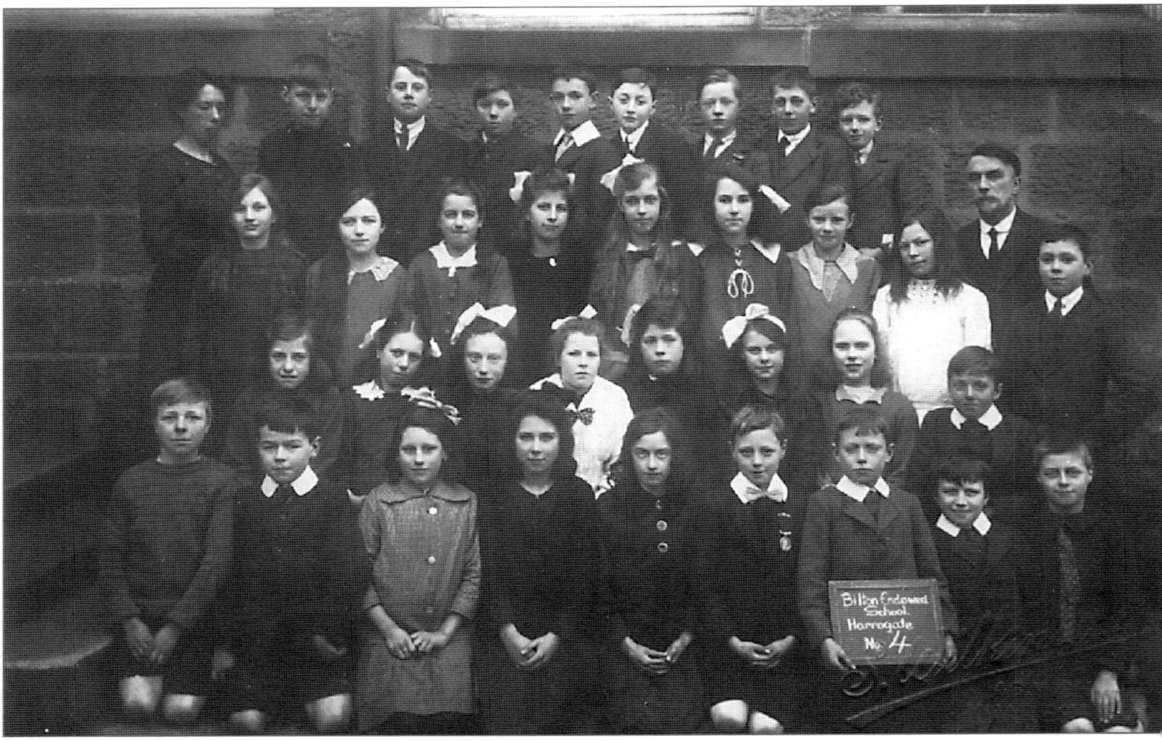

Bilton Endowed School, Bilton Lane, Class 4, *c*. 1920. The school was endowed in 1793 by the bachelor brothers Richard and Francis Taylor. The Infants' School in Church Square was endowed by William Sheepshanks who lived at The Mansion, Park Place, in the 1830s.

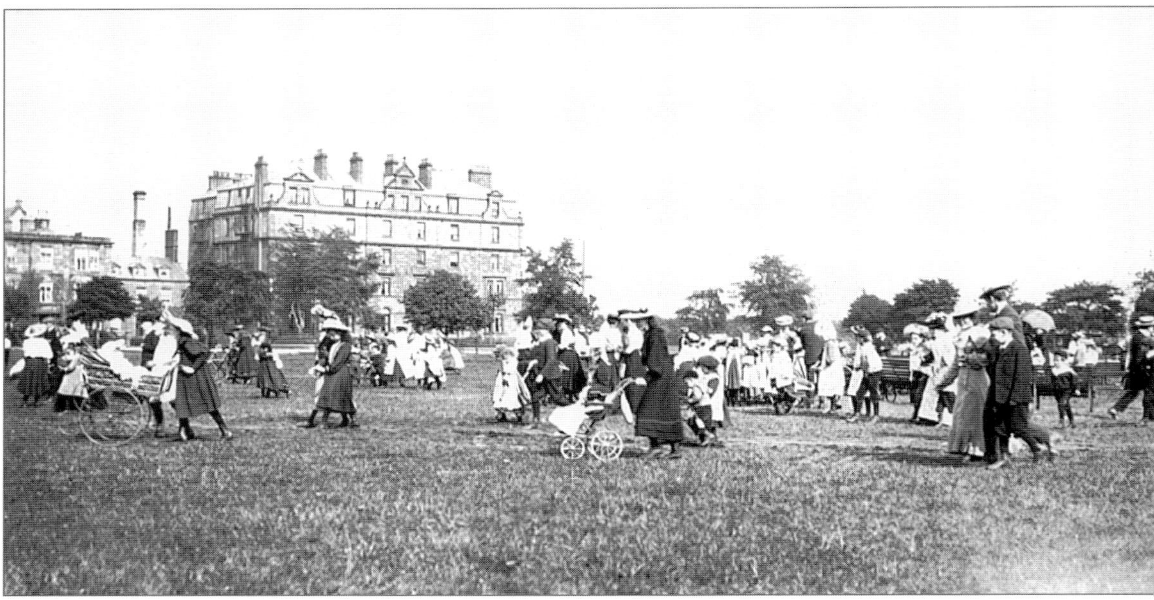

A special event for children, West Park Stray, with the Prince of Wales Hotel in the background, *c*. 1902. Under the 1778 Award the 200 acres of fine common stretching from the White Hart Hotel in Low Harrogate to the Granby Hotel in High Harrogate were to remain unenclosed for ever and 'all persons to have free access to the springs and be at liberty to use and drink the waters'.

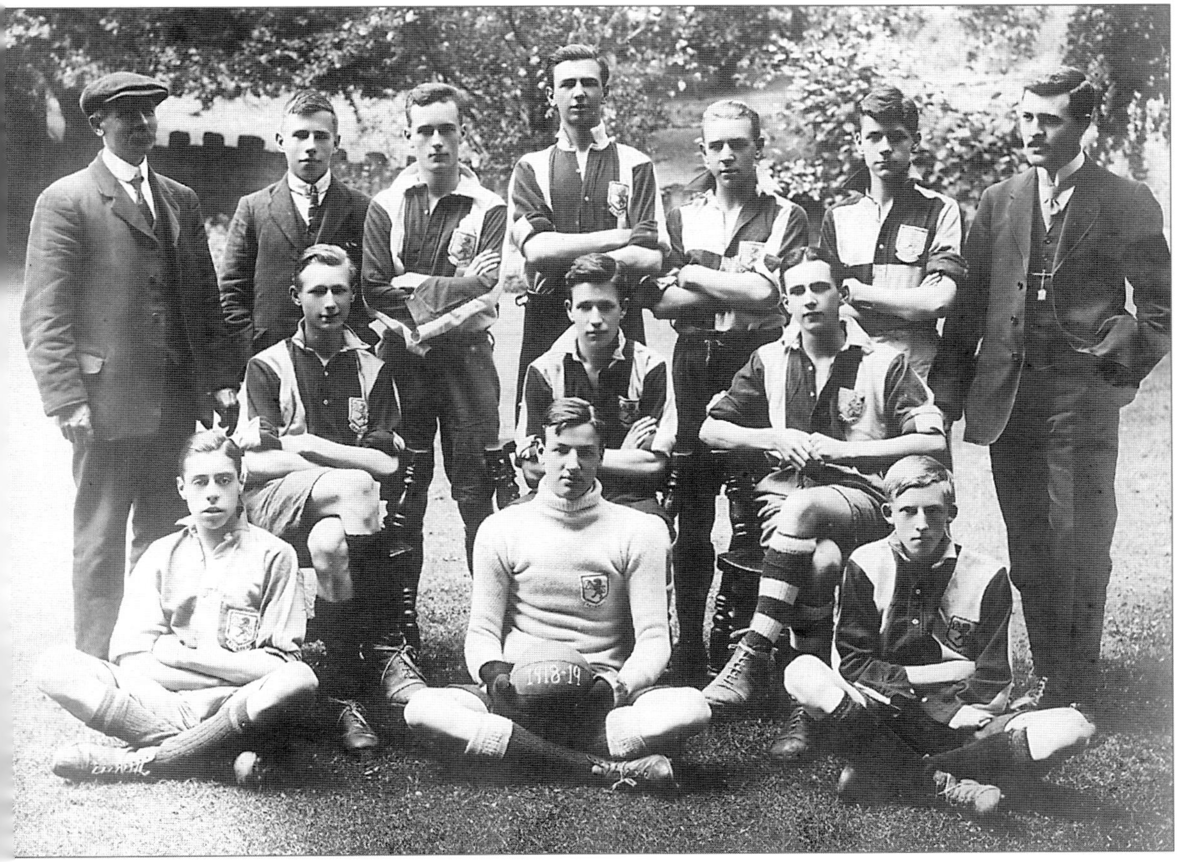

This football team, thought to come from the Harrogate area, was photographed in 1919 by a Sheffield man, G.T.Y. Dickinson, Fellow of the Royal Photographic Society. The names of the team may still have significance to some who recall the season of 1918–19. The two gentlemen far left and right respectively are J.W. Smith and S.T. Lewis, while the team are: ? Skerrit, A.F. Cooper, S. Newsome, E.J.G. Pinder, W.M. Clyde, I.T. Burdekin, A.H. Rodgers (captain), W.D. Baily, E.W. Kirk, A.M. Russell and S.R. Woods. Under a magnifying glass the badge appears to read 'Kursaal', an obvious link with Harrogate, but I would dearly like to know the origin. On the football scene the 'Blades' of Sheffield, Bradford City and the highly successful Shipley team of Crag Road United were all in the public eye when this team was going strong.

By the 1900s city parks provided boating, bowling, tennis, swimming, cricket and football. Cycling clubs, walking clubs and gymnastics were all part of a new open-air athleticism that gripped the nation. In Harrogate the huge, copper-domed Majestic Hotel had opened, then came the Grand in Cornwall Road, looking down on Valley Gardens. St Luke's Church had been built and the first sod cut by Alderman Fortune at the site chosen for Roundhill Reservoir.

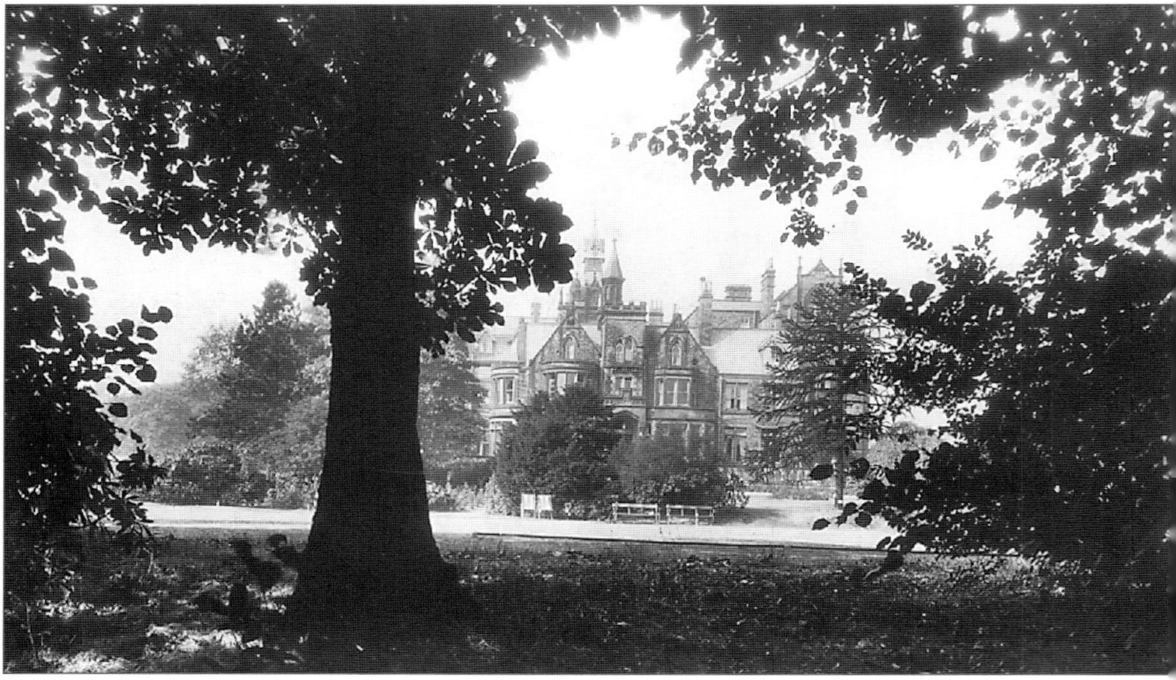

Harlow Manor, Cold Bath Road, 1936. Opposite was considered to be the site of the well of St Mungo who lived in 512 AD and was renowned for curing children. There is another St Mungo's Well at Copygrove Hall 8 miles away. Harlow Manor is included among fourteen hydropathic establishments and eighteen principal hotels listed in the 1930s.

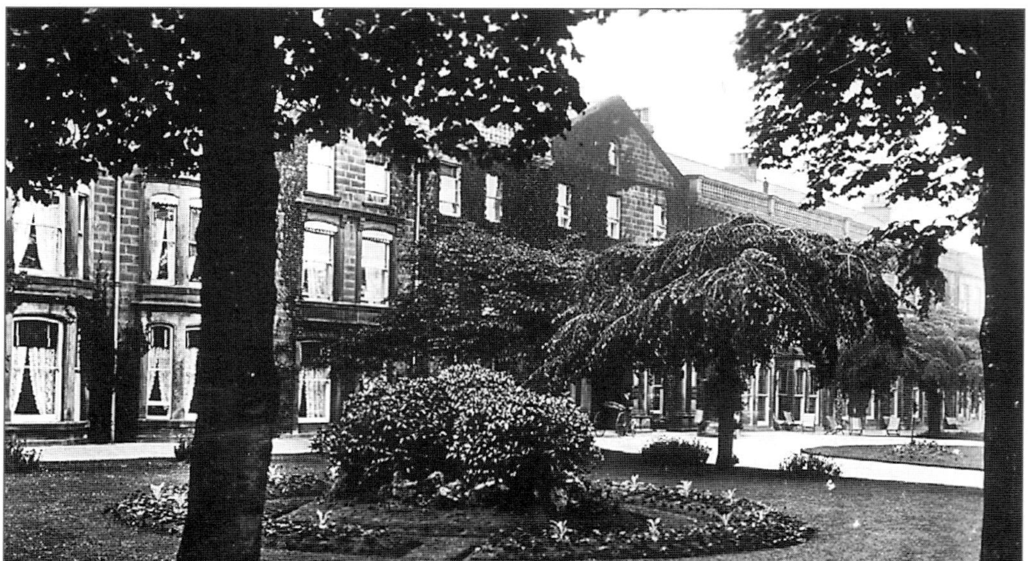

Queen Hotel, first called the Queen's Head, 1932. Dating from 1687, this could be the oldest hotel in Harrogate. In 1793 Clement Wolsley laid out a 1½-mile racecourse which ran in front of the Queen's Head. It had a flimsy grandstand, and races were held in August to suit visitors.

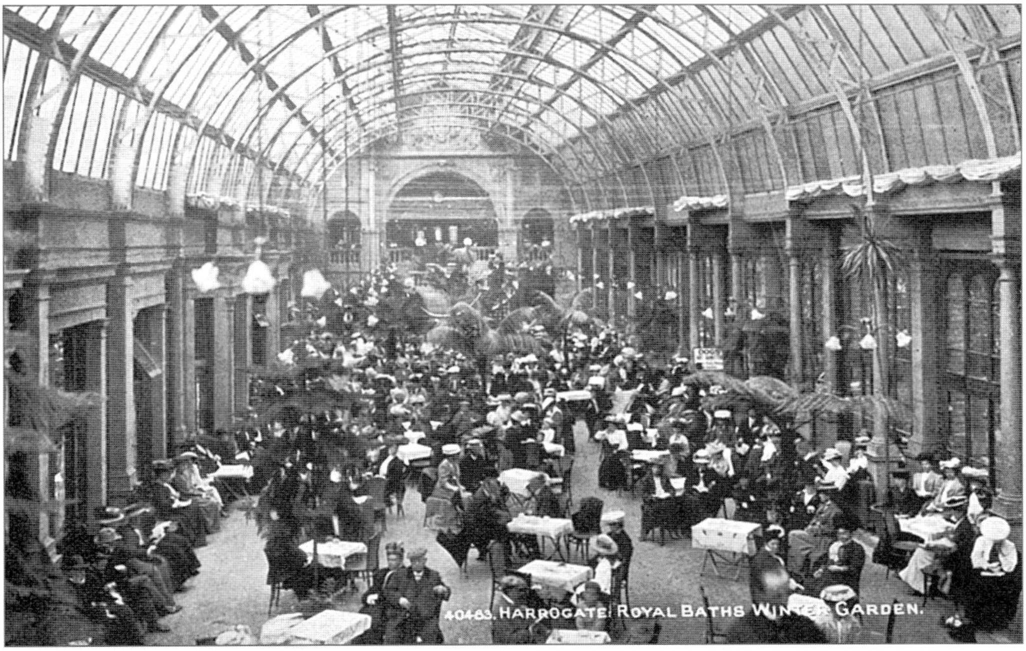

A crowded scene at Harrogate Royal Baths Winter Gardens, *c.* 1912. On the right, a firm notice states 'Dogs Not Admitted'. Facing south, this area was thrown open completely in fine weather, but exercise was possible in all weathers. In the 1930s the Municipal Orchestra played every morning throughout the year, with admission free to Baths patients, 3*d* to visitors.

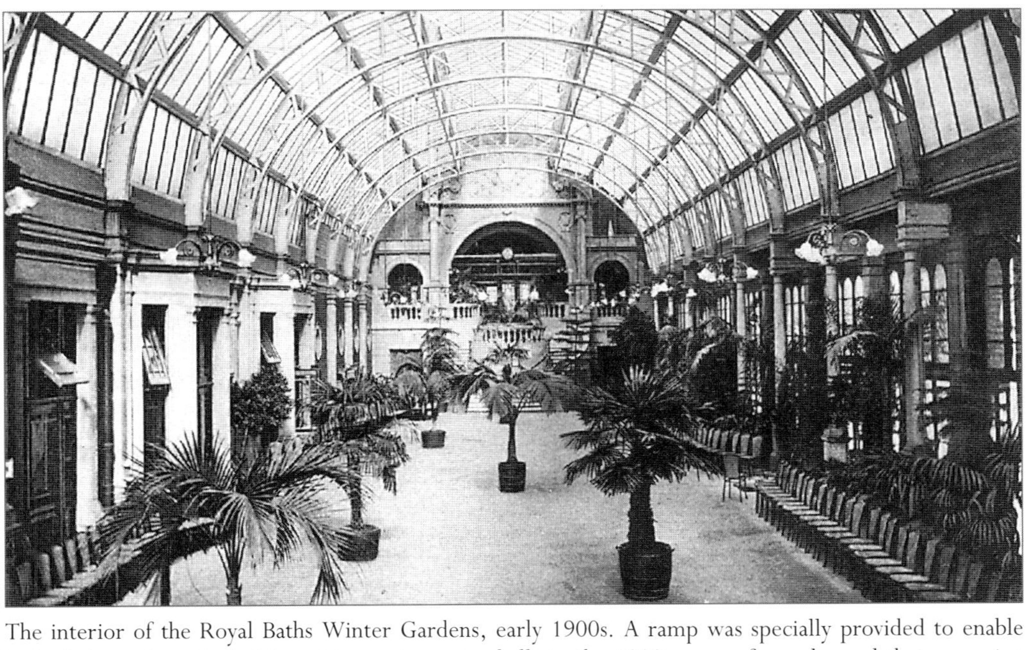

The interior of the Royal Baths Winter Gardens, early 1900s. A ramp was specially provided to enable bath chairs to be wheeled into this spacious, airy hall. In the 1920s rows of people read their morning papers amid potted palms while listening to music provided by a grand piano and violins.

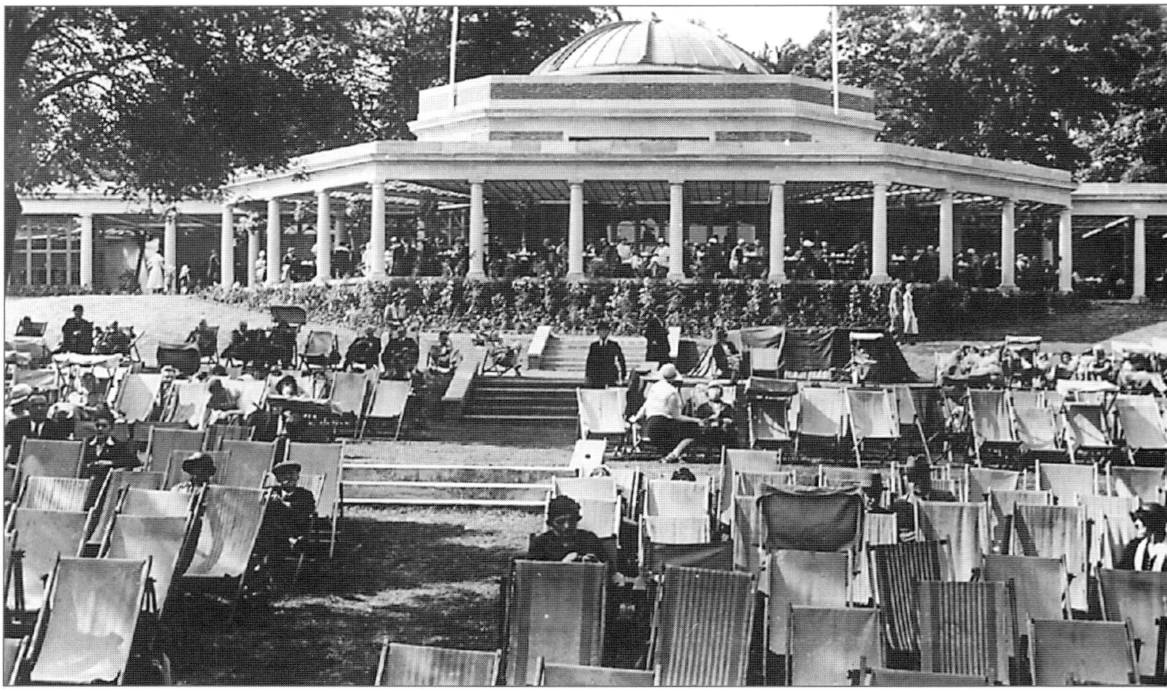

The Tea Pavilion, Valley Gardens, 1920s. Formerly called the Tea House and having a thatched roof, this splendid new building indicated the amazing popularity of the spa town. The Tea Pavilion is doing a roaring trade and the summer crowd is enjoying canopied deck chairs within a sun trap.

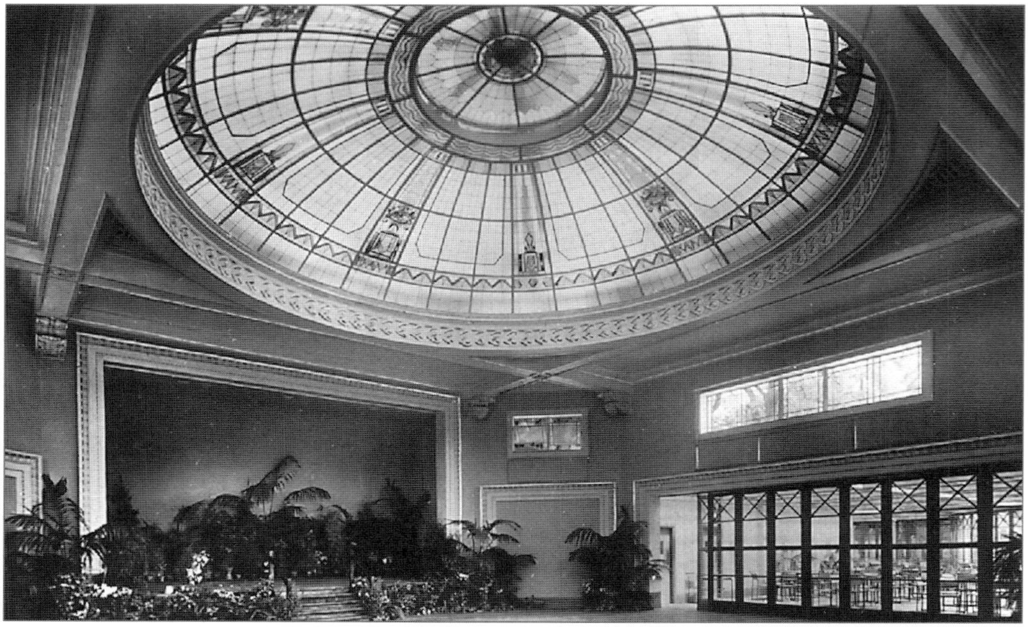

Interior of the Tea Pavilion in Valley Gardens showing the magnificent circular glass ceiling, *c.* 1930. The stained-glass scene in the Royal Pump Room 'to commemorate the discovery of the medicinal waters of Harrogate' was inscribed with literary panache: 'For an angel went down at a certain season and troubled the water.' These were all part of lasting, glowing memories some visitors took home.

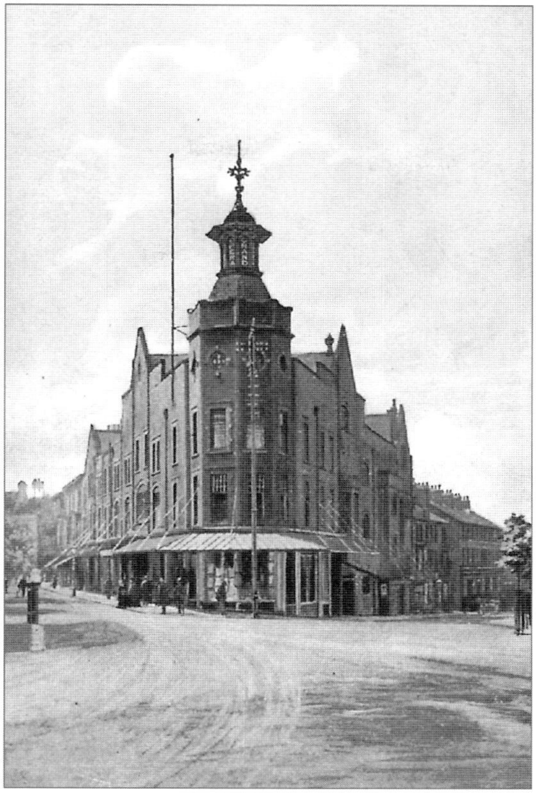

The Grand Opera House, 1906. This fine red-brick building, designed by architect F. Tugwell, was opened in 1900 by the Mayoress Mrs J.H. Myrtle. Its octagonal tower was crowned with a cupola on which white bricks spelled out the name 'Grand Opera House'. With the arrival of the 'talkies' in the 1920s the cinema claimed a large part of its audience so it had to switch to repertory and became the Harrogate Theatre. The White Rose Players, some of whom went on to fame and fortune in London, continued until 1955 when the theatre closed. After some years the Corporation bought and restored it. The entrance foyer has a striking art nouveau frieze depicting the theme of drama and the theatre.

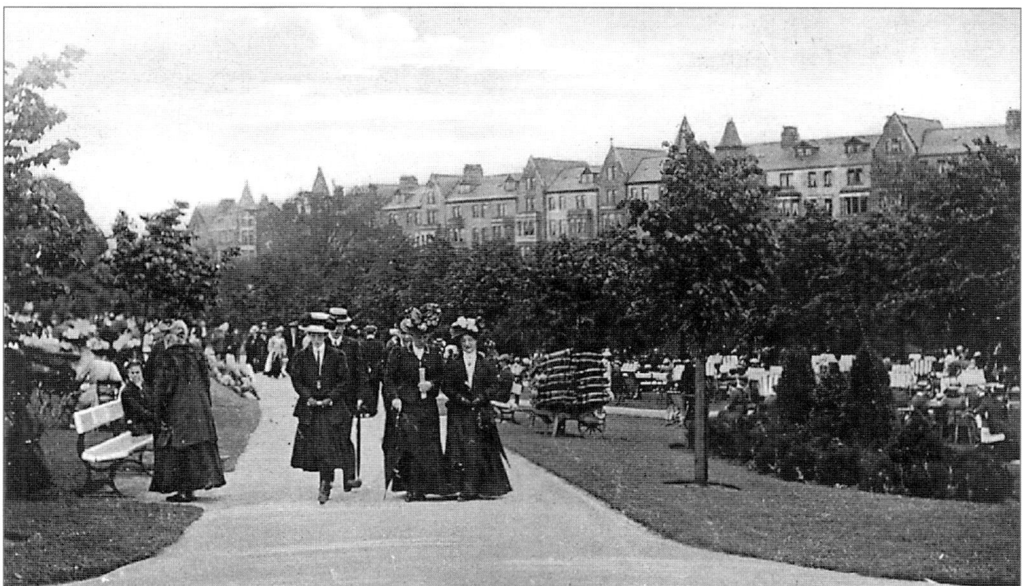

Crowds congregating near the Shady Walk, Valley Gardens, a popular promenading area leading to pine woods, 1910. The natural beauties of this wild dell were further enhanced by skilled landscape gardening. Additional ground eventually allowed the Gardens to stretch from the Royal Pump Room to Bogs Field.

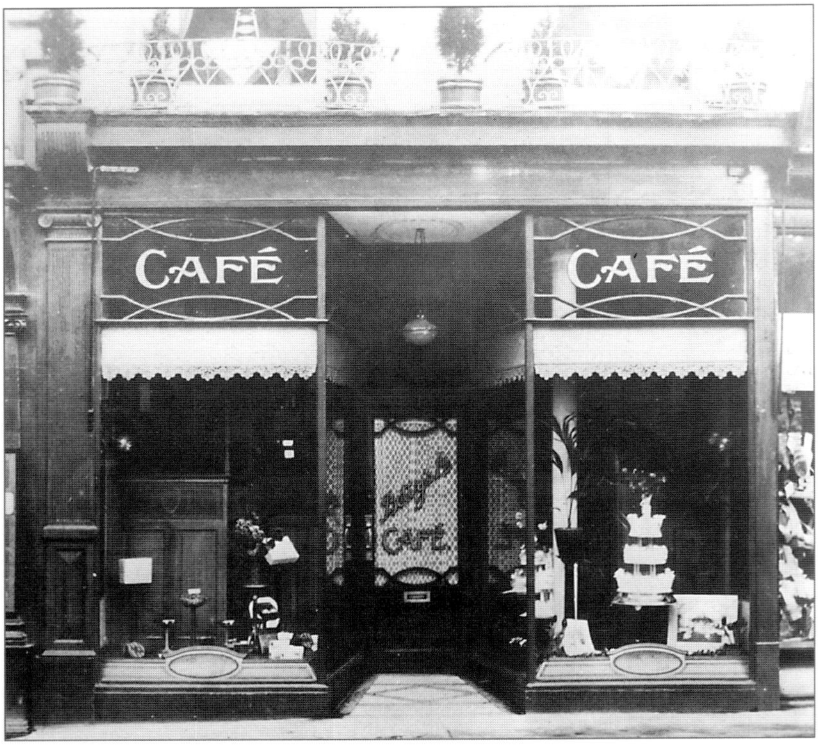

Betty's Café Tea Rooms, Cambridge Crescent. Harrogate's smartest café, Betty's on Cambridge Crescent, was opened by Frederick Belmont in 1919. Thanks to the in-house bakery on the fourth floor, the café and shop were filled with delicious aromas of freshly baked bread and cakes. Very soon Frederick's natural Swiss flair for hospitality and his mouthwatering cakes brought him royal patronage and popular acclaim. By 1992 a new bakery was built in Starbeck, complete with its own orchard to meet the growing demand for Betty's range of cakes, chocolate and bread.

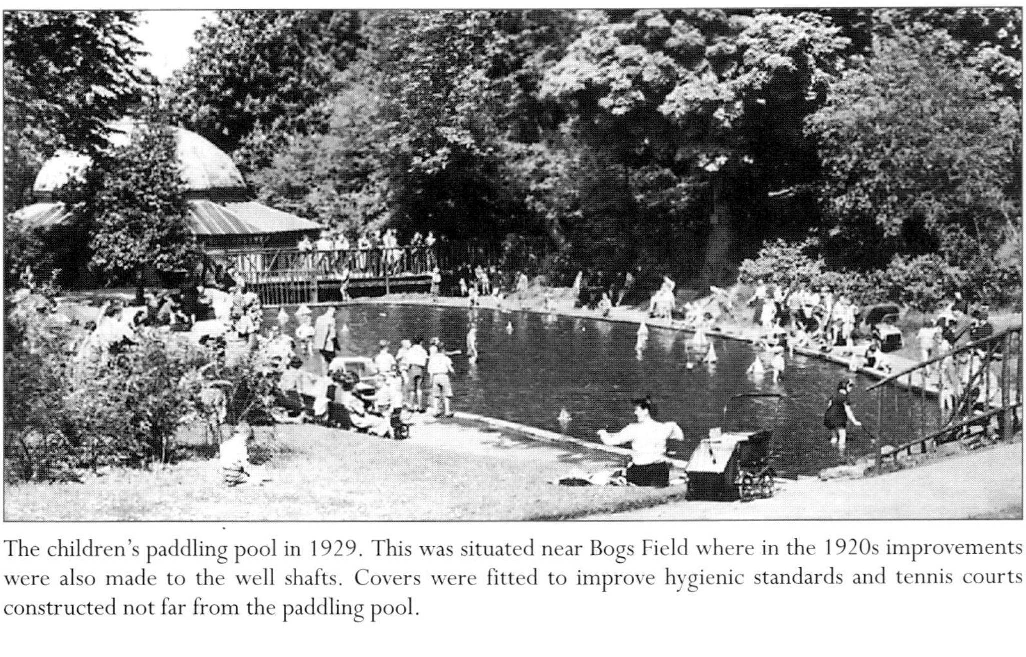

The children's paddling pool in 1929. This was situated near Bogs Field where in the 1920s improvements were also made to the well shafts. Covers were fitted to improve hygienic standards and tennis courts constructed not far from the paddling pool.

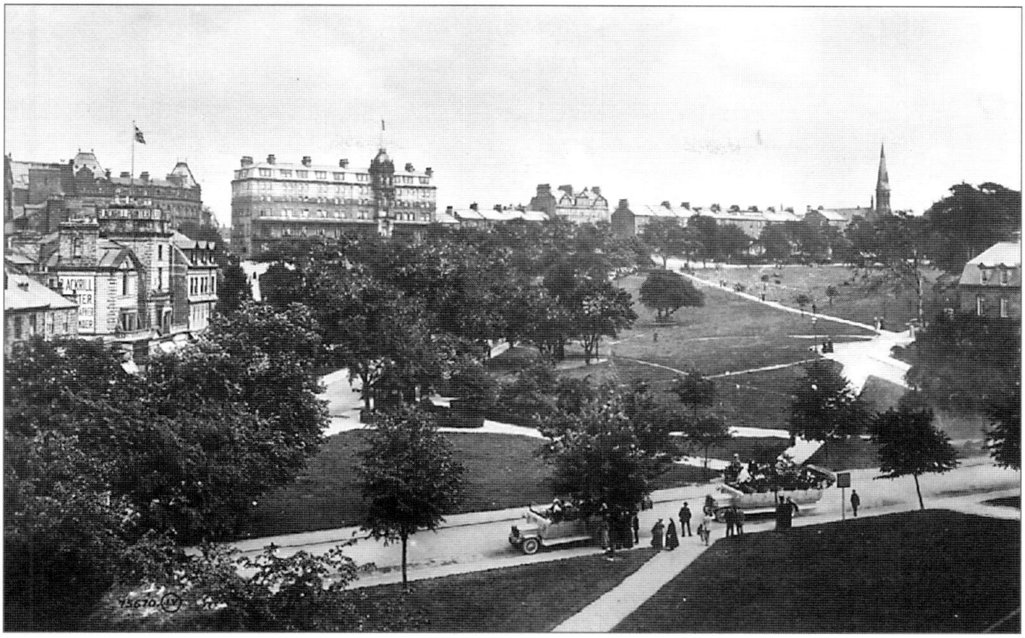

The Stray, 1918. A 1778 Award declared this 200 acre stretch of Common extending from Low to High Harrogate 'open and unenclosed', with free access to the springs. This land, which may never be built upon, was frequented by horse riders and the fashionably dressed. Note the two early motor charabancs. During the Second World War crops were grown on the Stray.

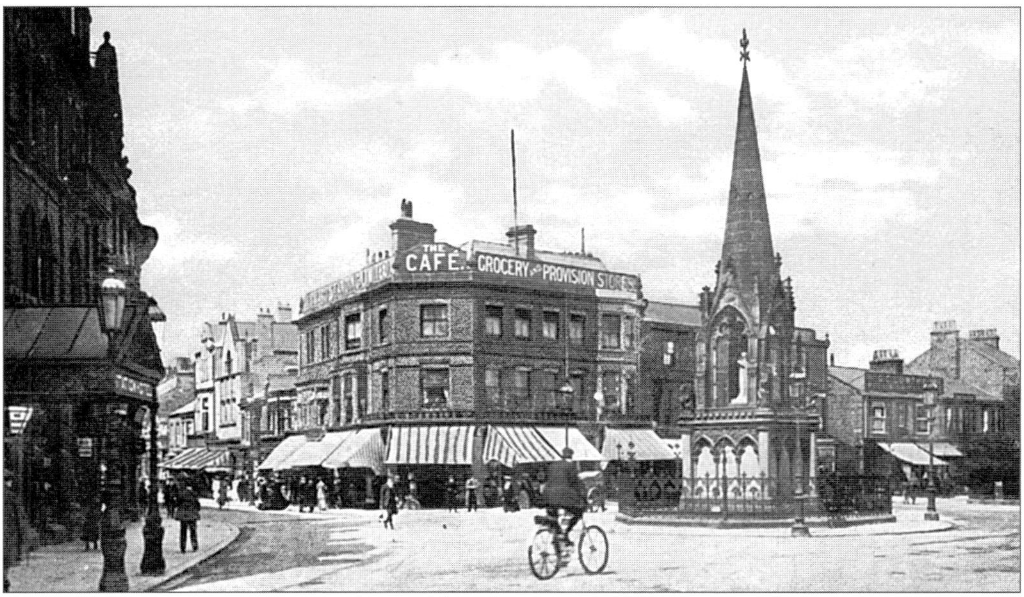

Station Square with the London North Eastern Railway station on the left, early 1900s. Across from the Victoria Monument is G.G. Lowther's provisions store almost adjoining another café and grocery. People wishing to reside in Harrogate approached John Day and Sons, estate agents, who had established themselves alongside the builders and developers. Between 1860 and 1890 the population trebled.

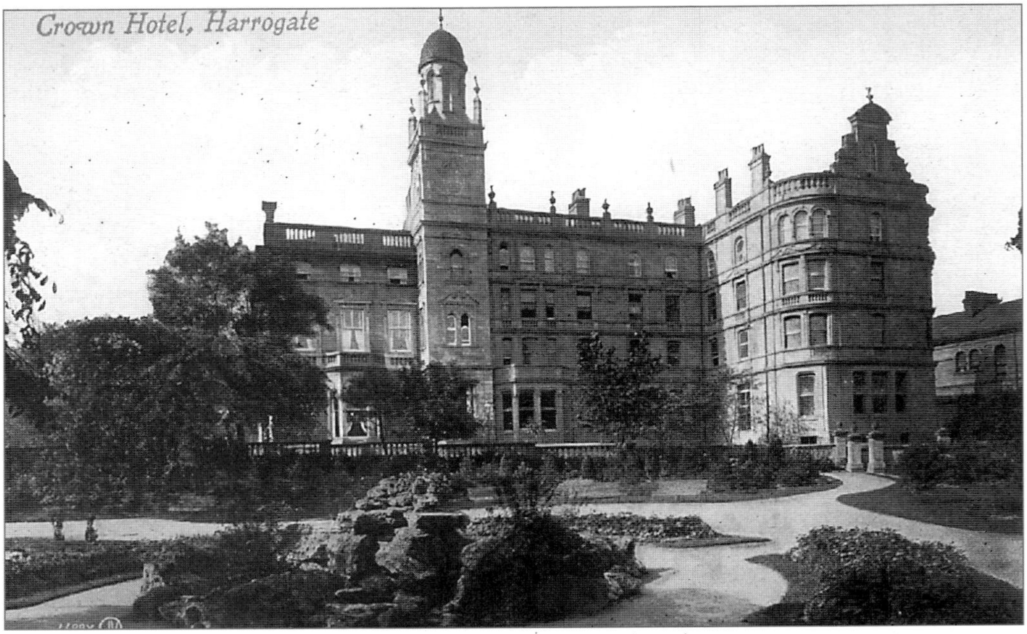

The Crown Hotel, Low Harrogate, situated next to the Royal Pump Room, 1927. Joseph Thackwray was the first owner. It was built in 1847, the year after the laying out of Royal Parade, and enlarged again forty-three years later. Low and High Harrogate were described as 'the parents of the prosperous town' and the opulent appearance of the Crown indicates the rise to popularity.

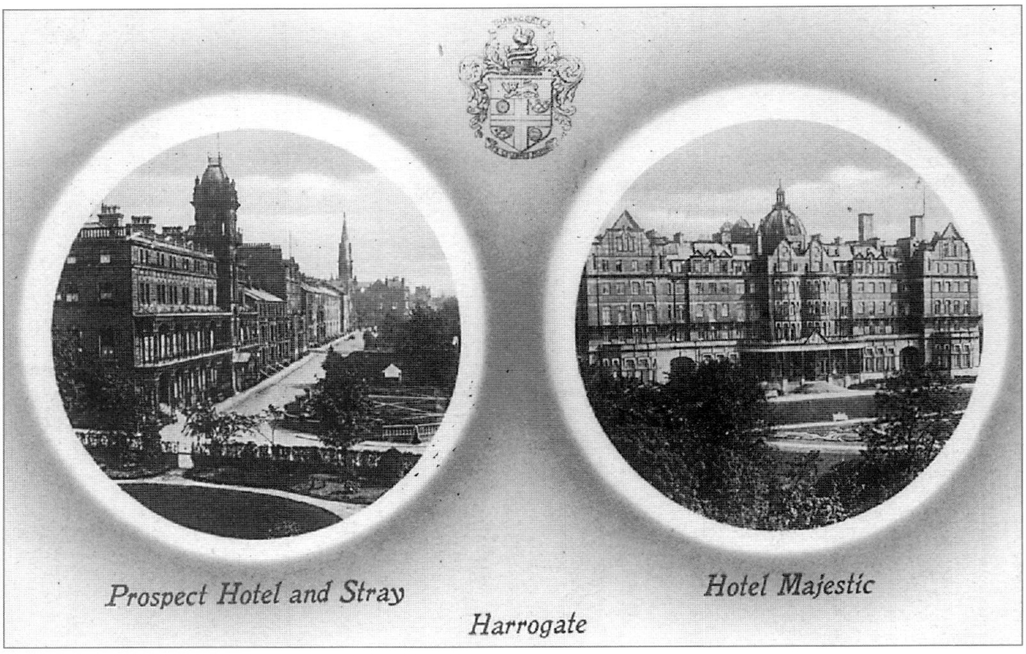

'A collector's piece' is how this 1935 postcard of the Prospect Hotel and Hotel Majestic topped by Harrogate's heraldic device was described. At the Majestic on Ripon Road winter terms were 21*s* a day, summer 30*s*. The Prospect charged 15*s* and the Granby from 16*s* 6*d*. A week's accommodation at the North Eastern opposite the railway station cost 94*s* 6*d*.

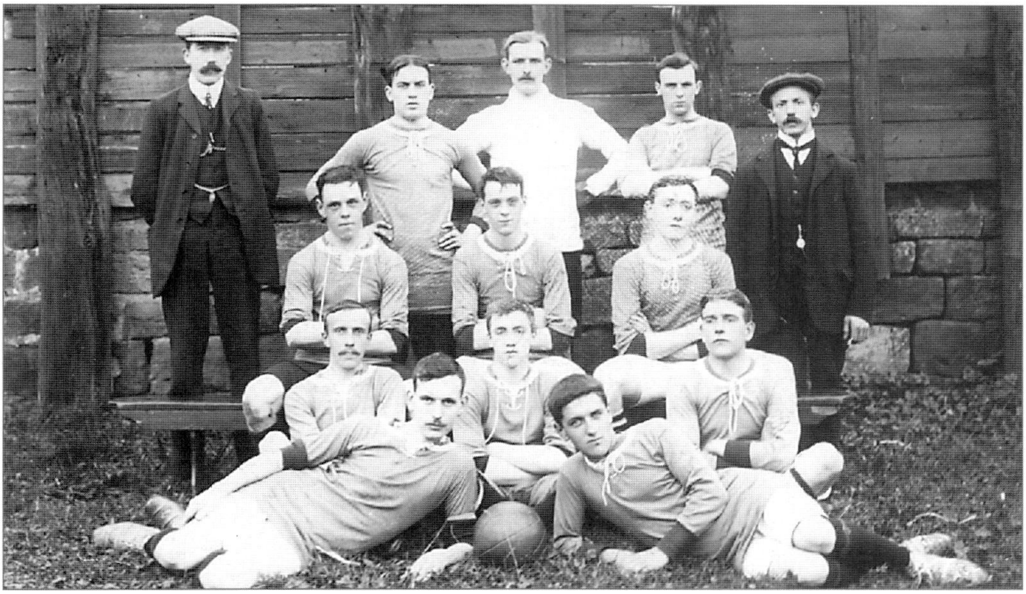

Harrogate and District Football Association Inter-League team, 1910. Football was played on ground behind the County Hotel. In earlier days the Stray was the scene of rural sports. Jingling matches were popular in which twenty men were blindfolded. One man had a bell; his eyes were not covered. Weaving in and out of the others, he was eventually captured, betrayed by the sound of the jingling bell.

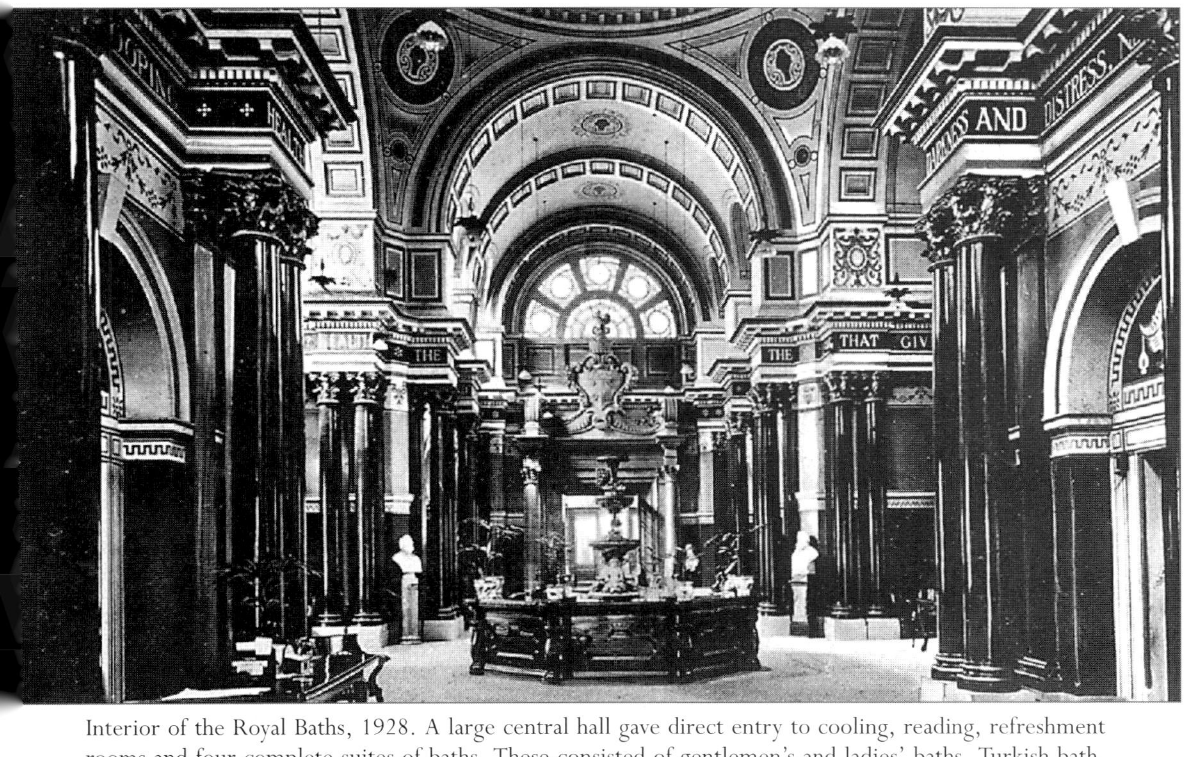

Interior of the Royal Baths, 1928. A large central hall gave direct entry to cooling, reading, refreshment rooms and four complete suites of baths. These consisted of gentlemen's and ladies' baths, Turkish bath, inhalation, pulverisation and dry massage room. An inscription in Roman capitals ran round the walls. Part of it read: 'Health is the vital principle of bliss.'

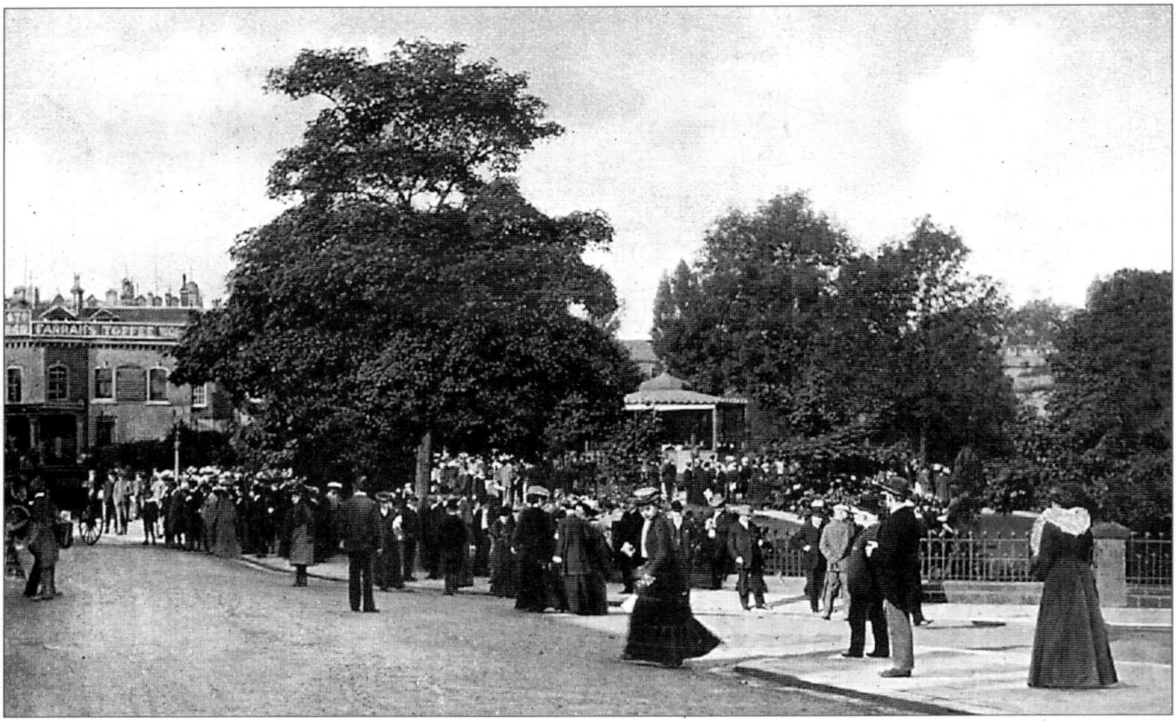

Crescent Gardens, *c.* 1905. Although the photograph indicates the time as only 7.45 a.m., crowds have gathered for their daily ritual of water drinking before breakfast. In the background is Farrah's Toffee Works with its proud boast 'Established 1840'.

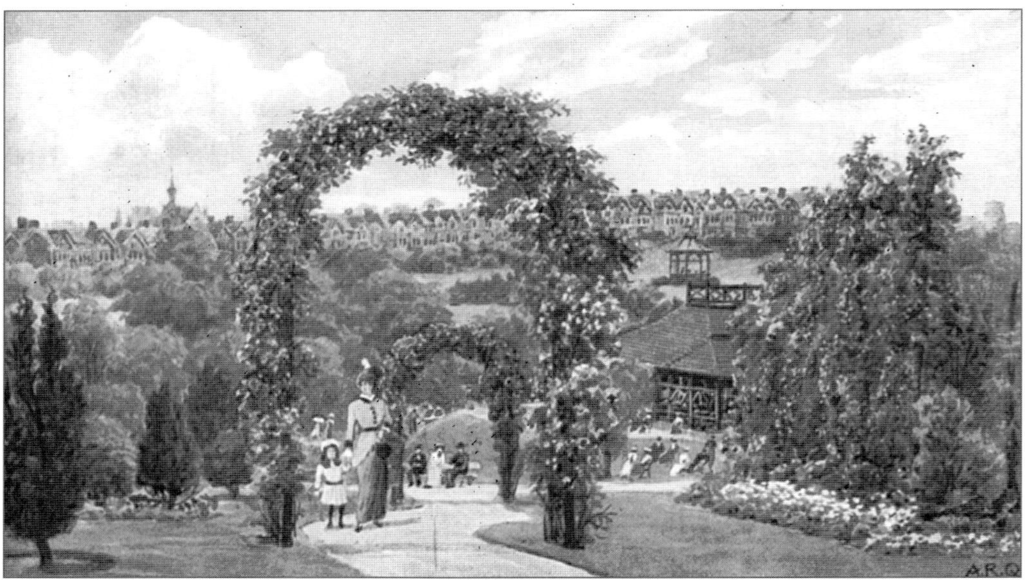

Artist A.R. Quinton's impression of laden rose arches at the height of summer in the 'world famous' Valley Gardens, *c.* 1900. Mrs Brogden, who sold wool from a tiny hut and wove woollen slippers on this spot before the 18-acre gardens were made, would have been amazed at the crowds flocking to the Tea Room. In this water-conscious town, Taylors, in business for over 100 years, blended their tea to suit water supplies in different parts of the country.

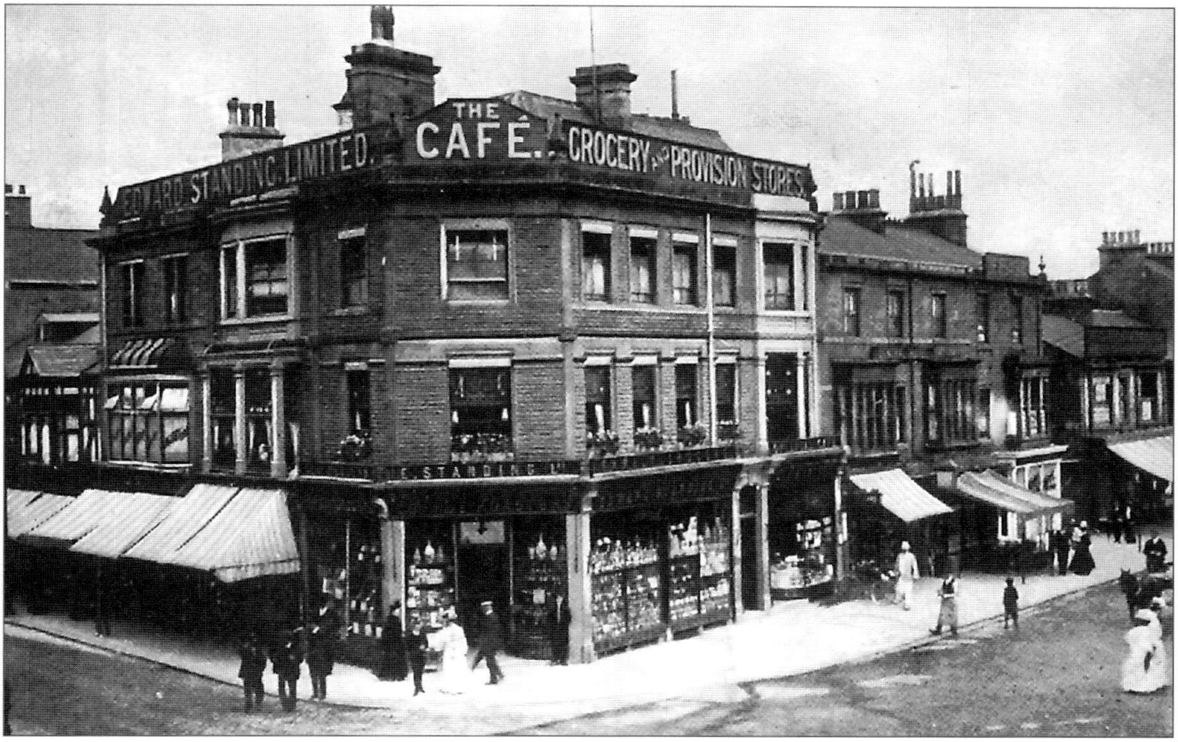

Edward Standing's café, grocery and provisions store, on the corner of James Street in the early 1900s. Built in the early nineteenth century, James Street was named after a landowner, James Franklin. At first it was residential but as the town population increased, shop fronts began to appear. There was greater demand for provisions and cafés, and Standing's was established in about 1883.

Here was served the famous Harrogate Tart made from 3 egg yolks, a pint of hot milk, a whole fresh egg, 3 oz flour, 3 oz caster sugar, 4 oz ground almonds. The flour, mixed to a smooth paste with cold milk, had the egg yolks stirred in and the beaten egg and sugar added vigorously. The butter was melted in the hot milk then stirred very gradually into the egg mixture. This was cooked in a double boiler until it resembled smooth cream but was not allowed to boil. The ground almonds were beaten in and traditionally poured into a baked pastry flan case. Some people liked it in individual glasses with ratafia biscuits.

Edward Standing Ltd have stamped the reverse of this view with 'Tea and Coffee Specialists. Our 2/- tea is perfection. We shall be pleased to forward a free sample on application.' Those were the days when the customer was always right. Certainly, real McCoy Harrogate Tart was delicious with a nice cup of tea.

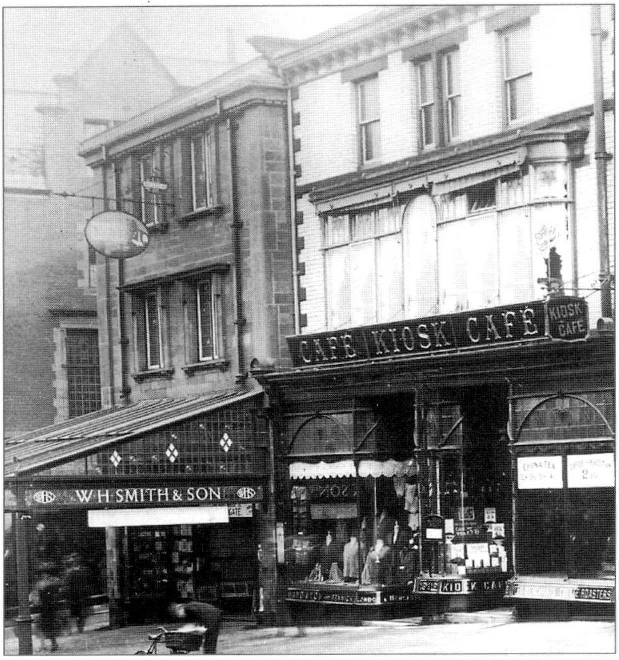

The Kiosk, Harrogate. In 1886 two brothers, Charles and Llewyn Taylor opened a family tea and coffee-merchants in Leeds. Over the next few decades they opened a chain of 'Kiosks' across Yorkshire which became famous for their tea blends and freshly roasted coffees. The Kiosk in Parliament Street, Harrogate, became a popular meeting place for the gentlemen of the town. Today only one 'Kiosk' remains – Taylors Tea Rooms in Stonegate, York.

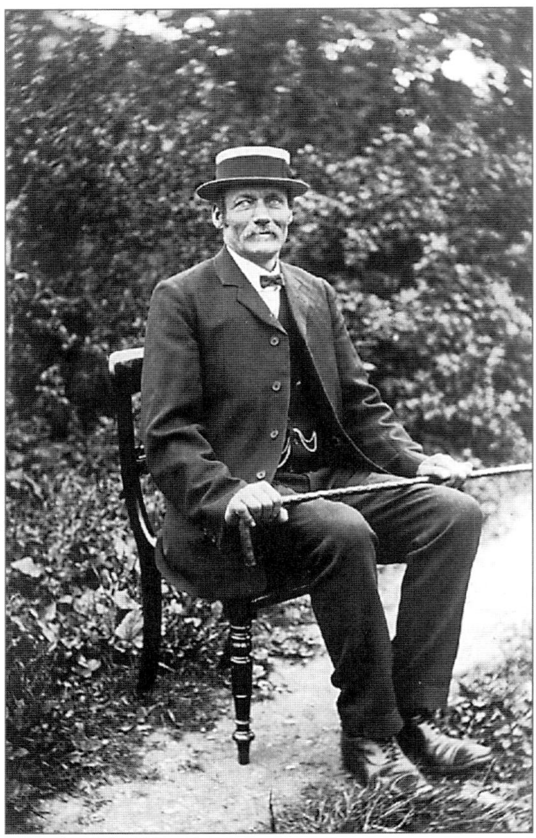

Sam Barlow, early 1900s. Aware of the different mineral waters, in retirement Sam adopted the discipline of baths and treatment taken on alternate days, with waters drunk daily. The cost of sulphur baths and drinking water was 12*s* a week. It was possible for patients wishing to continue their cure to have the particular waters they required sent on to their home address. The eighty-eight wells were divided into four classes: strong sulphur, mild sulphur containing alkaline salts, saline chalybeate; pure chalybeate. Sixteen were used for internal ministration and became known as Harrogate Water, the rest for bathing. Sam's example was followed by Alfred Osman who founded pigeon racing as a sport in Great Britain and started its journal *Racing Pigeon*. 'Taking things quietly towards the end of his life, he went off to Harrogate to take the cure', reported the *Daily Telegraph*.

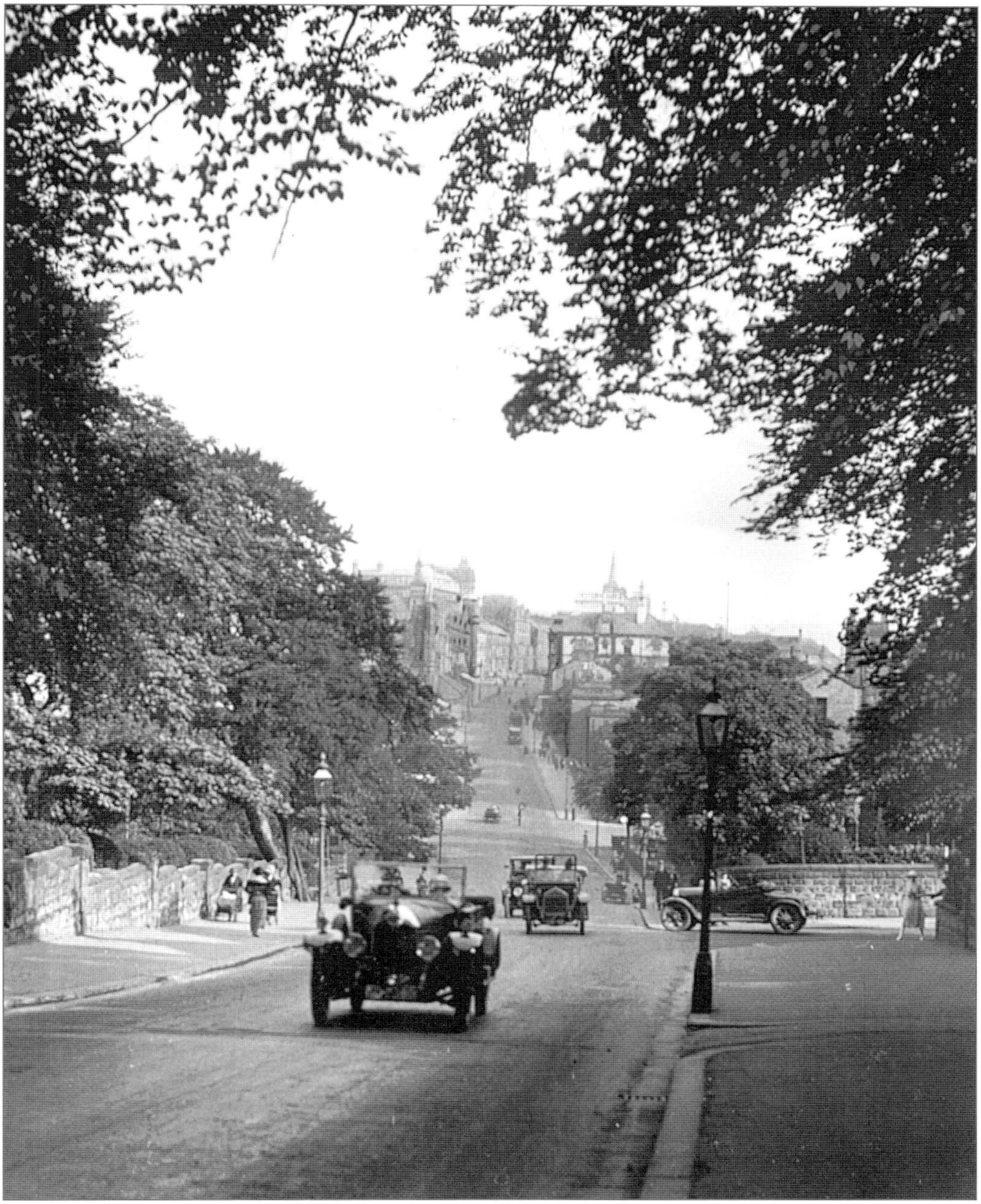

Leaving Harrogate by the Ripon Road, as shown in this photograph, the motorist passed through Killinghall, on to Ripon and thence to Fountains Abbey. It was possible also to reach Fountains by a pretty walk from Wormwald Green station. This view reveals a gracious town, some interesting vintage motor cars and the fashions of around 1921. Many of the trees, especially on the Stray, were planted by Alexander Wedderburn, first Earl of Rosslyn and son of a Scottish judge, who lived at Wedderburn House built in 1786. At a very busy Harrogate Conference in 1946 I recall lodging in a beautiful house that once belonged to a lord. En suite arrangements featured a sunken, white, marble bath. I awoke next morning, gazing at a ceiling covered with rosy cherubs sporting on clouds against a cerulean blue sky. 'Am I in heaven?' seemed a reasonable question, but this was merely an expression of traditional Harrogate grand style around the turn of the century, its motto 'a citadel famous for its springs'.

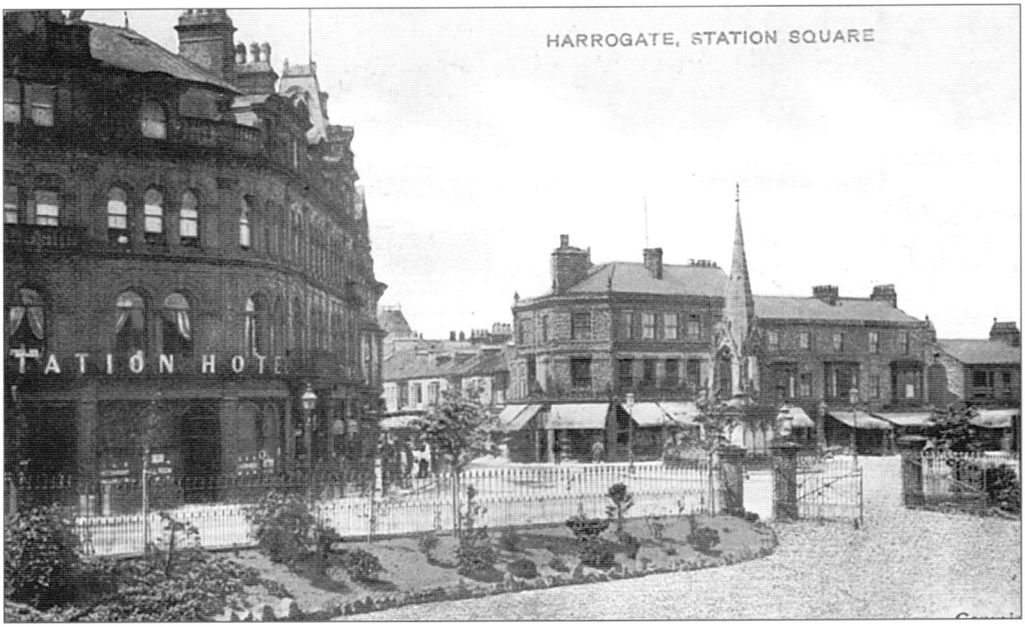

Station Square and Gardens with the Station Hotel and Victoria Monument, *c.* 1913. Its elegance was not marred by advertisements other than one for Maples furniture, whose high-class cabinet making was prized in Harrogate.

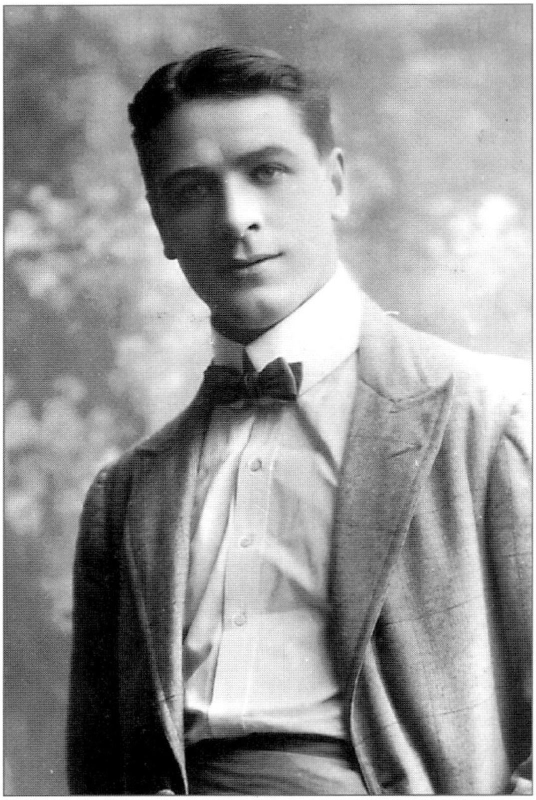

Actor Mr Matheson Lang was one of many famous people who passed through or stayed at the famous spa town in the nineteenth and twentieth centuries. William Allingham's Journal for 29 August 1863 reveals that when he called at the home of Alfred Lord Tennyson he was told: 'Mr Tennyson is ill. He will be coming to London from Harrogate.' The nineteenth century actor Charles Macready for a time owned the Granby Hotel. Writers have described Harrogate and the country around in novels, poems and non-fiction works, examples being: *Her Mad Month* (Baroness Grundy), *Hard Lines* (Hawley Swert), 'The White Doe of Rylstone' (William Wordsworth), 'Number 7, Brick Row' (W. Riley), *Records of Harrogate* (Walter J. Kaye). Many well-known doctors have been associated with the town since 1631, when St John's Well was discovered by Dr Michael Stanhope who wrote about the medical properties of the well.

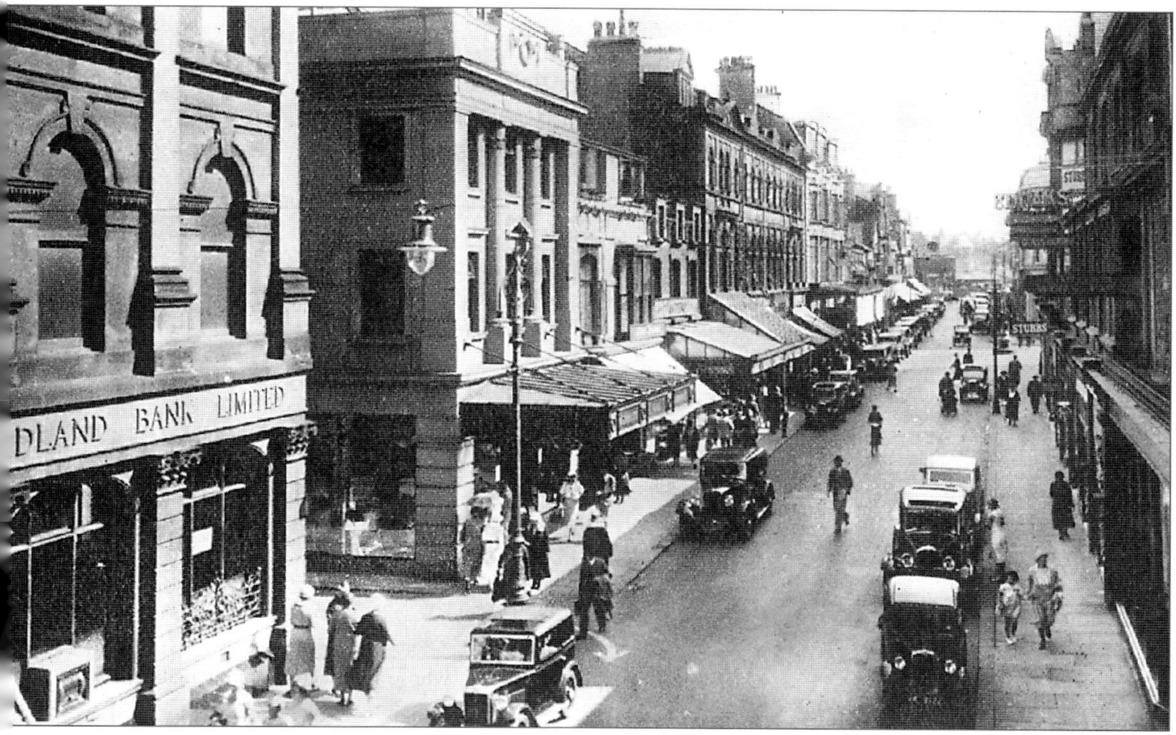

A bustling James Street, which was first envisaged as a grand approach to the town's amenities, in the mid-1930s shows an increasing number of motor cars. This once-residential street is now entirely given over to shops, many with arcades and sun blinds. Stubbs, on the right, agents for Kodak, catered for the growing number of amateur photographers among tourists. You could buy a Soho Myna folding camera for only 15*s*. Near Standing's Café was J. Baxter, 'cigar, tobacco and fancy goods dealer', briar pipes being one of his specialities.

In 1900 Alex Maclean was a jeweller at no. 33A, with linen draper Thomas Stubbs next door, while at no. 13 Charles E.J. Eynon, dispenser of medicines and manufacturer of medical and toilet preparations, also had a photographic department with a dark room. There were also ladies' outfitters, cabinet maker John Thompson and boot maker James Paley.

In Parliament Street were the Wharfedale Dairies, Singer Sewing Machines and John Richardson and Sons, wine and spirit merchants. At the top of Parliament Street the Café Imperial opened, adjoining Montpellier Parade, where in 1892 Hunter's long-established premises also attracted many customers. At 16 Parliament Street in 1901 C.E. Taylor and Company Ltd kept a large assortment of decorated tea canisters for Christmas presents and were prepared to post freshly roasted coffee and pure China tea 'specially chosen for invalids' to all parts daily.

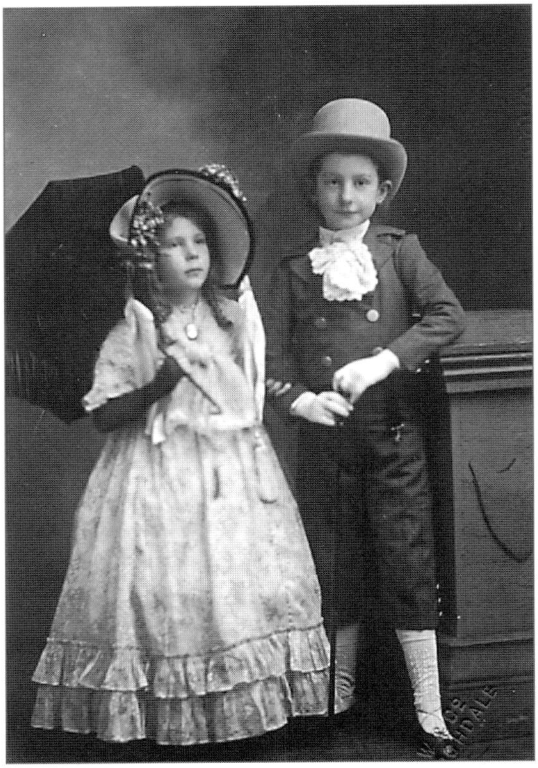

At a Harrogate Fancy Dress Ball in about 1920 two children appeared as Mr and Mrs General Tom Thumb. The fame of the midgets from the American Lilliputian Company sponsored by Phineas T. Barnum lingered on. After appearing in Paris the midgets had entertained the Royal Family at Windsor Castle in 1865. It was Queen Victoria who had conferred the title of General Tom Thumb on the dwarf Charles S. Stratton. Harrogate had many fancy dress balls and firework displays. One grand affair was at the opening of the Royal Spa Concert Room in 1835. This was indeed a far cry from the days when actors had to perform in the barn attached to the Granby Hotel. In the 1920s the Harrogate Theatre, intended as a Grand Opera House, had become a Repertory Theatre. It closed in 1955 but has since been bought by the Corporation.

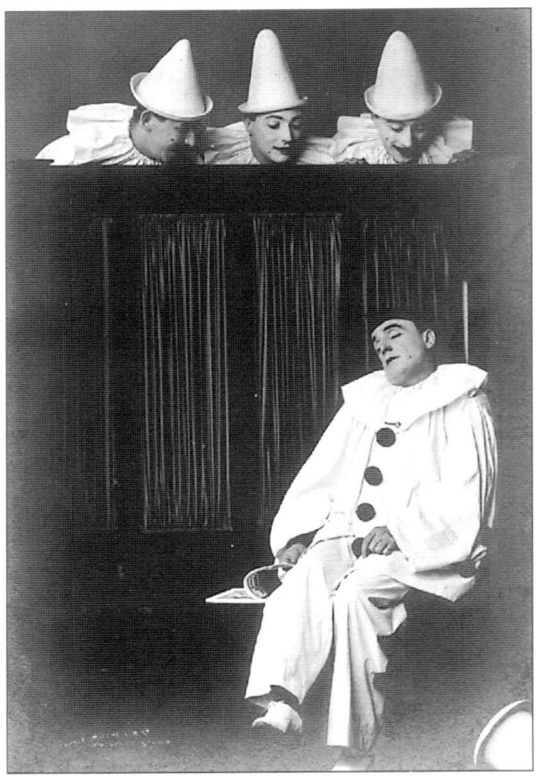

Tom Coleman's Harrogate Pierrots, amusingly posed at E. Michell and Company's Prospect Studio. These jolly pierrots, performing in the street, catered more for working class crowds rather than the rich and the famous arriving with servants, cooks, maids, stable boys and dressmakers, as they had in the previous century. The railway brought a wide diversity of people to Harrogate. The fashionable season began in May and continued until late September. In the 1760s a theatre was built in High Harrogate and rebuilt to more commodious standards in 1788 for the staging of plays. Pierrots were still popular in the 1930s when the population had reached over 39,000, swelled by visitors all year round.

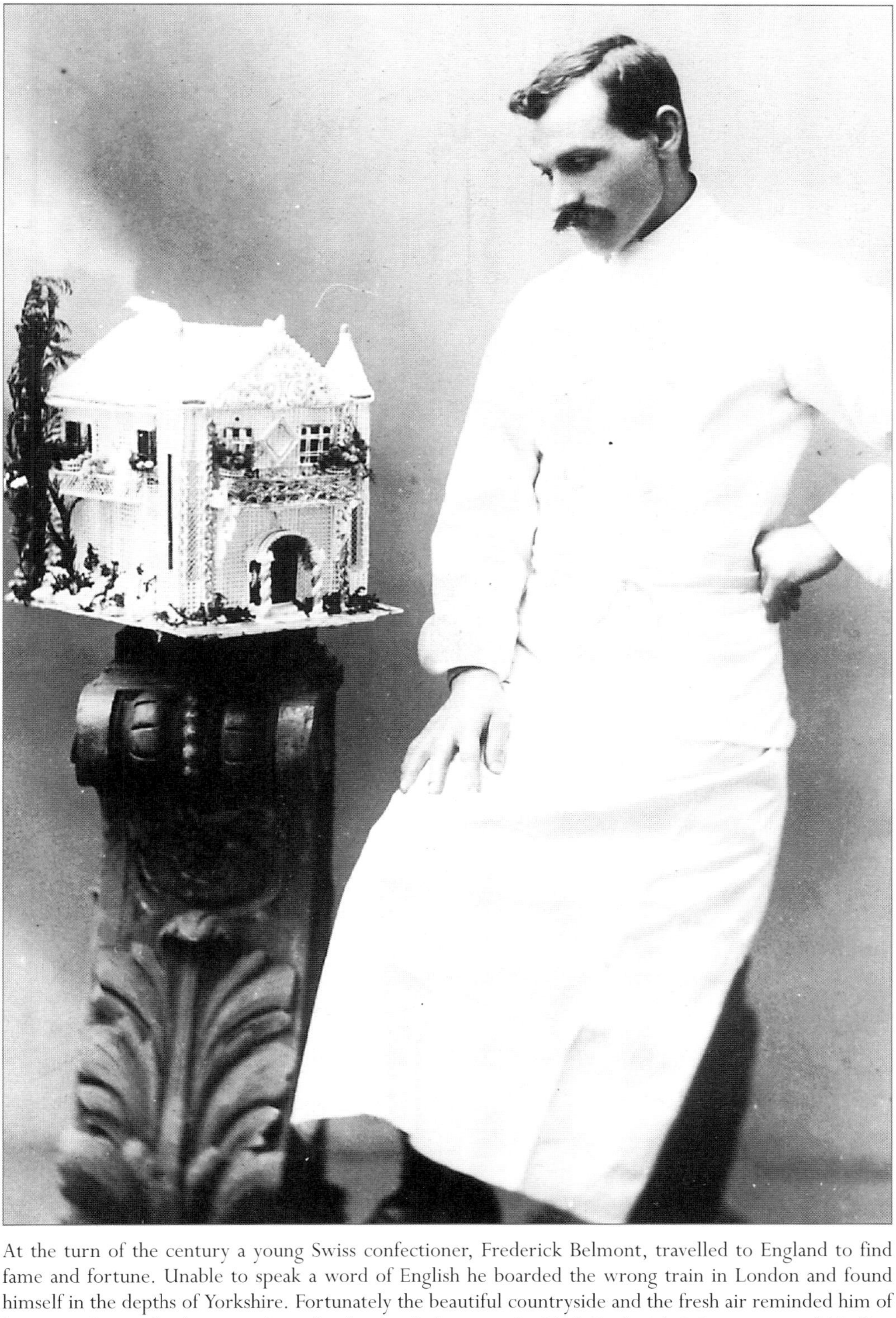

At the turn of the century a young Swiss confectioner, Frederick Belmont, travelled to England to find fame and fortune. Unable to speak a word of English he boarded the wrong train in London and found himself in the depths of Yorkshire. Fortunately the beautiful countryside and the fresh air reminded him of his native Switzerland, so much so that he decided to stay. In 1919 Frederick Belmont opened his first Betty's Café Tea Room in Cambridge Crescent, Harrogate, to immediate popular success.

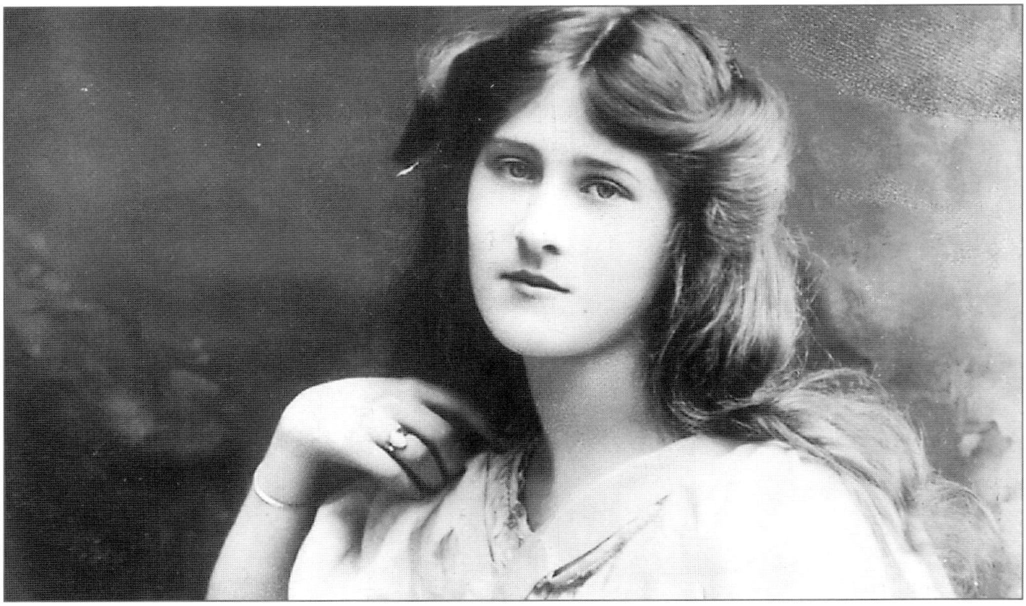

Music-hall artiste Phyllis Dare appeared in 1910 with her sister Zena on the stage of the Empire Theatre, where clever and versatile acts were performed beneath a beautifully carved proscenium. The 'stars' of yesterday were photographed in the Philco series and made into greetings cards.

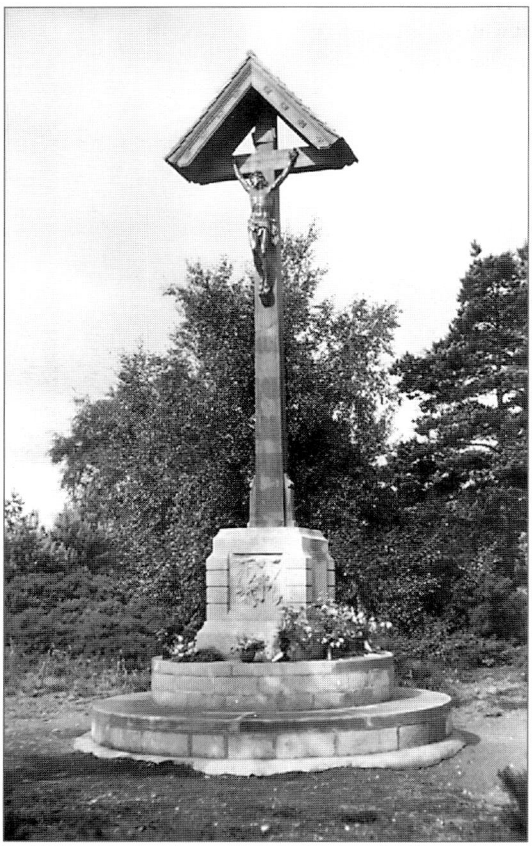

The Calvary, Harlow Moor, 1929. Erected by ex-servicemen to honour their comrades who were killed during the First World War, this memorial, sited on the moor at a point where paths diverge, was known locally as the 'Calvary'.

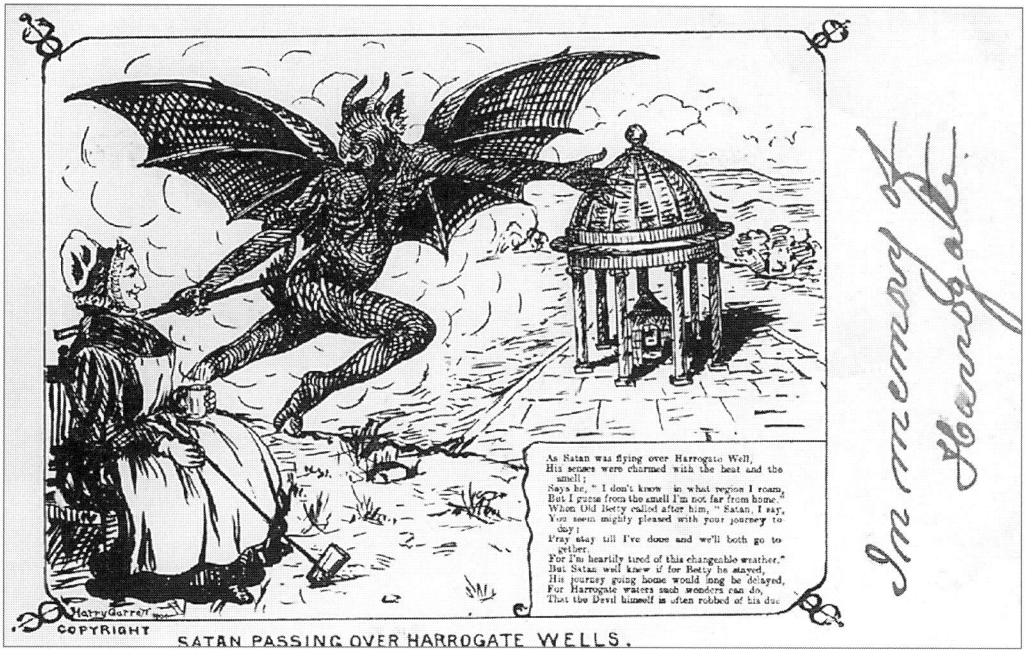

This amusing 1905 card inscribed 'In Memory of Harrogate by Jenny Carter' reads:

> 'As Satan was flying over Harrogate Well
> His senses were charmed with the heat and the smell.
> Says he, 'I don't know in what region I roam
> But I guess from the smell that I'm not far from home.'

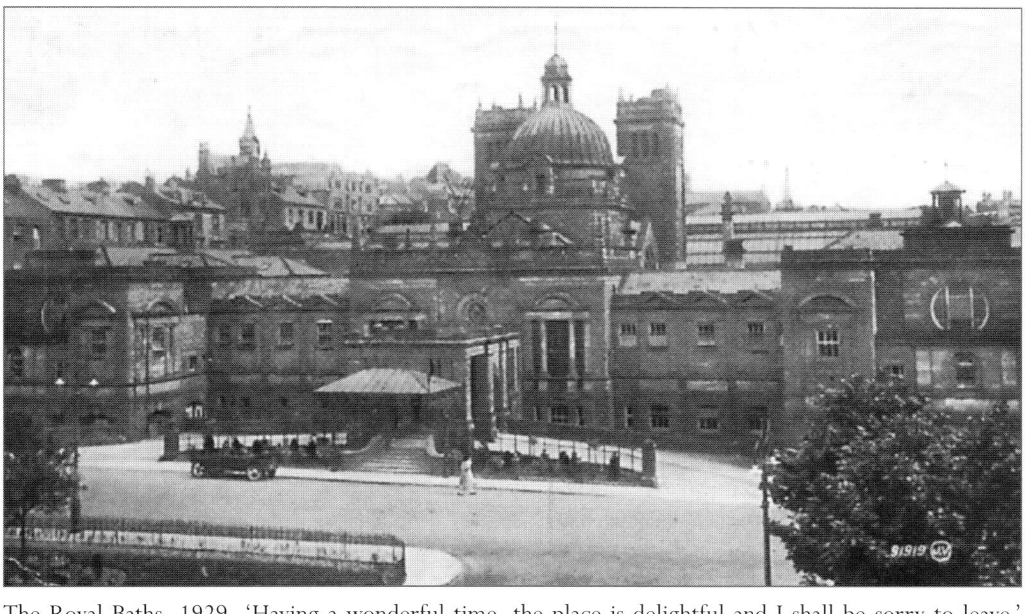

The Royal Baths, 1929. 'Having a wonderful time, the place is delightful and I shall be sorry to leave,' wrote Nellie from 3 Belmont Road. At the Royal Baths Assembly Room she would no doubt see a carved stand made for the Great Exhibition of 1851, holding bottles of the mineral water that made Harrogate famous.

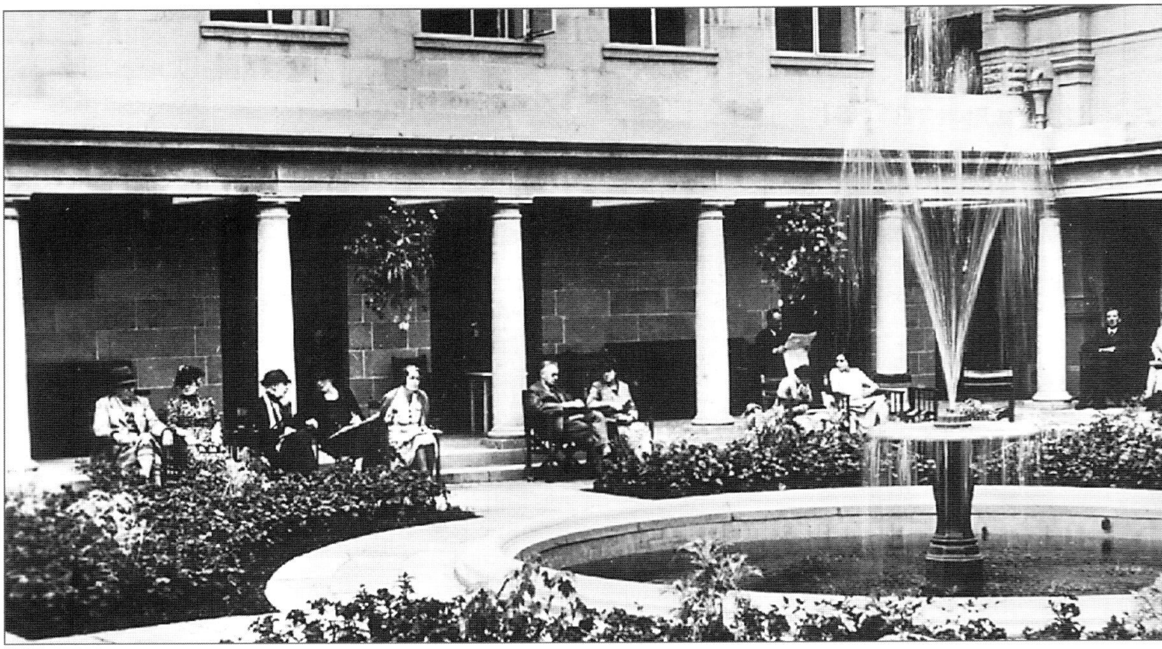

Fountain Court, Royal Baths, 1948. After two centuries of fame, demand for taking the waters was waning and the town realised it was no longer well served by its bath chair image. The Fountain Court, along with other facilities, was opened by the Lord Mayor of London Sir Frank Bowater on 10 July 1939.

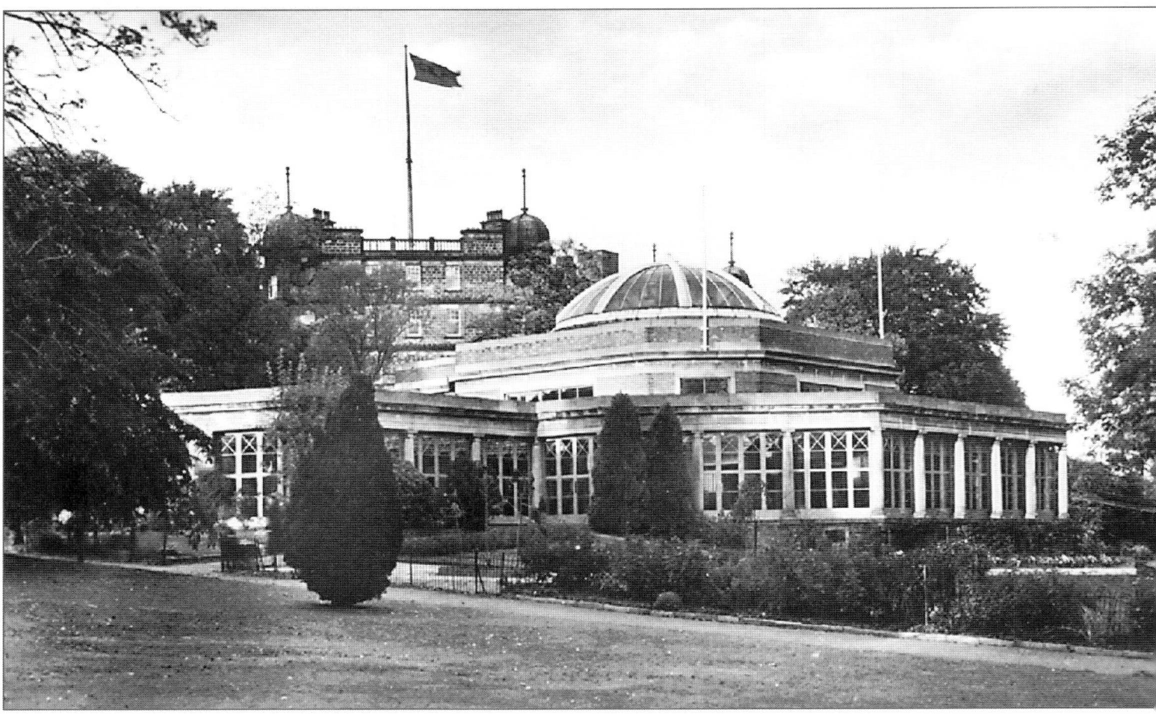

The Sun Pavilion, situated in a deep, natural dell enhanced by landscape gardening, 1938. Leading to this is the Sun Colonnade where the famous Harrogate Spring Flower Show is held. The 600-ft long glass-covered walk was opened in 1935 by an eminent physician, Lord Horder.

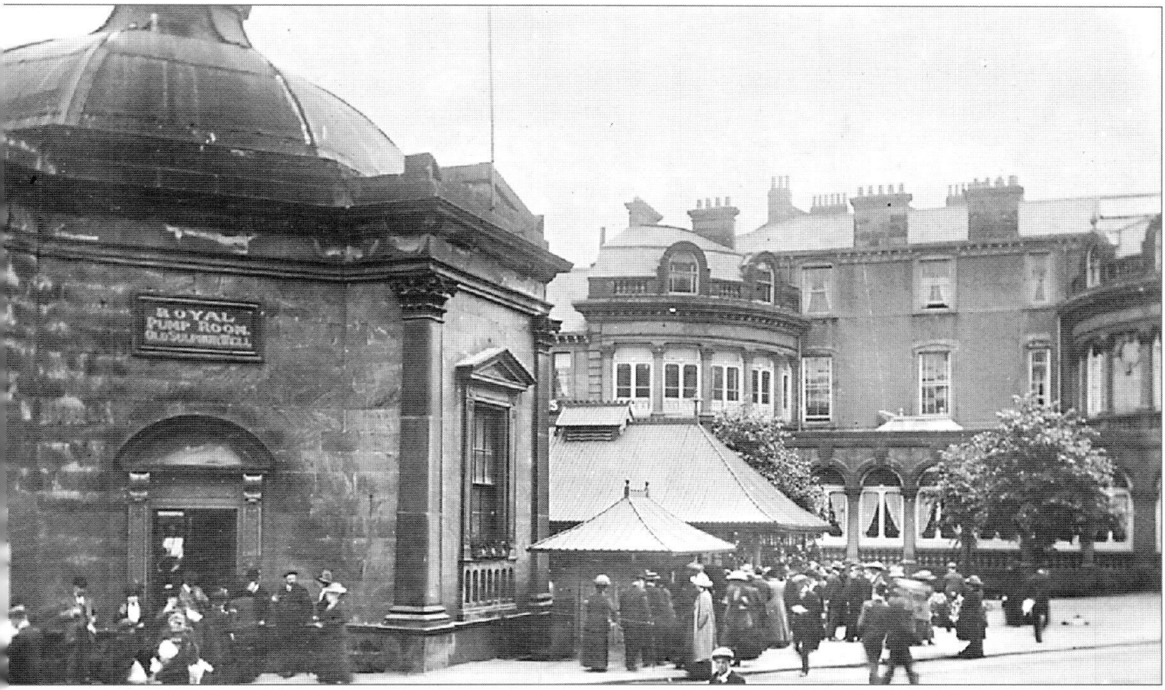

Outside the Royal Pump Room and Sulphur Well, 1902. Here a crowd gathered regularly as early as 7.30 a.m. to drink the waters, following their doctors' orders. In 1925 it was estimated that 260,000 drinkers used the Pump Room.

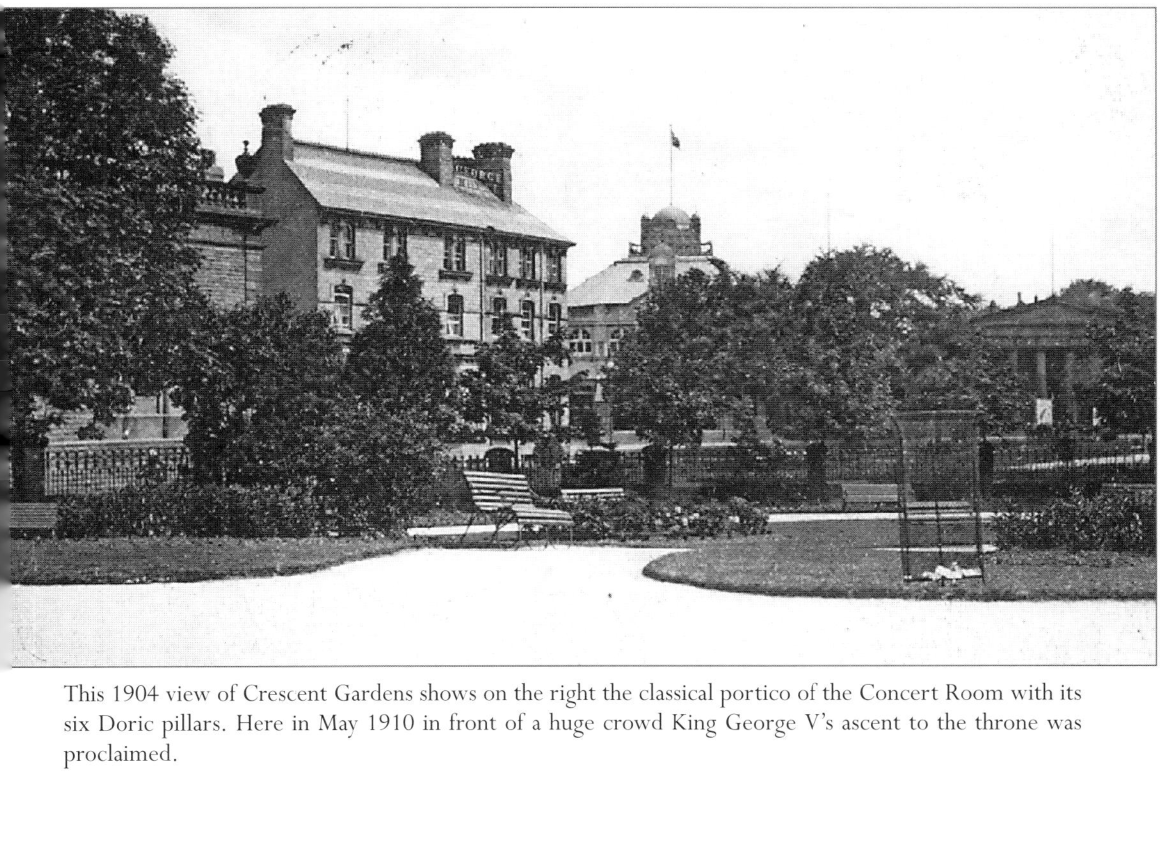

This 1904 view of Crescent Gardens shows on the right the classical portico of the Concert Room with its six Doric pillars. Here in May 1910 in front of a huge crowd King George V's ascent to the throne was proclaimed.

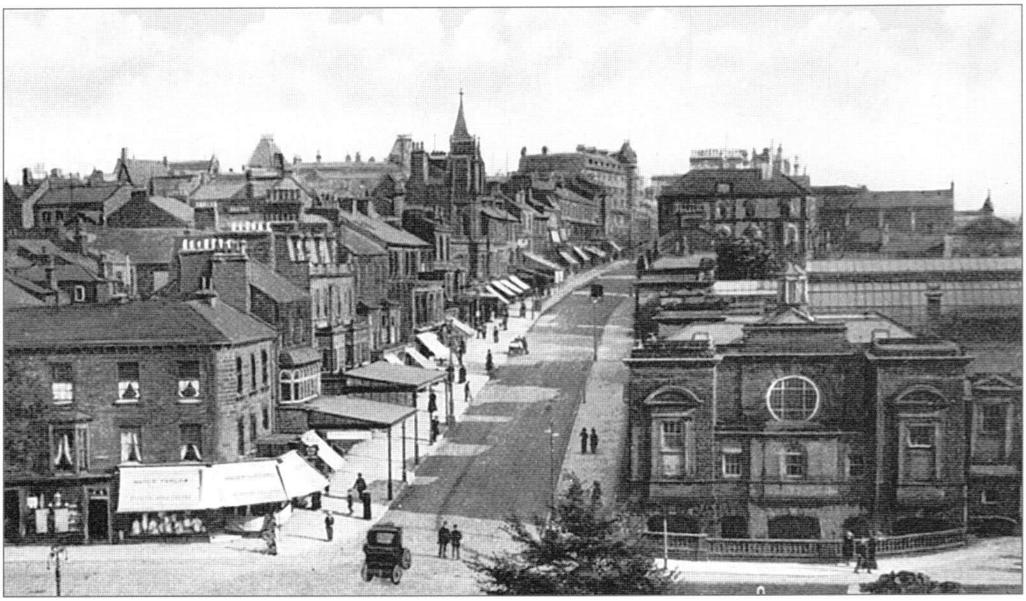

Parliament Street and Royal Baths, *c.* 1907. In the far left on the corner is the shop of clothing specialist Madge Farlow, which years later was occupied by Louis Cope. At a time when traffic was scanty a solitary motor car trundles up Parliament Street totally disregarded by two pedestrians in the middle of the road.

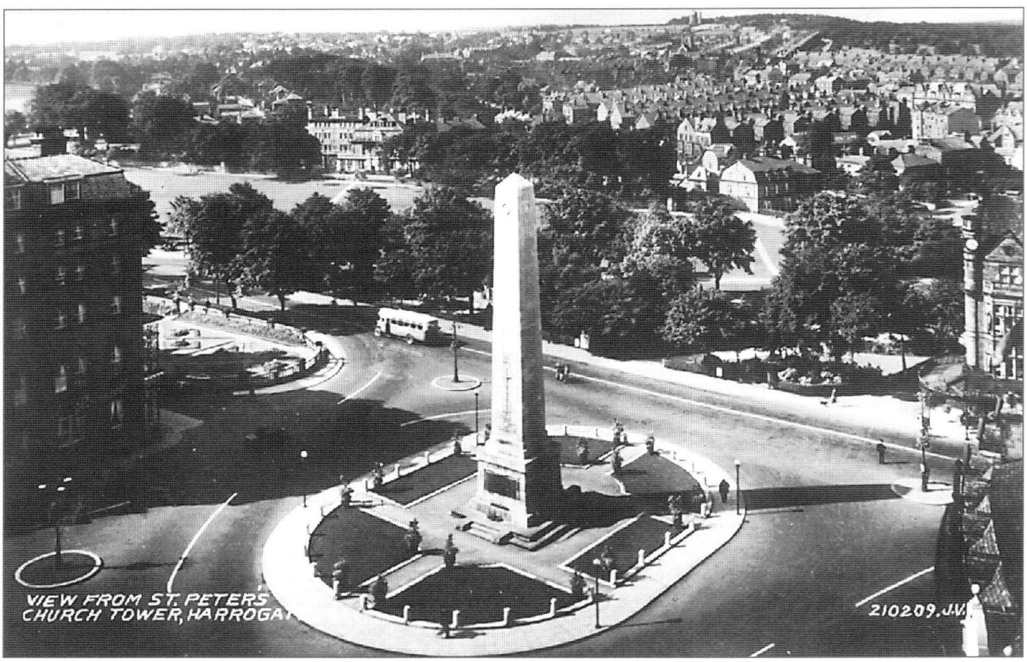

This view from St Peter's Church tower in about 1940 shows a well-wooded, planned town spreading in all directions. St Peter's, situated in Cambridge Street, was one of eighteen churches and chapels of different denominations. Built in 1876, St Peter's has treasures: Caen stone onyx pulpit, Berlinson and Grylls stained glass, and carving by Thompson of Kilburn whose sign is a mouse incorporated in his work.

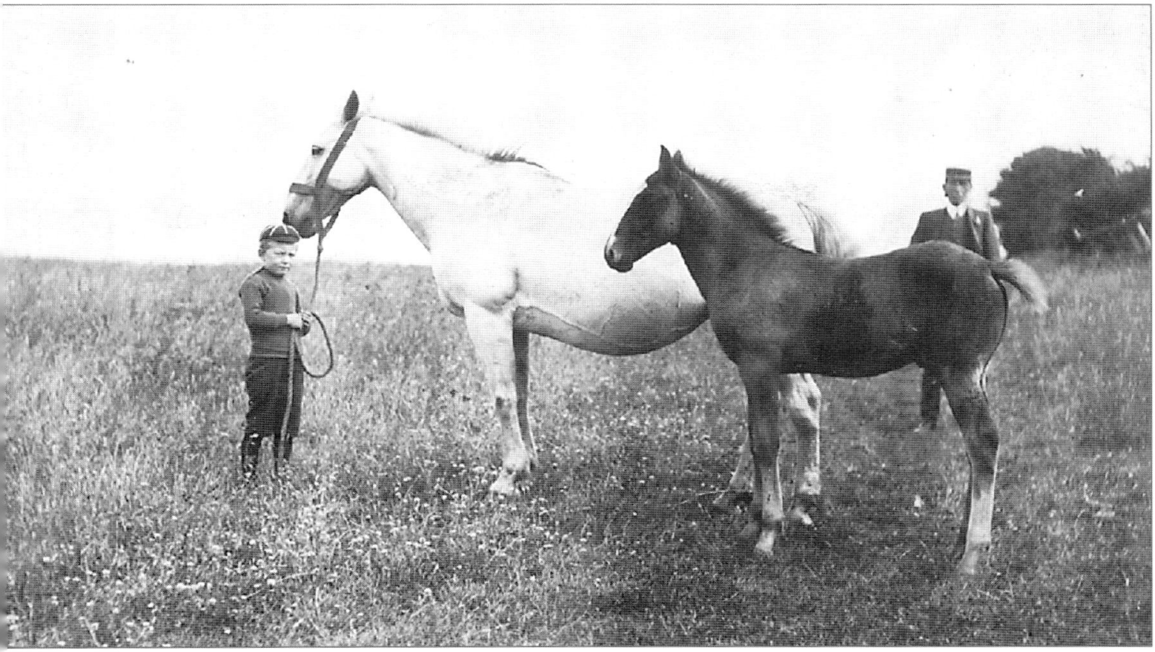

The Yorkshire boy in this early 1900s photograph was eager to work with horses but farming a small-holding of 7 acres was uneconomic. In 1897 John Dickinson of Timble near Harrogate wrote: 'I don't want to part with the horse as it would be a step down walking to Harrogate again. I have been unlucky in farming.'

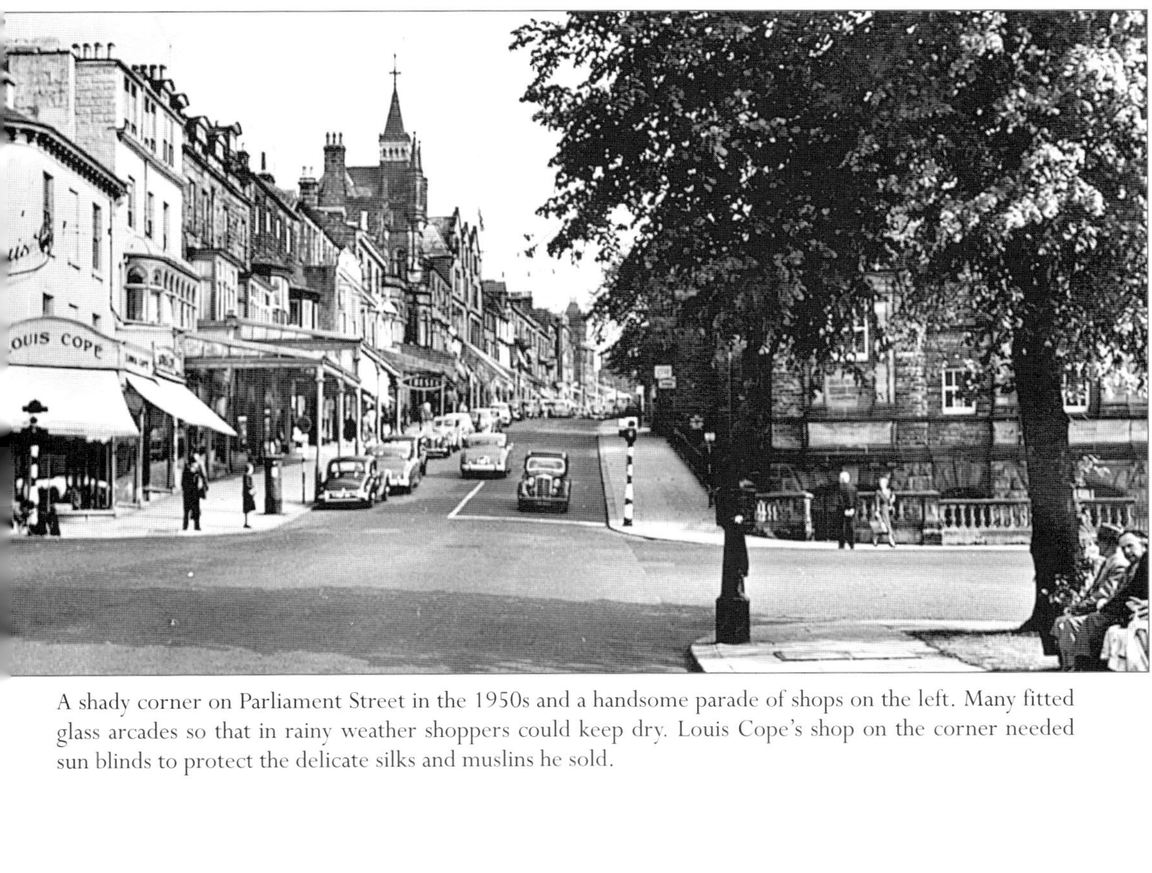

A shady corner on Parliament Street in the 1950s and a handsome parade of shops on the left. Many fitted glass arcades so that in rainy weather shoppers could keep dry. Louis Cope's shop on the corner needed sun blinds to protect the delicate silks and muslins he sold.

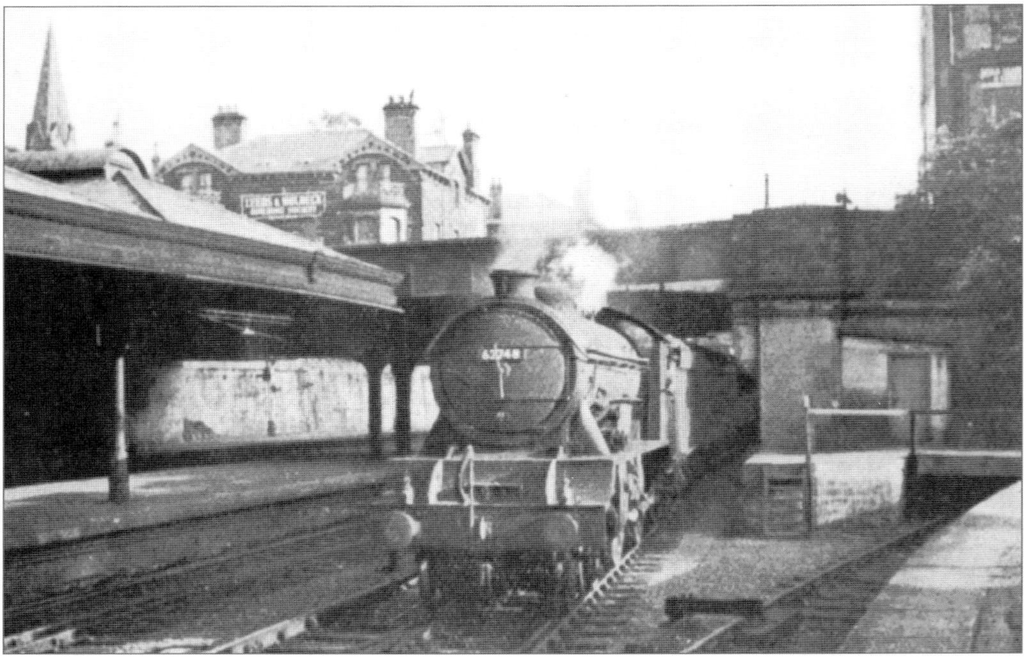

Hunt Class 4–4–0 locomotive No. 62748 heads the Leeds to Harrogate train at Harrogate station, 1955. The original Thirsk and Leeds Railway opened throughout the route in 1849. Its union with the Harrogate loop line was at Bilton Junction close to the boundary hedge of the old Forest of Knaresborough, the path being part of an old packhorse route.

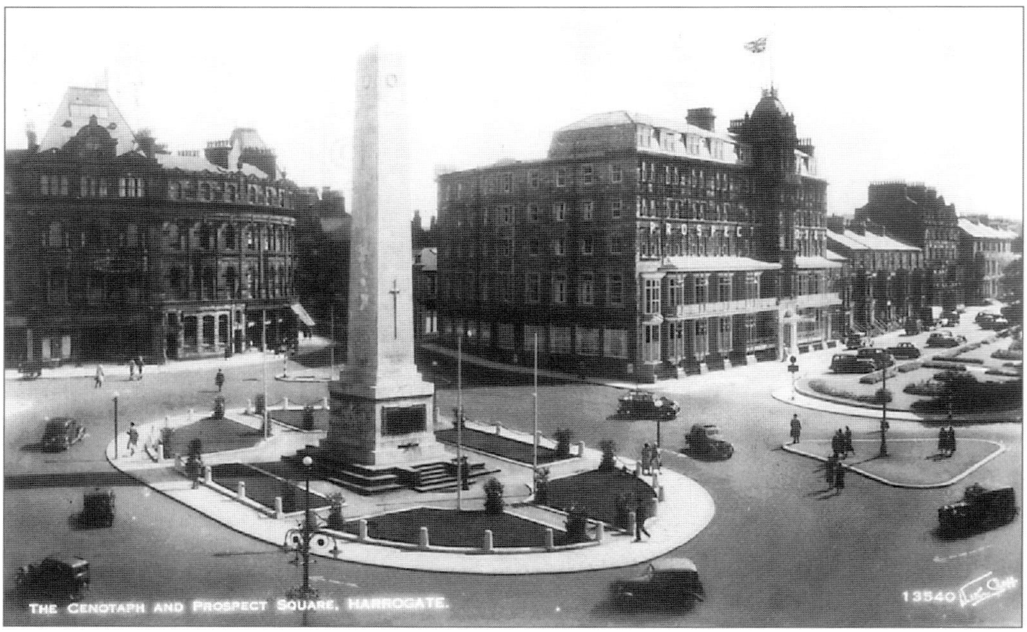

The Cenotaph and Prospect Square, 1952. The Prospect Hotel on the right and other fine buildings indicate splendid accommodation, a great asset in promoting conferences and exhibitions. Another advantage was the bracing, dry, sunny and healthy climate. Records show Harrogate to be one of the sunniest places in Britain, especially in winter.

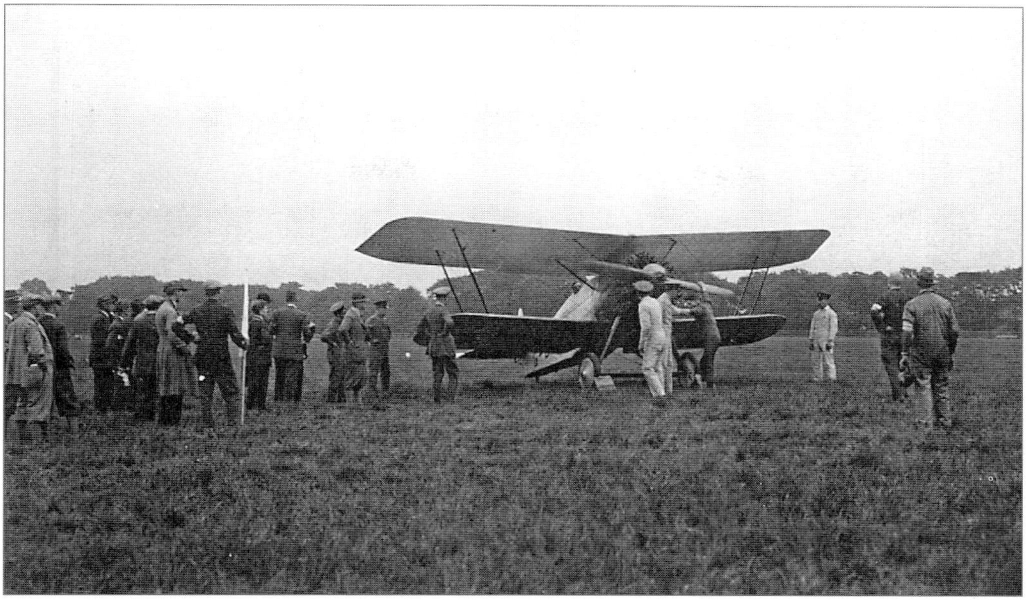

Landing near the Wetherby Road, F.L. Barnard was the first arrival on the Stray on 23 July in the 1925 Round Britain Air Race. He had left Hendon at 9.48 a.m. and in spite of bad weather completed the flight in 1½ hours, making a perfect landing in his 395 h.p. Siskin V. Shortly afterwards he was followed by airmen Captain J.L. Baggs, Flight Lieutenant H.W. Jones, Major H. Hemming and Captain F.T. Courtney. As they arrived they were driven along the course in a motor car before the cheering crowds.

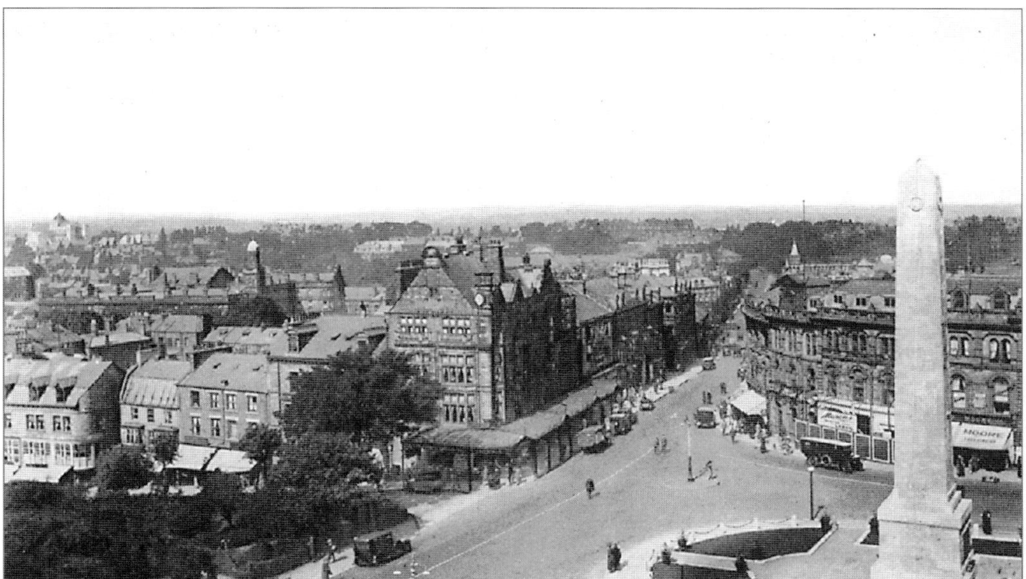

Bird's-eye view from Prospect Parade, *c.* 1926. Montpellier Parade is on the left, and on the corner is the Café Imperial with its iron colonnade. The Joy brothers of Cold Bath Road also established premises in the Parade, producing hand-made shoes. Mason's and Moore's shops graced Cambridge Crescent, designed by J.H. Hirst. The close proximity of the moors to the town is apparent.

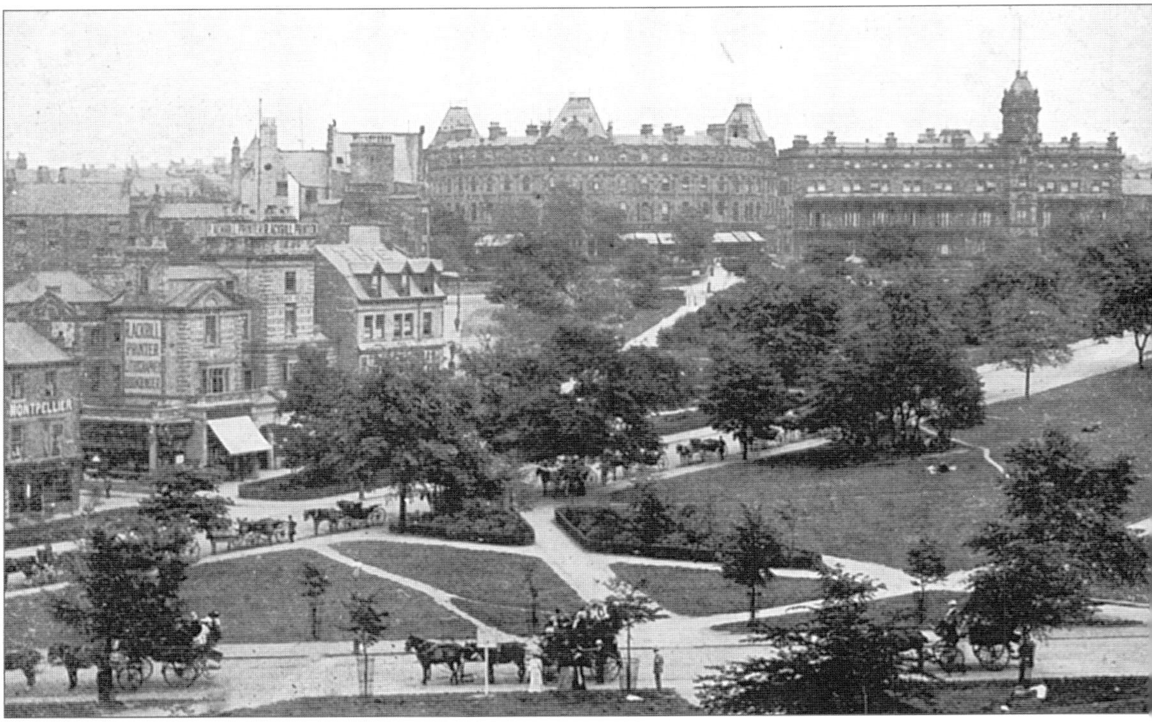

Prospect Hill, 1909. The premises of R. Ackrill, printer, lithographer and bookbinder are seen on the left, forerunner of today's Ackrill Press. The many types of horse-drawn vehicle are interesting, from landaus to four-horse wagonettes. Occasionally even bath chairs would be pulled by a donkey.

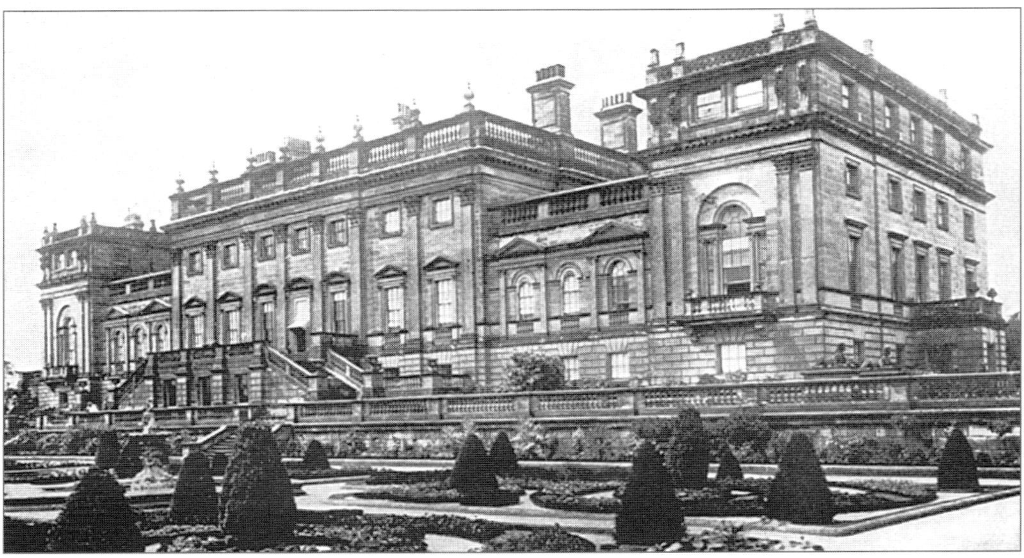

Harewood House, near Harrogate, one of the finest houses in the north, *c.* 1926. Built in the 1760s, it was designed by the York architect John Carr with some influence from another great architect and designer, Robert Adam. Capability Brown laid out the extensive parkland, which caused Harewood village to be removed to a new position outside the confines of the spacious grounds.

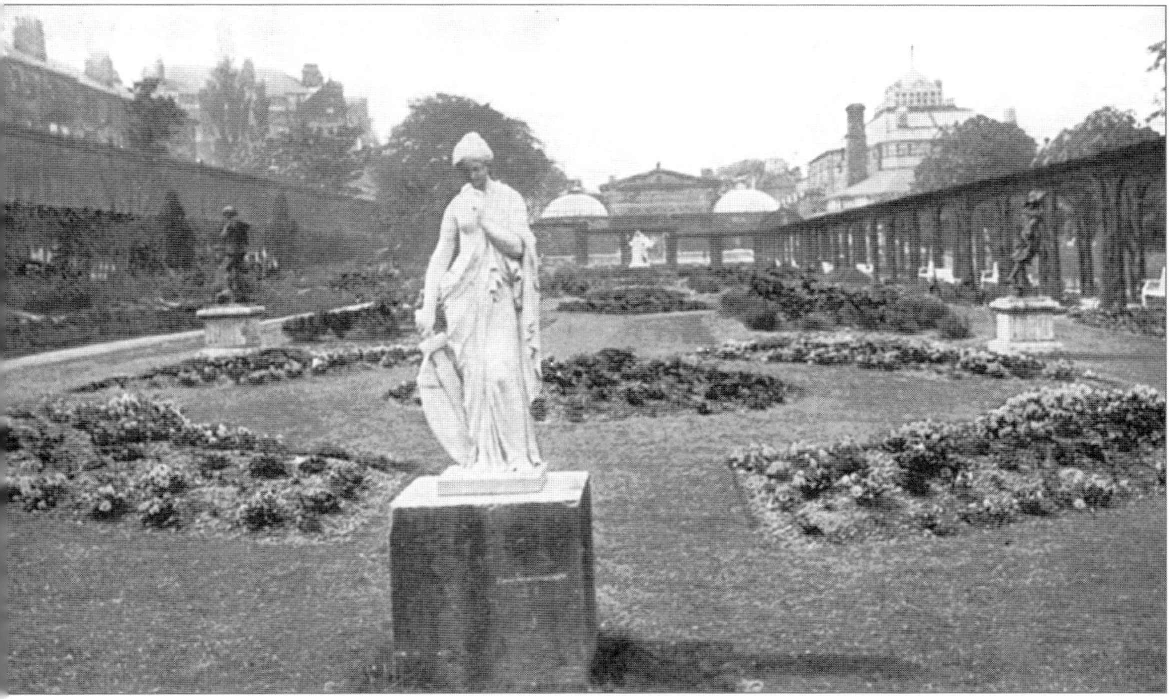

The statuary in the Royal Hall Gardens, and the glorious array of bedding plants, seen here in about 1940, made this one of the most impressive in a town noted for floral display. Today's *Harrogate and District Guide* refers to 'endless acres of immaculate gardens always a blaze of colour throughout the whole year, lush green open spaces and stunning architecture'.

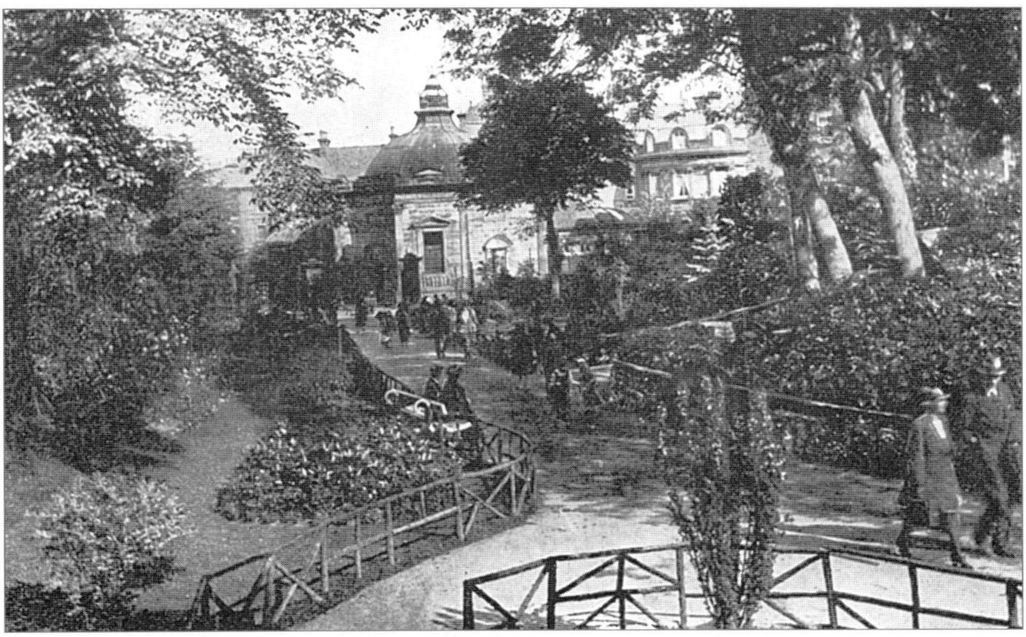

Entrance to the Valley Gardens, *c.* 1935. After drinking at the Sulphur Well, people often made for the Sun Colonnade down one side of the gardens or dined under the glass-domed roof of the Pavilion, still in use as a concert hall. The Magnesia Well was housed in a green-domed building in the Gardens.

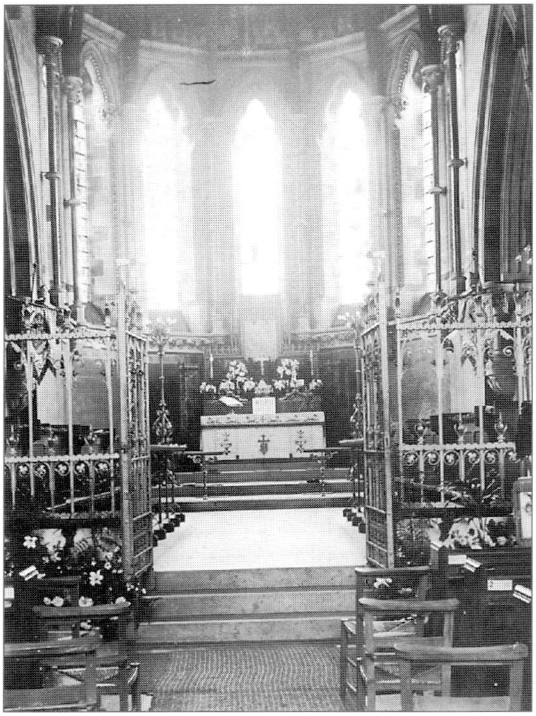

St Peter's Church high altar, *c*. 1900, showing the golden gates given by the architect Hirst of Bristol. The 1860s and beyond saw the development of Harrogate. Elegant villas, hotels, shops and churches arose, planned mainly by the Victoria Park Company formed under the inspiration of Richard Ellis and other businessmen. Master builder George Dawson worked with J.H. Hirst and together they erected many beautiful classical buildings which have endured and which undoubtedly stamped the high tone of the town upon visitors and populace alike. St Peter's in Cambridge Street was built without a tower but the now familiar tower was erected in 1924.

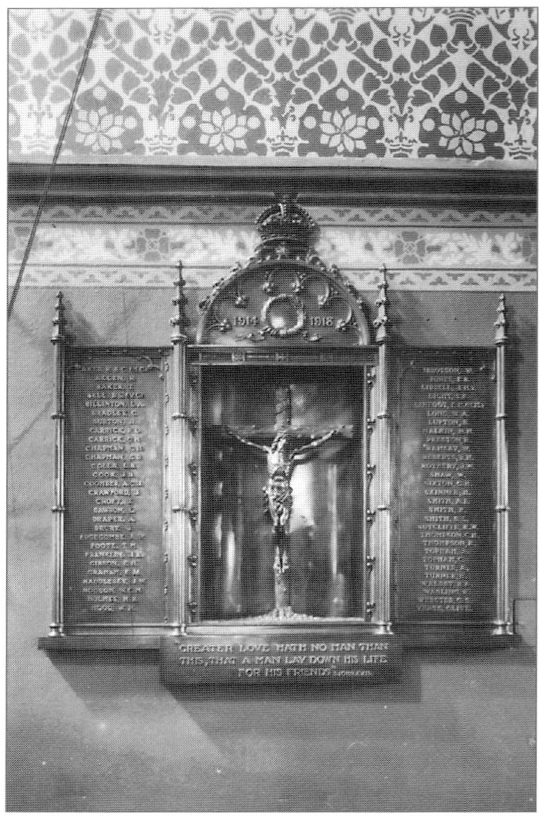

The War Memorial in St Peter's Church, photographed in about 1930, commemorates the fallen of the First World War. Beneath the crucifix is lettered: 'Greater love hath no man than this that a man lay down his life for his friends.' The panels on each side, listing the names of the young men of Harrogate who never returned, follow the style of the First World War street shrines which for many years neighbours kept bright with flowers. Almost every household had lost someone and it was a solemn duty to keep the sad memories green. Being open to wind and weather, these poignant, simple wooden structures have rotted away.

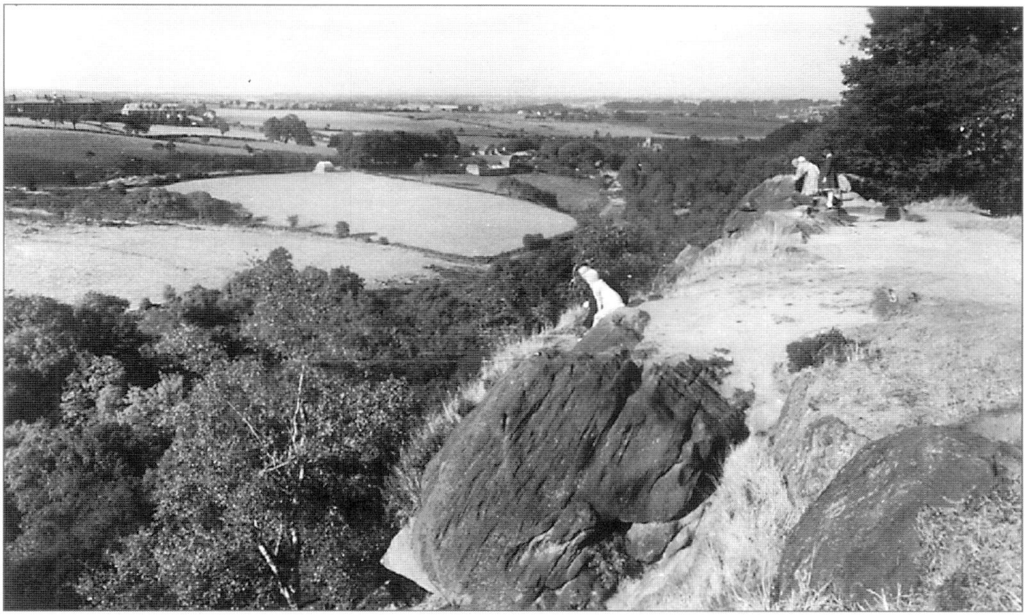

Birk Crag, 1927. This was still a favourite walk, 'Birk' referring to the birch trees. There were also lichens, gorse, ferns, heath and whortleberries growing there: 'a piece of genuine mountain scenery, a narrow glen half a mile in length through which run the waters of Oak Beck' (William Grainge). Oakdale Bridge crossed the beck and ancient Irongate was a pack horse bridge over which iron was carried through the Forest of Knaresborough.

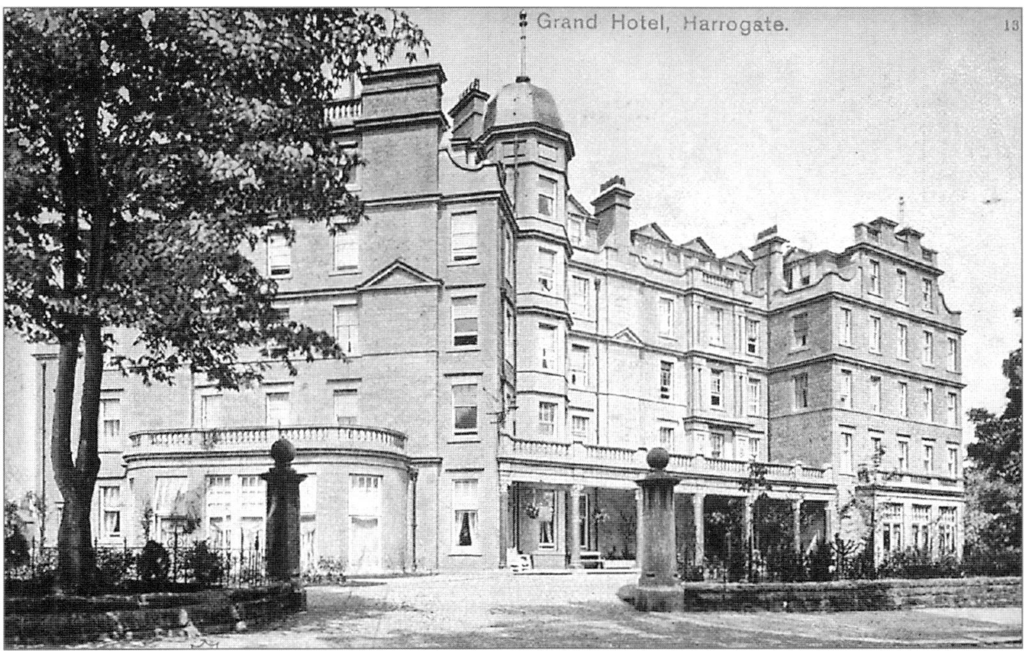

The Grand Hotel, Cornwall Road, 1914, was built in 1903 (three years after the Majestic Hotel) and certainly lived up to its name. They were on a par for standards of excellence. The Majestic, a popular venue for conferences, suffered a devastating fire in 1924 and German bomb damage to its conservatory on 12 September 1940.

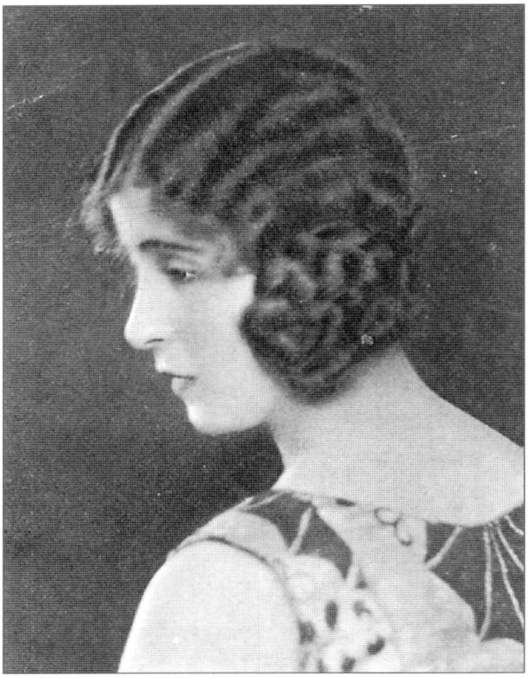

Miss Irene Cowden of Harrogate, *c.* 1928. She was described in the London *Mail* as the most beautiful girl in Yorkshire. She won many beauty contests and became an actress, appearing in *The Merry Widow* at Daly's Theatre. She worked for the Northern British Film Company in many lead roles including Mercenary Mary. Note Miss Cowden's hair style, carefully 'Marcel' waved and regularly shampooed with Amami, much advertised at the time, 'Friday night is Amami night' being the slogan.

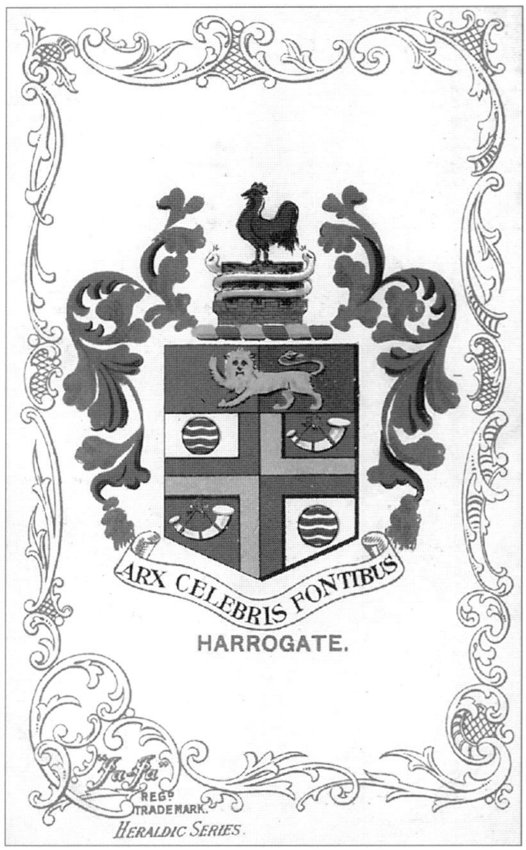

The Heraldic Series of about 1930 included 'The Queen of Inland Watering Places'. From 1884 to 1974 Harrogate flaunted this crest with its Latin motto '*Arx Celebris Fontibus*' (borough famous for its springs). Overlooking Crescent Gardens are the Council Offices, where the old motto can still be seen above the door. These were opened in 1931 on the site of the Victoria Baths built by John Williams. The Improvement Commissioners took these over in 1838 and replaced them with the new Victoria Baths. Following Local Government boundary changes in 1974 a new motto, 'To Be of Service', was adopted and a new coat of arms with the quarterings as follows: horn, white rose, spa waters, castle. Apple tree and wheat with a red lion centre complete the crest. In embracing Ripon, Knaresborough and Boroughbridge, the town became Greater Harrogate, its boundaries extending almost to York.

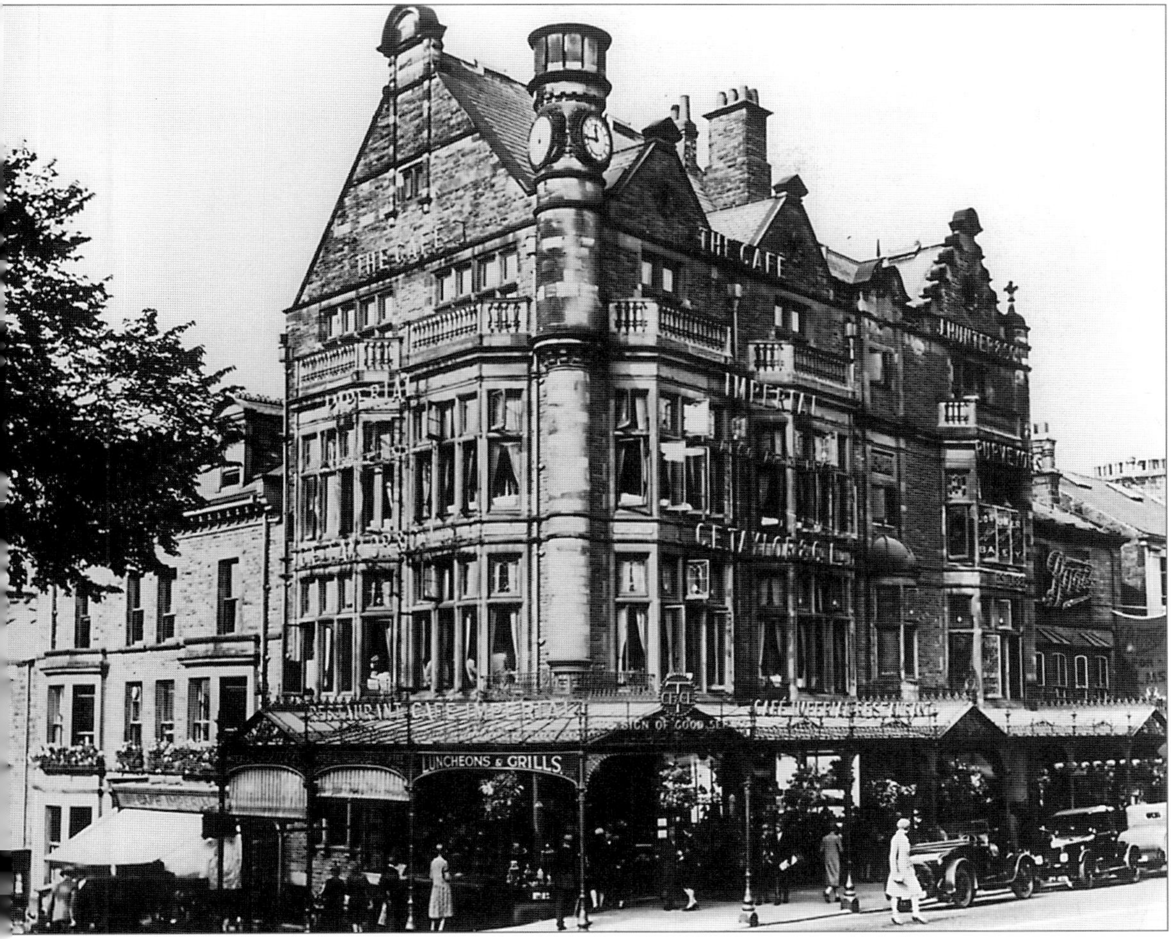

The Café Imperial, Harrogate. The Café Imperial was the grandest venture of Charles and Llewyn Taylor who were encouraged by the success of their tea and coffee 'Kiosks'. The Café Imperial served exotic teas from all over the world to the accompaniment of string quartets.

In 1962 Taylor's jointed forces with Betty's Café Tea Rooms and both companies are still owned by the direct descendants of Frederick Belmont. Today there are four Betty's Café Tea Rooms: Harrogate (now situated in the original Cafe Imperial building), York, Northallerton and Ilkley, a Taylors Tea Rooms in York and a family tea and coffee merchants in Harrogate.

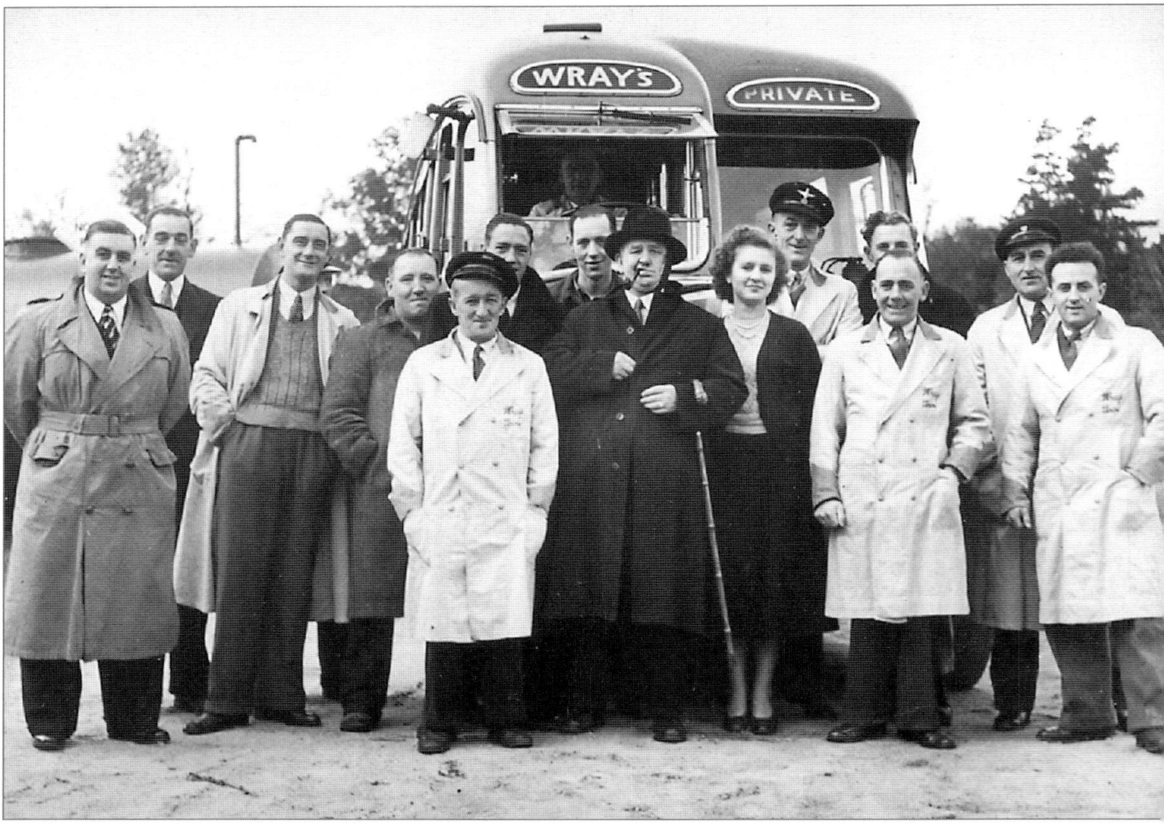

The driving team of Wrays of Harrogate, *c.* 1942. The company was established in 1929 under Alec Wray (centre, smoking a pipe) who was the first person to hold a car auction in Yorkshire. They operated from Shaw Mills in Nidderdale, later moving to Dacre Banks where they still have a depot, but Head Office is now in Montpellier Street, Harrogate.

The first vehicles were Model T Fords with slatted seats and tarpaulin covers, somewhat reminiscent of the 'covered wagons' of the Wild West, a far cry indeed from the present-day Volvo luxury coaches. In those days Harrogate visitors were delighted with fairly modest tours: for example, the Abbeys tour, How Stean Gorge, and Brimham Rocks. At the time of this photograph petrol rationing imposed severe travel restrictions.

Now in the third generation, under Managing Director Malcolm Wray, grandson of the founder, the firm is a national and international tour operator. Long distance and long duration tours offer thirty boarding points within the Harrogate, Knaresborough, Ripon, Wetherby and Leeds area, with Ilkley and Otley from the Wharfe Valley. Destinations include France, Italy, Holland and Belgium. 'The Connoisseurs of Coaching' gave pleasure at a time when it was badly needed, especially during the Second World War, and indeed have continued to do so ever since 1929.

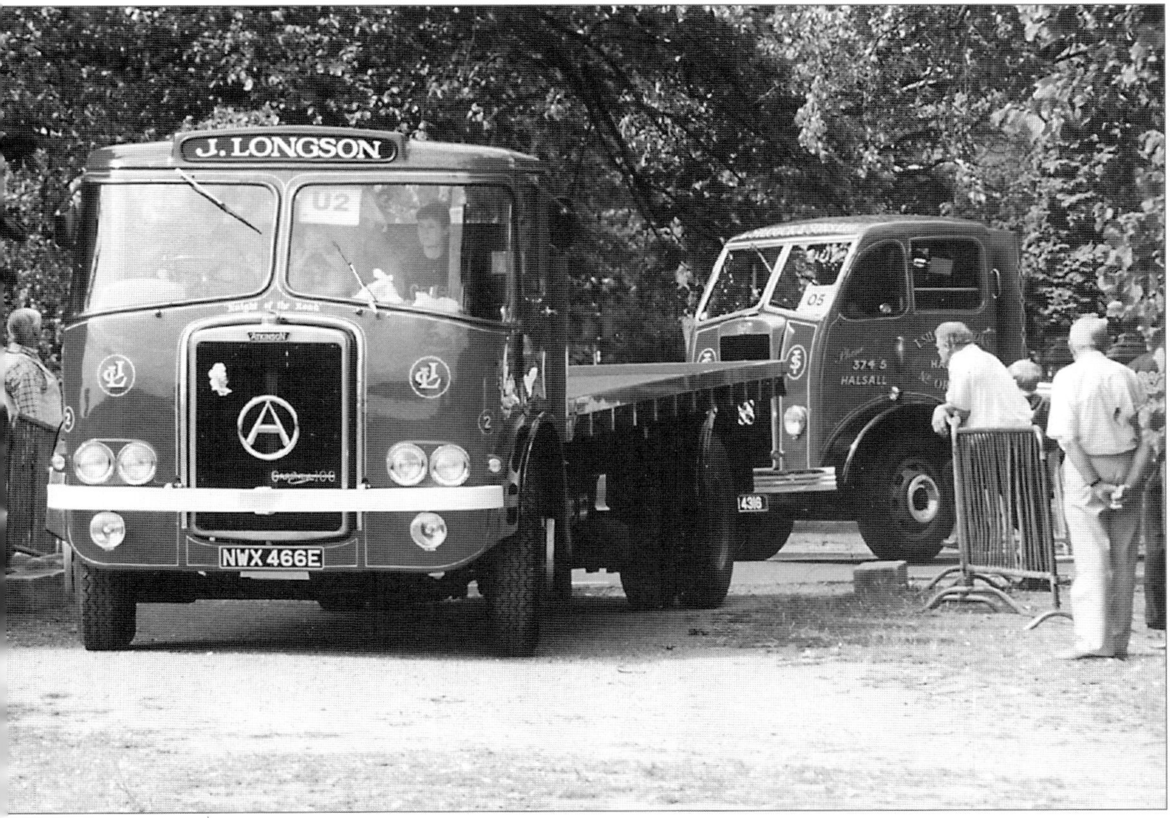

Trans-Pennine Vintage Vehicle Run, August 1970. This increasingly popular event, inaugurated in 1968, features more than 3,000 commercial vehicles. After travelling from Manchester to Harrogate they draw up on the Stray. The line-up includes a wide range of steam and vintage vehicles, some dating back to 1920.

On the route to Harrogate moorland scenery, with its thorn trees, rocks and dry stone walls, conjures up history. It is the task of John Clifton, master dry stone waller, to keep miles of walls in good repair. John commenced his apprenticeship by attending a course run by the Yorkshire Dry Stone Walling Guild. 'Many of these walls,' said John, 'are well over 100 years old . . . for every yard of wall you put up, you shift a ton of stone.' The hawthorn or May tree has symbolism beyond the memory of man, as boughs of the blossom were used for May Day sports, to decorate houses, on top of the Aldborough Maypole and to crown the May Queen.

On the moors around and beyond Harrogate at the turn of the century, a pole with a bunch of heather tied on top indicated an inn where good drinking water could be had. This was a variation of the medieval sign used at taverns and could be the origin of the phrase 'Good wine needs no bush'. This proverb means that if a commodity is intrinsically good, it needs no outward display.

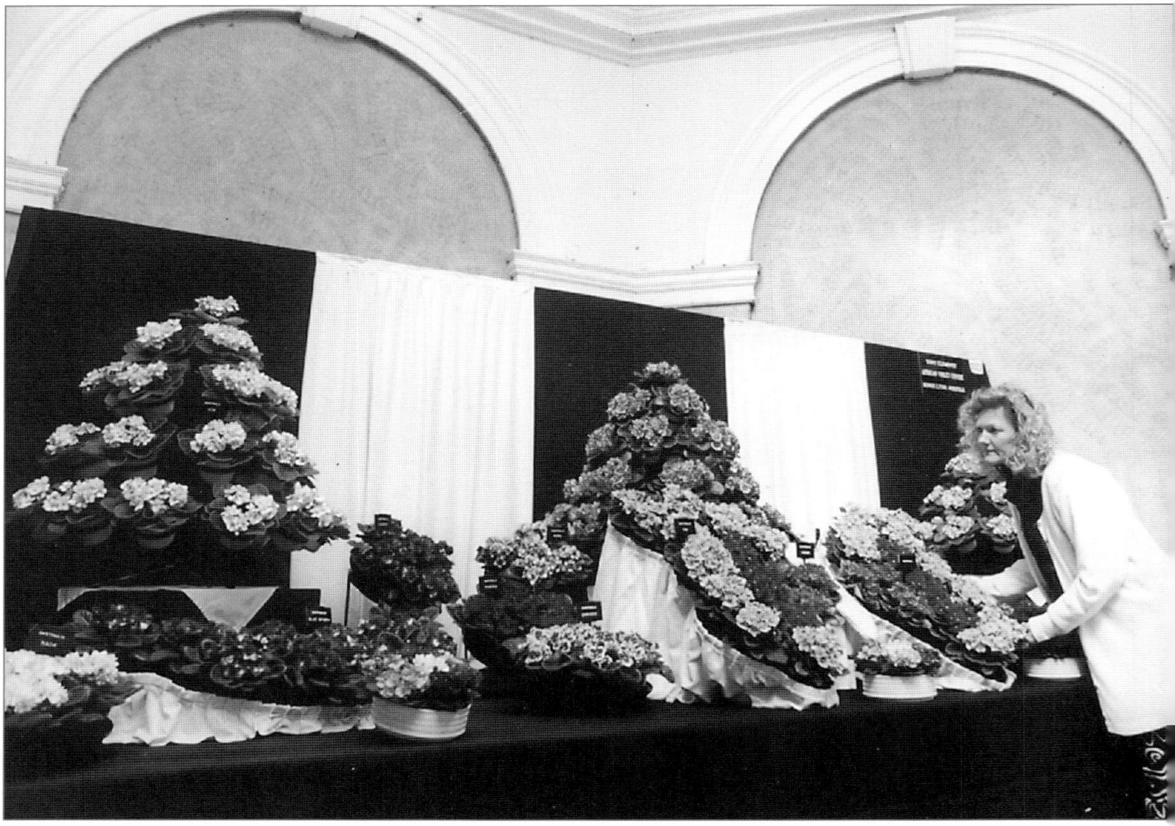

Harrogate Flower Show, 1970. The Harrogate Spring Flower Show has always been one of Britain's best-loved horticultural expressions, home to the largest display of modern daffodils in the north of England. It never fails to draw crowds who also appreciate the carpet of early spring crocuses on the Stray. Valley Gardens, along the streamside walk, is known worldwide for its dramatic floral displays and Harlow Carr Botanical Gardens, with its 68 landscaped acres, is the headquarters of the Northern Horticultural Society. Such is the scene set by modern-day Harrogate with its exhibition halls and International Centre.

A hundred years ago the locals enjoyed passing attractions. It was reported in 1881 that Wombwell's Menagerie camped on the outskirts of the Stray with fifty horses, two elephants and several camels. When fairs were held, gingerbread stalls were set up along with swing boats, whirligigs, shooting galleries, boxing booths and two Frenchmen with a dancing bear. Sports on Swinsty Moor to celebrate the completion of Swinsty Reservoir in 1887 included foot races, tug of war, sack race, bed run, wheelbarrow race and a race for women. 'A good knife and fork tea was provided followed by a magic lantern show at the Huts.' On another occasion it was 'dancing and singing in Uncle George's granary till 5 o'clock in the morning'. The big event of the year was a trip to Scarborough when 'an exceedingly long train' left Darley station at 6 a.m.

SECTION TWO

KNARESBOROUGH & RIPON

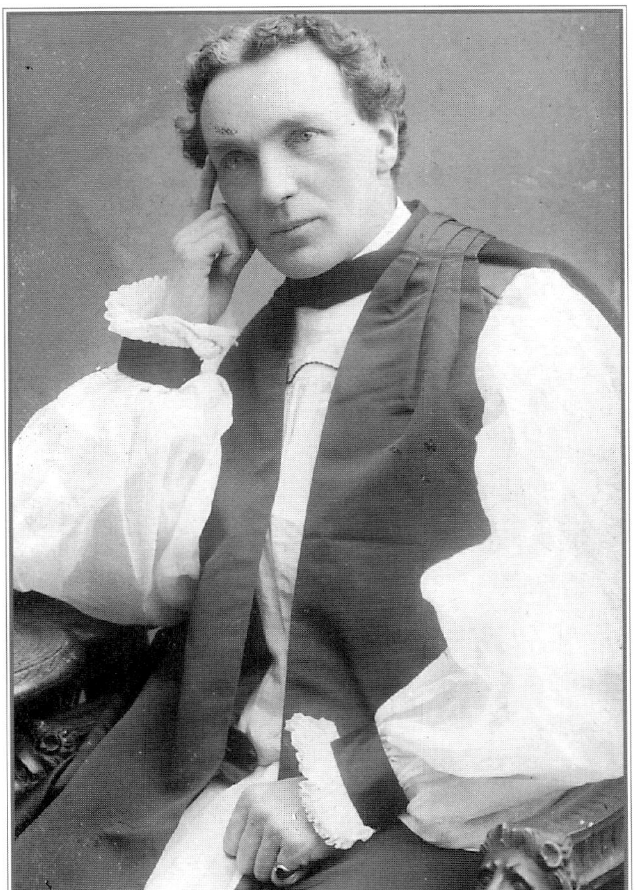

The Right Revd Lucius Frederick Moses Bottomley Smith, Suffragan Bishop of Knaresborough (1905–34).

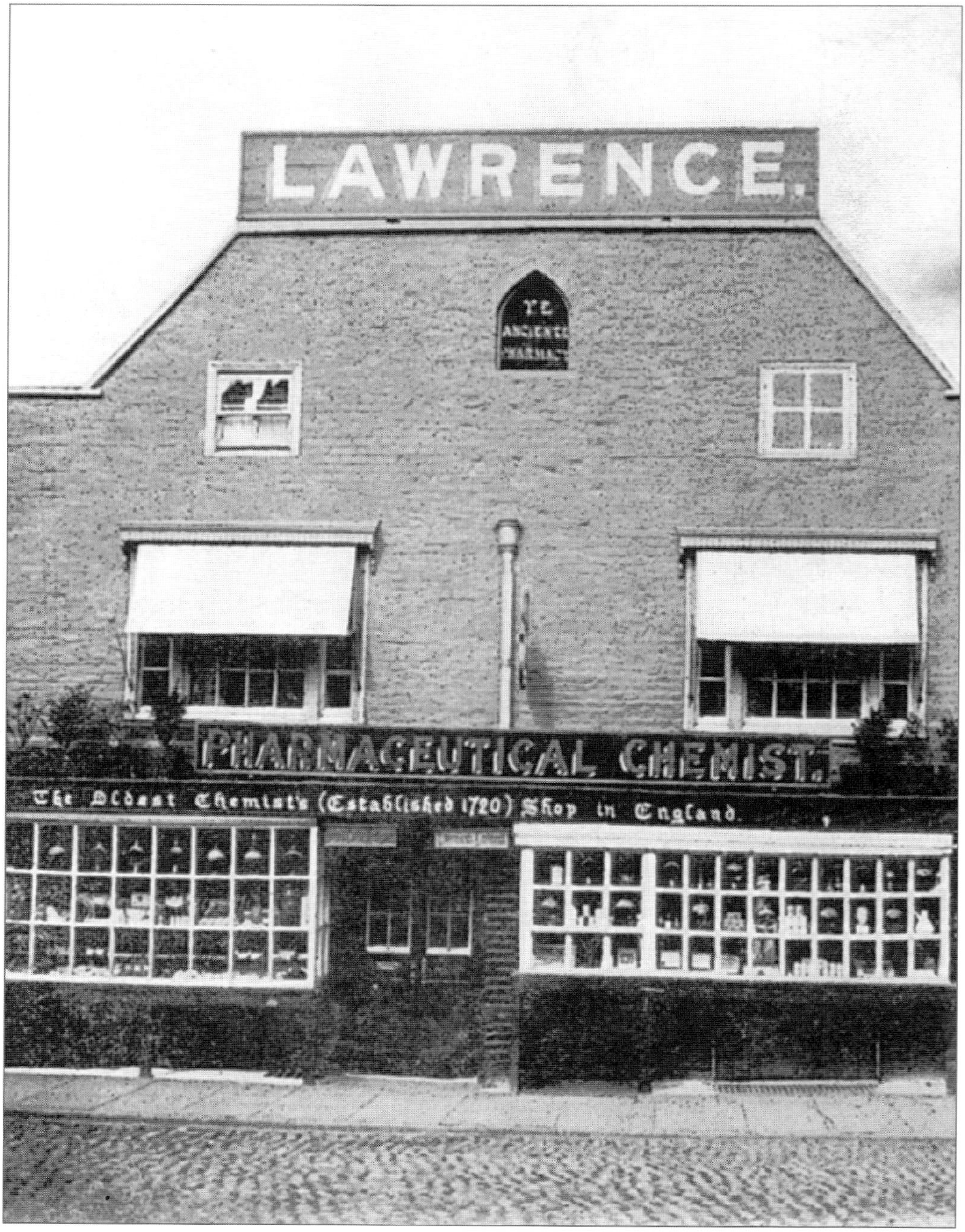

The oldest pharmacy in England, early 1900s. The interior of this Knaresborough chemist's shop, originally established in 1720 as an apothecary, had low, oak beams in the ceiling. The original pharmaceutical dark brown and green bottles were ridged to indicate poison. There were also enormous Winchesters, cylindrical glass, narrow-necked bottles which held over 2 litres of chemicals of different colours. The old couch remained where patients were bled by the application of leeches and where early dentistry was performed, as the chemist was also the local dentist. Mr W.P. Lawrence retired in 1965, his family having been chemists here for more than 100 years. Lawrence's Old English Lavender Water is still made from a well-guarded eighteenth-century recipe.

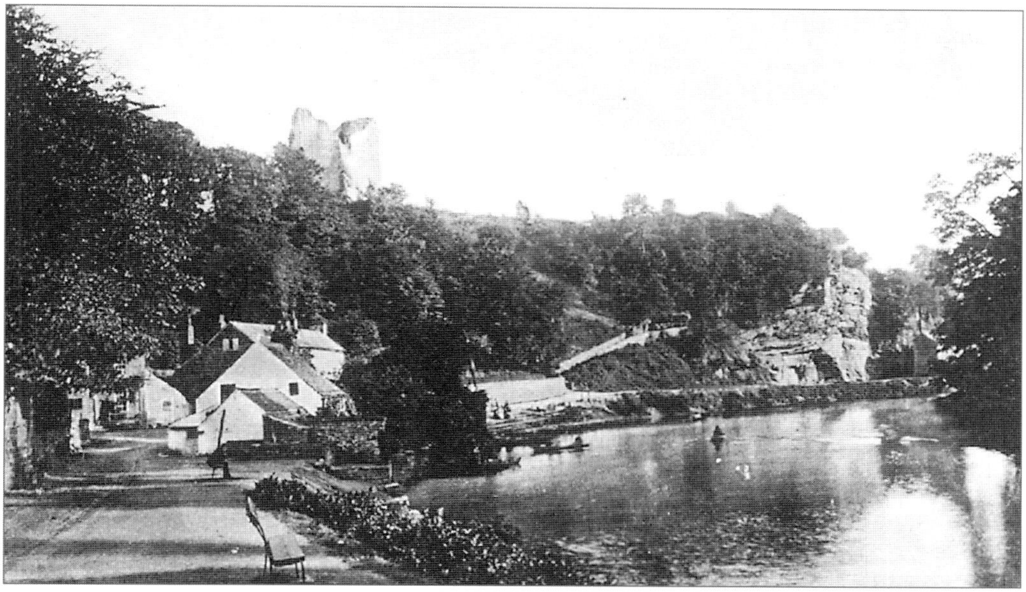

Knaresborough Castle on Castle Hill, photographed in 1906, was built soon after William I conquered England and sent his Commissioners to record all property in the Domesday Book. The four knights who slew Thomas à Becket in Canterbury Cathedral fled to this castle, which was later destroyed by Cromwell's troops. King John used the castle when he was hunting in Knaresborough Forest.

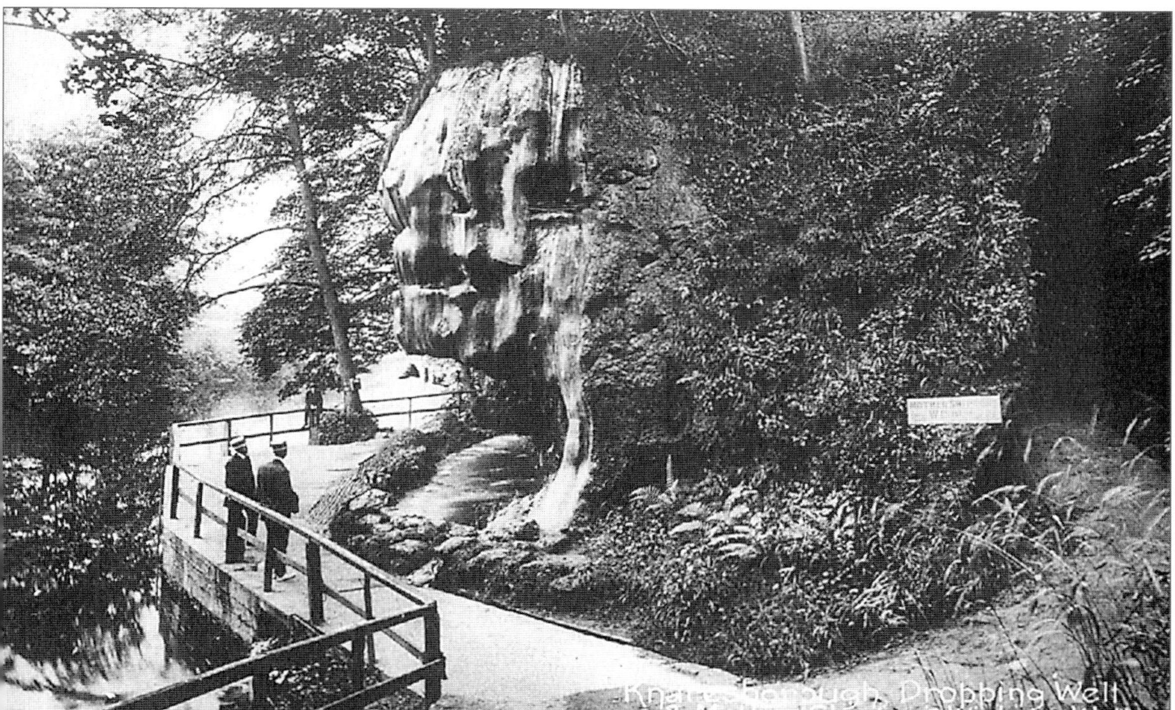

Knaresborough Dropping Well and Mother Shipton's Wishing Well, 1904. Situated on the long walk by the river, this was a fascination to all, as articles suspended in the falling waters became encrusted with limestone and within months assumed a brown petrified appearance.

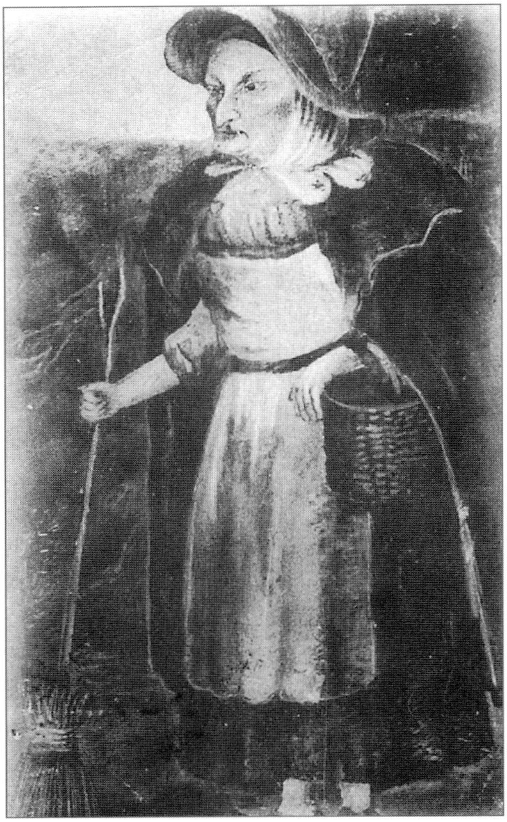

Mother Shipton, 1900. She was reputed to have been born in a cave near the Dropping Well on 6 July 1488. Her real name was Ursula Southeil. She married Toby Shipton in 1512 and became a famous prophetess. Since her birth many grotesque happenings had been associated with her and Toby made money out of her reputation. He set up as a fortune teller near the well and because of his wife's odd appearance ('her body crooked and her face frightful') he fostered the idea that she was a white witch with extraordinary powers. In old prints she is depicted as travelling in a small, four-wheeled carriage pulled by a deer. Mrs Shipton had a stay in London at Wapping where she wrote one of her prophesying poems which was published in an 1840s edition of *Blackwood's Magazine*.

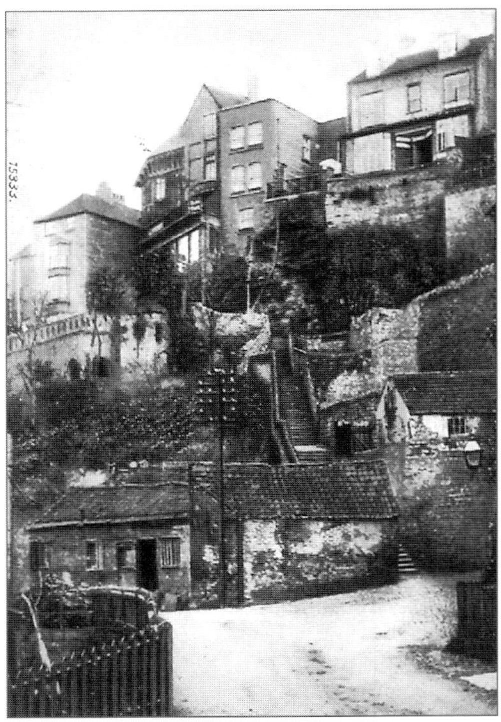

Gallon Steps at Knaresborough, 1906. Only 3½ miles from Harrogate, the Royal Borough of Knaresborough, once noted for linen manufacture, stands on top of a hill overlooking the River Nidd. Roman coins have been found within the Borough. Precipitous rocks and glens characterise the Nidd so there are many steps in this area. In a town surrounded by thick woods, over the years tier upon tier of cottages have been built on the rock face. Delightful views of the town can be seen in a favourite walk via Bilton, recommended for tourists in the early 1900s. The Royal Park of Bilton once belonged to the Honour of Knaresborough and was stocked with deer. Originally afforested for the purpose of royal sport, Thruscross, Clint and Killinghall, with their various hamlets, were in the Forest of Knaresborough which covered an area 20 miles by 8 miles around the castle.

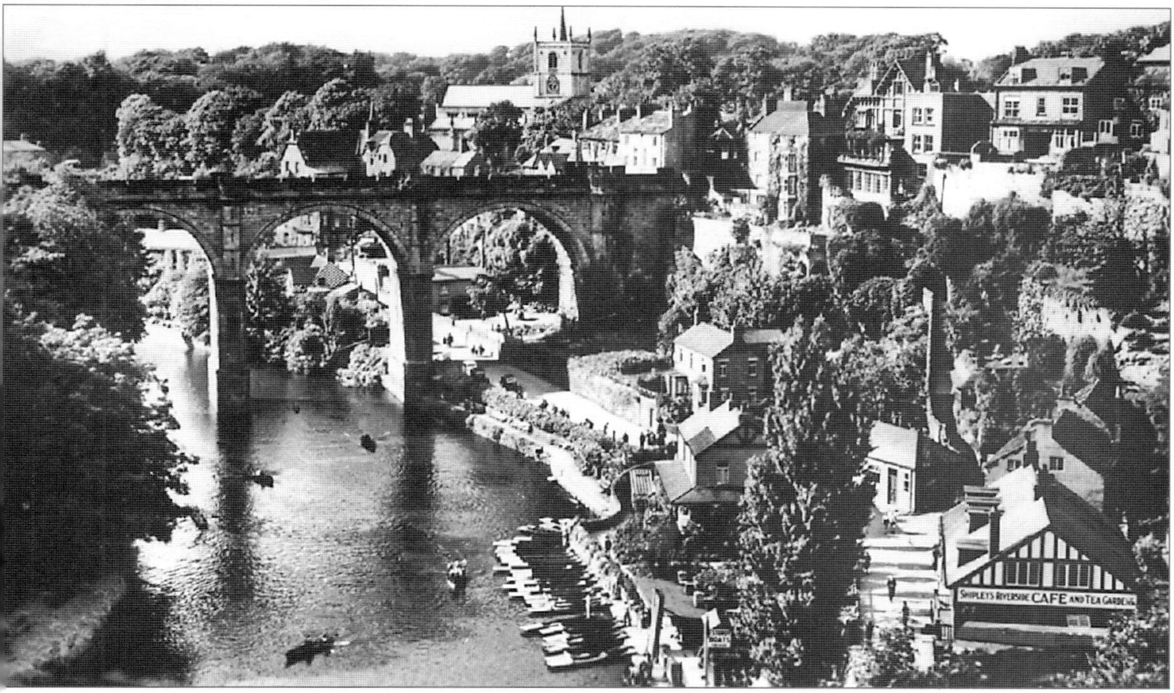

This 1962 view of Knaresborough viaduct and river from Castle Hill shows the town to great advantage. In a very popular boating area note the signs 'Sturdy Boats' and 'Shipley's Riverside Café and Tea Gardens'. What was acclaimed as Surprise View attracted many an artist.

The name Knaresborough derives from the Anglo-Saxon Knarres-burg, meaning a fortress on a rock. The huge sandstone hill about 100 ft above the River Nidd was the site of an early fort and later was no doubt used by the Romans as a good look-out point. The market town grew up in Norman times in the lea of the castle. In the late 1920s visitors to the ruined castle paid 6*d* to see the ancient Guard Room with its many relics, the King's Chamber or Banqueting Room and the Dungeon. By special arrangement the site of the ancient portcullis could be viewed. Baron Serlo de Burgh's castle was partly demolished by Cromwell's troops.

The view also shows the parish church, its architecture Perpendicular and Early English. Mentioned as early as 1114, the church was restored in 1774. The Slingsby family was connected with this church, where there are two interesting fifteenth-century paintings on wood of Moses and Aaron.

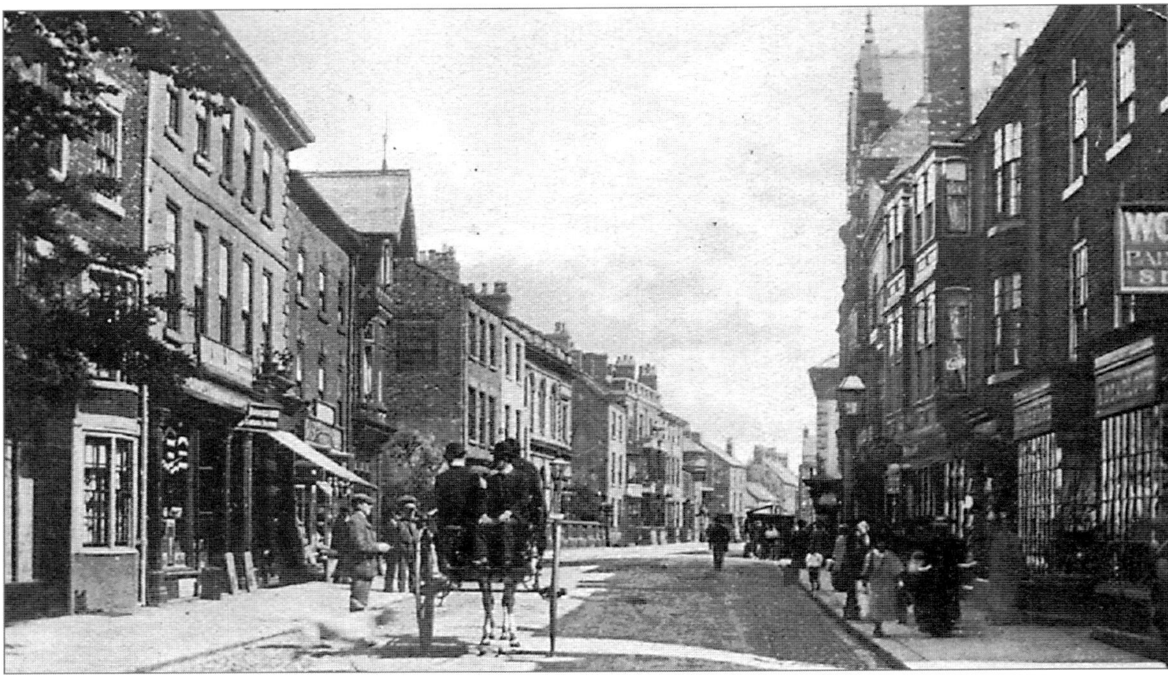

The High Street, Knaresborough, 1915. On the right is the long-established business of Mr Wood, painter and sign writer, opposite a bookseller and stationer's shop. Transport was mainly by horse and carriage but in the distance, far right, there appears to be an early motor bus.

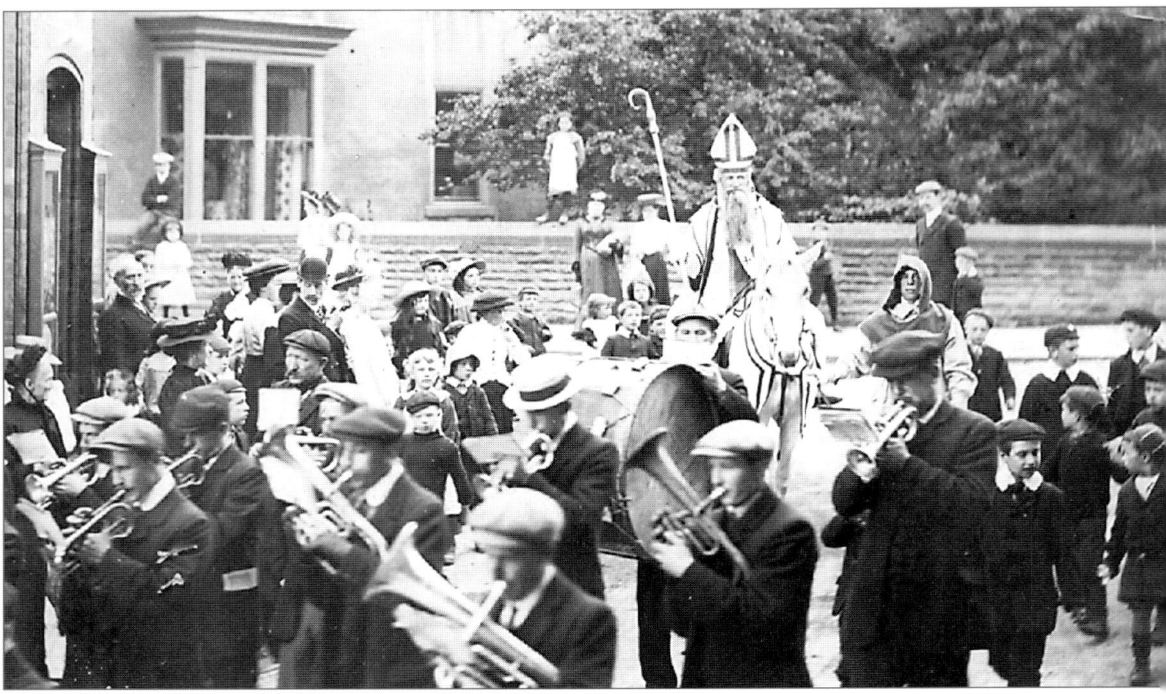

The Annual St Wilfrid's Procession takes place on the first weekend in August. This early 1900s occasion features a cloth-capped brass band with the usual end of procession stragglers in the shape of small boys from Ripon.

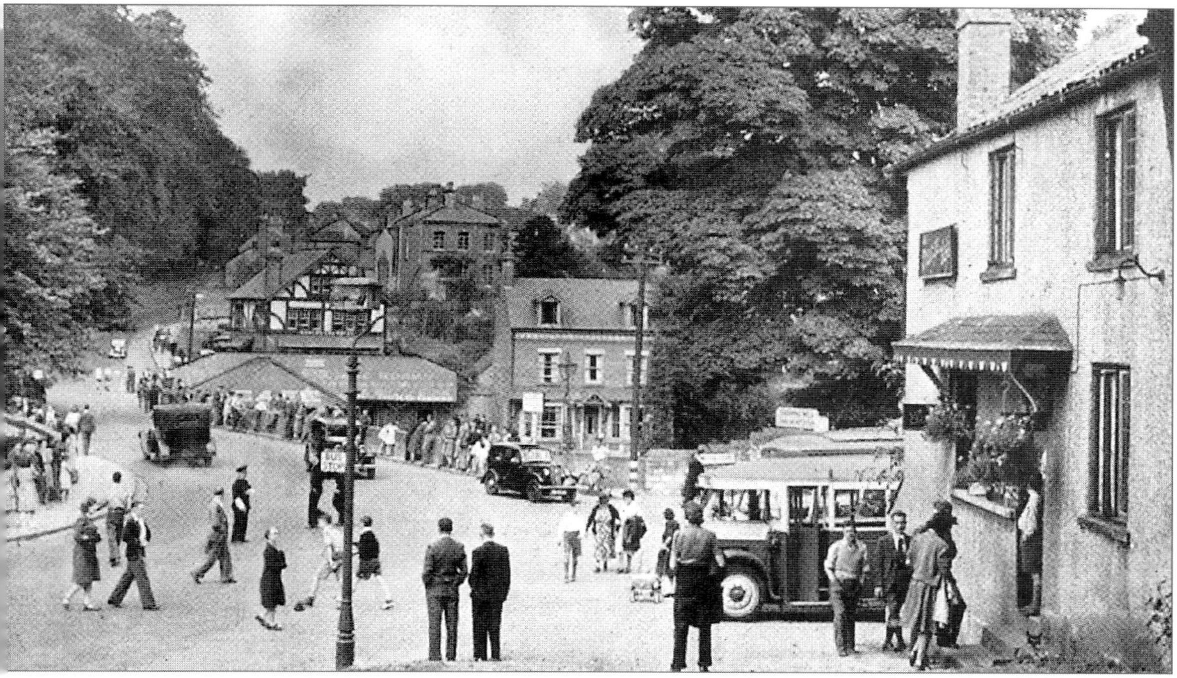

High Bridge, Knaresborough, late 1930s. This ancient bridge was enlarged in 1773, when it was known as Danywell Bridge. Now the main motor traffic artery into Harrogate, it needs constant upkeep. The path to the Dropping Well and on to the Low Bridge, once known as March Bridge, was tramped by hundreds on payment of a small entrance fee near High Bridge. There was a wealth of history to enthral tourists from Harrogate who often approached from the north side of the Stray.

It is strange to think that centuries ago Harrogate was less well known than Knaresborough. Making his comparison in 1649, John Taylor, Apothecary, refers to the 'Glory of Knaresborough, the English Spaw, proved by Reason and Experience, equall not inferior to the German Spaw . . . of all five fountains near unto the towne which doe participate of minerall vertues.' He continues: 'The other is further off, almost two miles from it beyond a place called Harrogate Head, in a bottom on the right hand.'

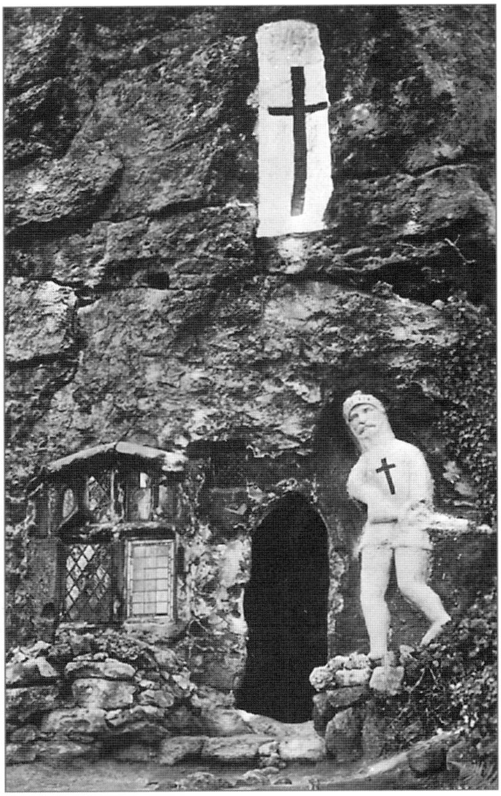

St Robert's Chapel, 1923. An excavation in the cliffs at Knaresborough, it may be unique as a medieval shrine. Robert, born 1160, the son of a Mayor of York, was a hermit. Although attributed to St Robert, it is actually the Chapel of Our Lady of the Crag. In 1916 the figure of the Virgin and Child was placed in the restored Oratory. The quaint armed figure outside does not represent St Robert. The cave has a further interest in that it was used by murderer Eugene Aram to hide his victim, an episode about which Thomas Hood wrote a poem.

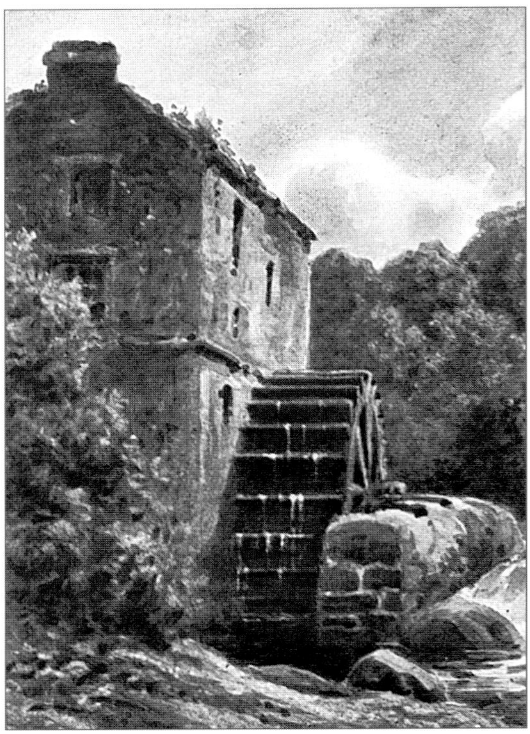

A 1920s watercolour of the Old Mill, Knaresborough. The Castle Mill, originally a cotton mill, was later in full use making linen. In its busiest days it produced over 20,000 yards of cloth a week and continued to do so until 1972 because the high quality cloth was so well favoured even by royalty. At one time the mill was powered by a grand waterfall on the walk between the Dropping Well and the imposing viaduct. In the eighteenth century the town's water supply was pumped from near the castle but before the pump was installed water was carried up in leather puncheons on the backs of mules or horses. Strong local ladies who would take up buckets of water at a penny a time objected to the pump as it damaged their trade. This custom led to the route being called Water Bag Bank.

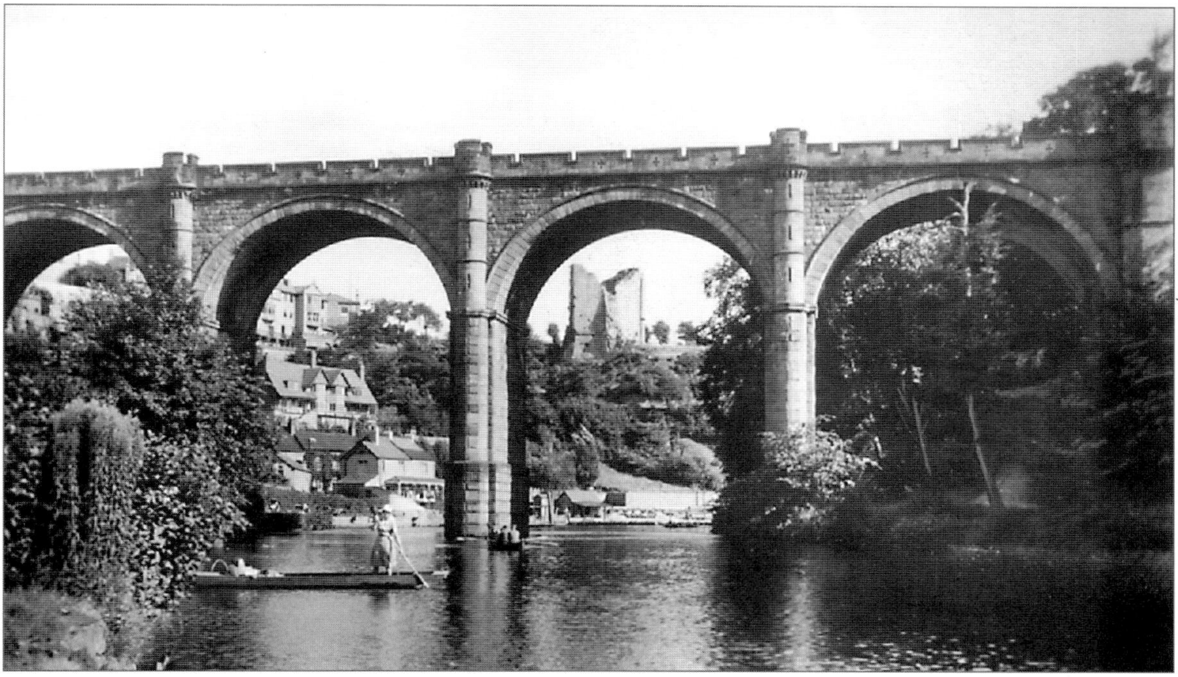

‘On the river’, Knaresborough, 1937, a superb photograph by the firm of Valentine. The centre arch makes a dramatic frame for the ruined castle. This is the railway viaduct spanning the River Nidd which is deep and at this point suitable for boating, craft being for hire near the road bridge.

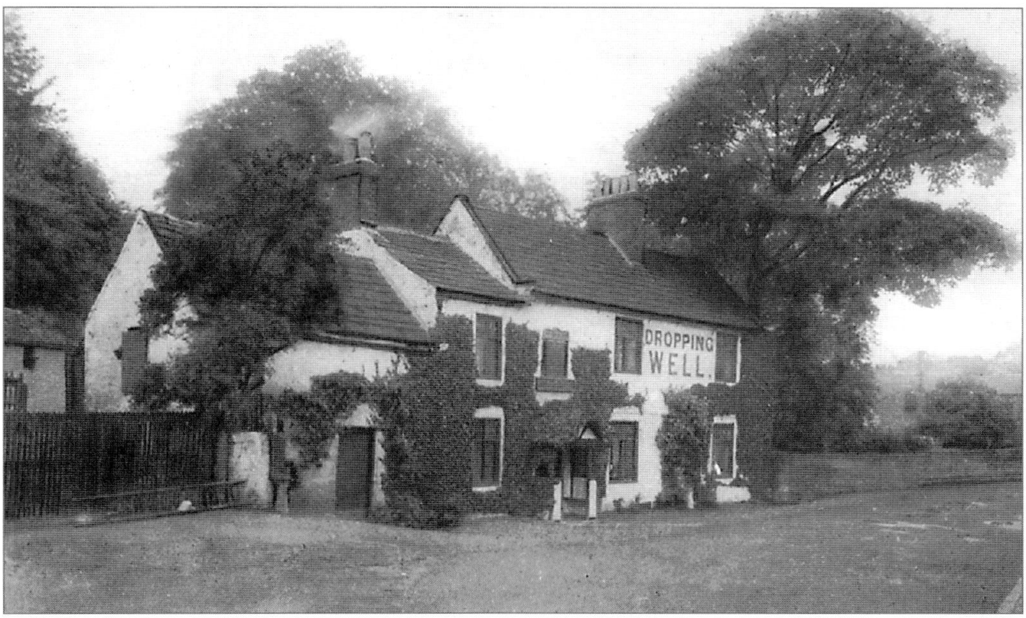

In 1901, when this photograph was taken, the Dropping Well was approached through the Mother Shipton Inn. The magnesium limestone waters flowing at the Dropping Well turned a collection of items to stone and these were kept at the inn. Every Boxing Day since 1968 a tug of war has been held between strong men from the Half Moon Inn and Mother Shipton Inn. The losers were dragged through the waters of the ford which was later replaced by Low Bridge.

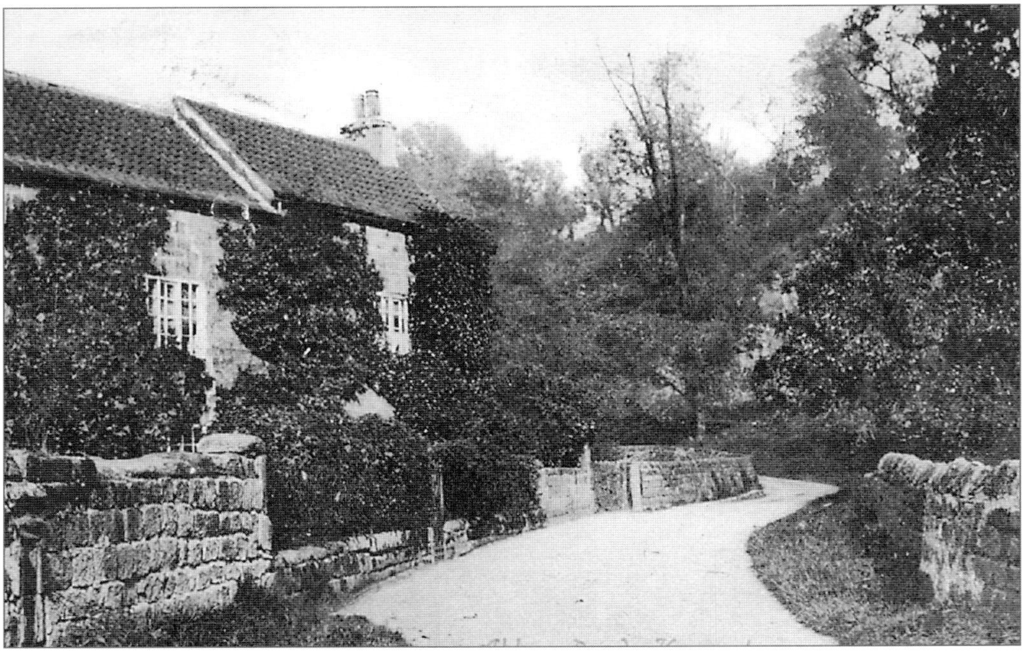

Abbey Road, Knaresborough, close to the House in the Rock and the Chapel of Our Lady of the Crag, 1905. In the vicinity there was once not an abbey but a priory dedicated to St Robert, who had gained a reputation as a herbalist and healer of wounds.

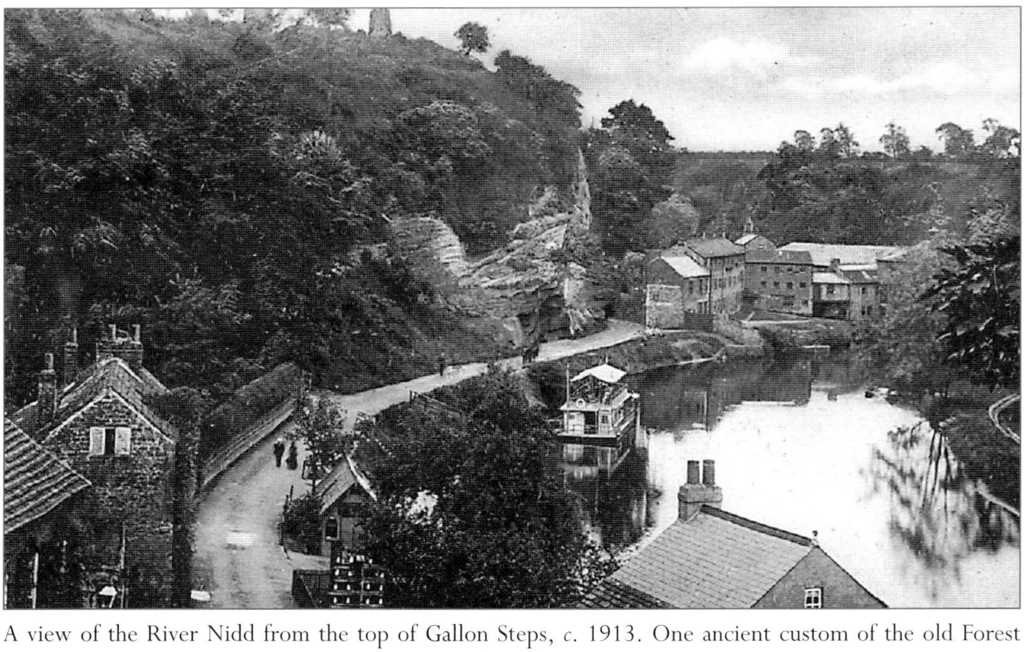

A view of the River Nidd from the top of Gallon Steps, *c.* 1913. One ancient custom of the old Forest Court of Knaresborough which dates from 1177 and survived into the late nineteenth century was the swearing in of men to serve on the jury. The Court of the Forest, called the Sheriff Torne or Great Court Leet, was held in the Castle twice a year, after Easter and Michaelmas. The officers were high steward, under steward, grave (court crier) and beadle.

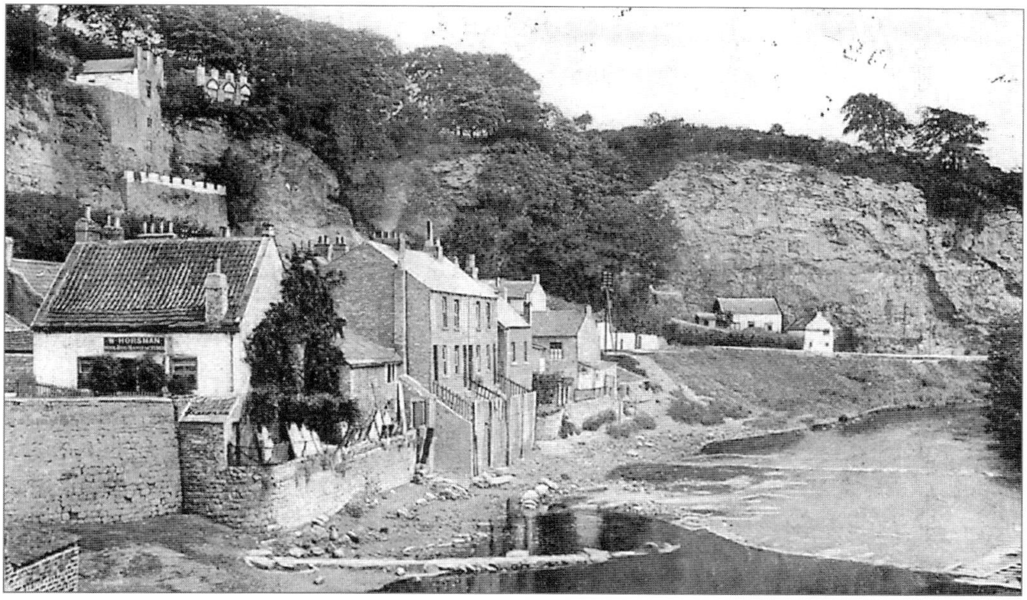

Fort Montague and Crag Top, Briggate, Knaresborough, 1916. Thomas Hill, a weaver, hacked from solid rock a house first known as Swallow's Nest. For twelve years from 1770 onwards he and his son laboured, changing the name to Fort Montague as they 'built greater'. A self-styled Lord, Thomas flew a flag and now and then sounded off a cannon, but sadly he did not live to see his fort completed.

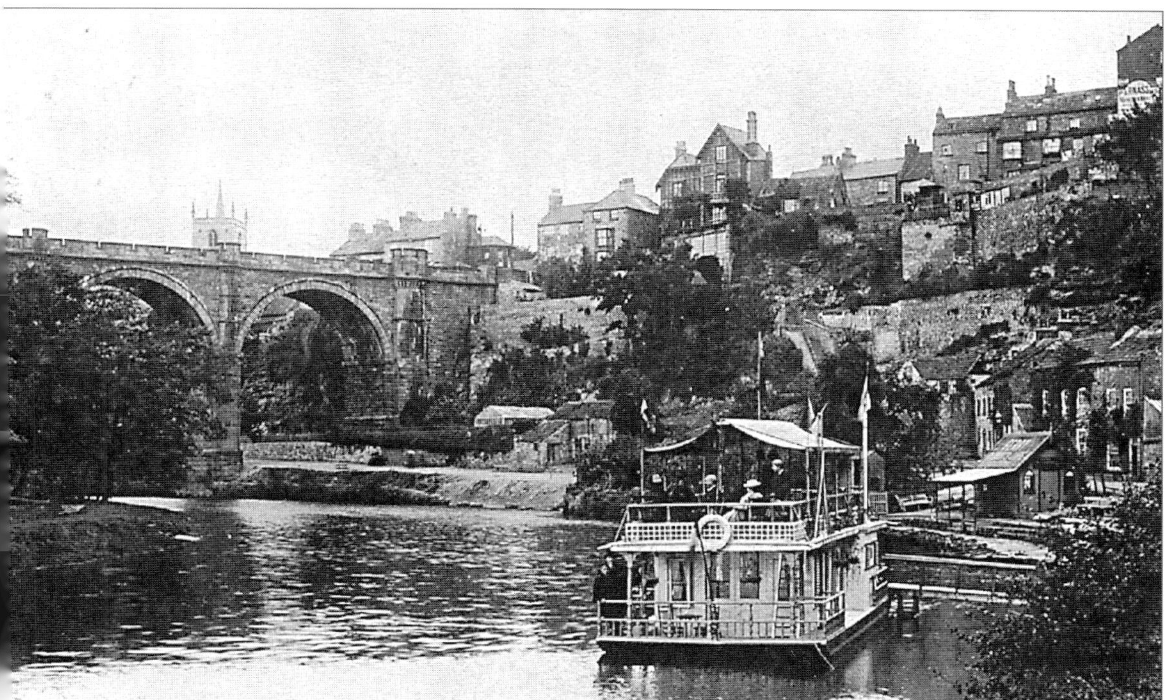

From this popular houseboat on the Nidd at River Side there was a good view of the viaduct, the castle and the parish church of St John with its quaint, pointed spire. In summer this area was crowded with boats and punts. At Conyngham Hall public park there were also tennis courts, putting greens and a small zoo.

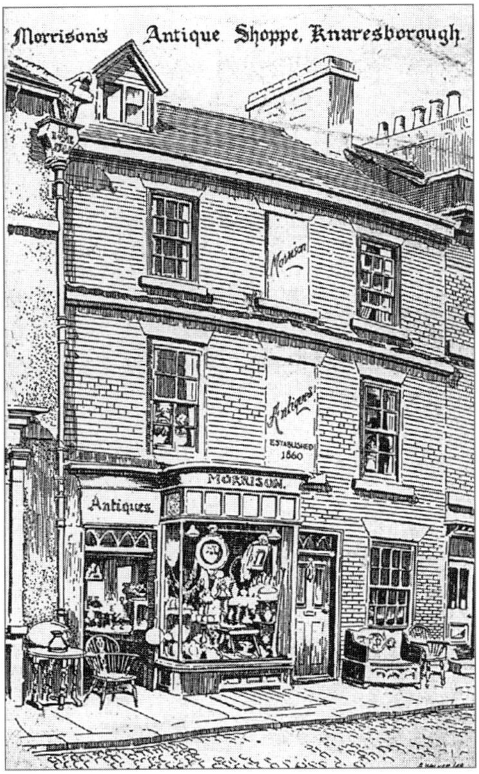

Morrison's Antique Shoppe, Knaresborough, established 1860. The dated down-spout in this trade *carte-de-visite* drawing by A. Walker shows that the building itself was there in 1741. Shops of this age, the many red-roofed houses and old cottages clinging to the crag above the river, are all reminders of Knaresborough's antiquity and its great forest. Another is King James's Grammar School, founded in 1616, which in 1901 moved to modern quarters. Some of its old rules are worthy of study and closely resemble those of the similarly dated school in the Forest of Bowland. Lessons commenced at 6 a.m. in summer, later in winter, but boys had to provide their own candles, paper and quills. They also had to practise regularly at the Butts with yew bow and arrow. Proficiency was essential as they could be called on in time of war to serve their sovereign.

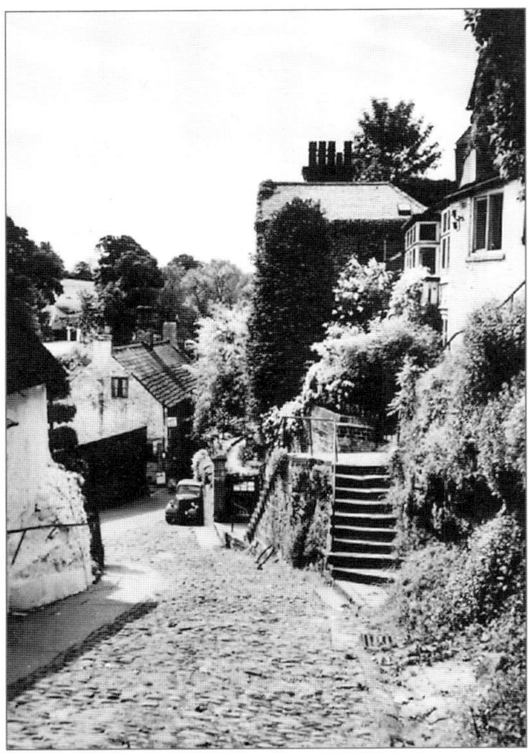

A steep cobbled street in Knaresborough, 1940s. The winter of 1948 was severe with February bringing blizzards, the snow so gleaming white that farm workers had to be equipped with sun glasses as they searched for sheep trapped in drifts. Drake Ghyll's 'Diary' in *The Dalesman* reads: 'They brought in a good ewe, heavy with lamb, which was blind. She must have been stricken the same.' When it became warmer on 1 March he wrote: 'The sheep are shedding their coats of icicles.' In the Dales it was very hard work on the farms as for weeks on end fodder had to be carried over fields deep with snow.

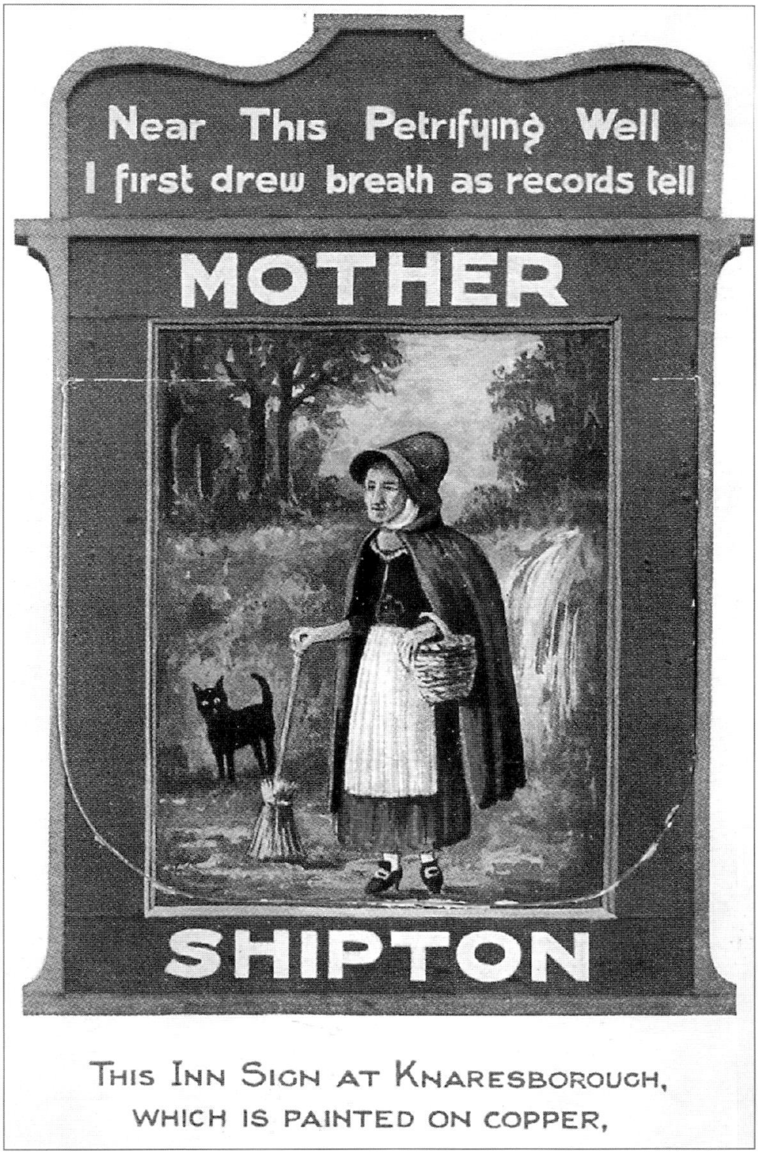

An inn sign at Knaresborough 1900, painted on copper and over 200 years old. Centuries after Mother Shipton's death in 1561, the details and date of which she herself had accurately predicted, thousands made pilgrimages to her place of birth as some of her prophesies appeared to come true.

In repairs to St Paul's the ball and crown were removed and, in the same year, when the Bow Church was repaired, its dragon on the spire was taken down. These events were recorded in Mother Shipton's lines of the sixteenth century:

> 'Eighteen hundred and thirty-five, which of us shall be alive?
> Many a king shall end his reign, many a knave his end shall gain.
> Many a statesman be in trouble, many a scheme the world shall bubble.
> Many a man shall sell his vote, many a man shall turn his coat.
> Right be wrong and wrong be right, by Westminster's candlelight.
> But when from the top of Bow, shall the dragon stoop full low.
> When the Church of Holy Paul shall come down both cross and ball?'

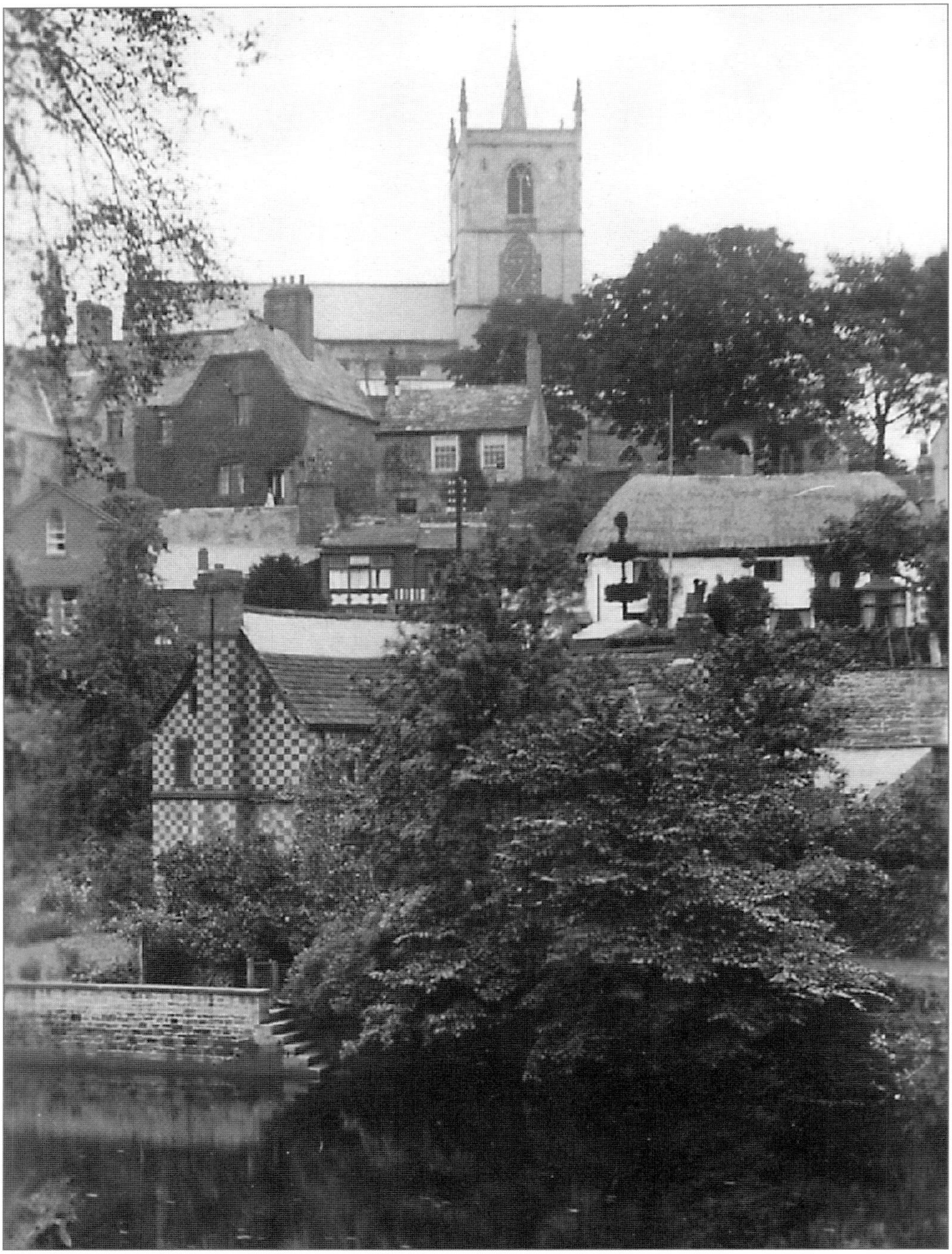

The parish church, Knaresborough, overlooking old buildings which include the Manor House, 1941. This view was a favourite subject for artists. Mention of the church was made in 1114. Of Perpendicular and Early English architecture, the oldest parts, dating from the mid-twelfth century, are the base of the chancel and part of the vestry. Attached to the choir are the Slingsby and Roundell mortuary chapels. The picturesque Manor House with its many gables and half-timbered exterior, under the cliff on the banks of the River Nidd, could be visited in the 1920s and 1930s at a cost of 6*d* and teas were provided. The beautiful oak panelling, much admired by tourists, was thought to date back to the year 1400.

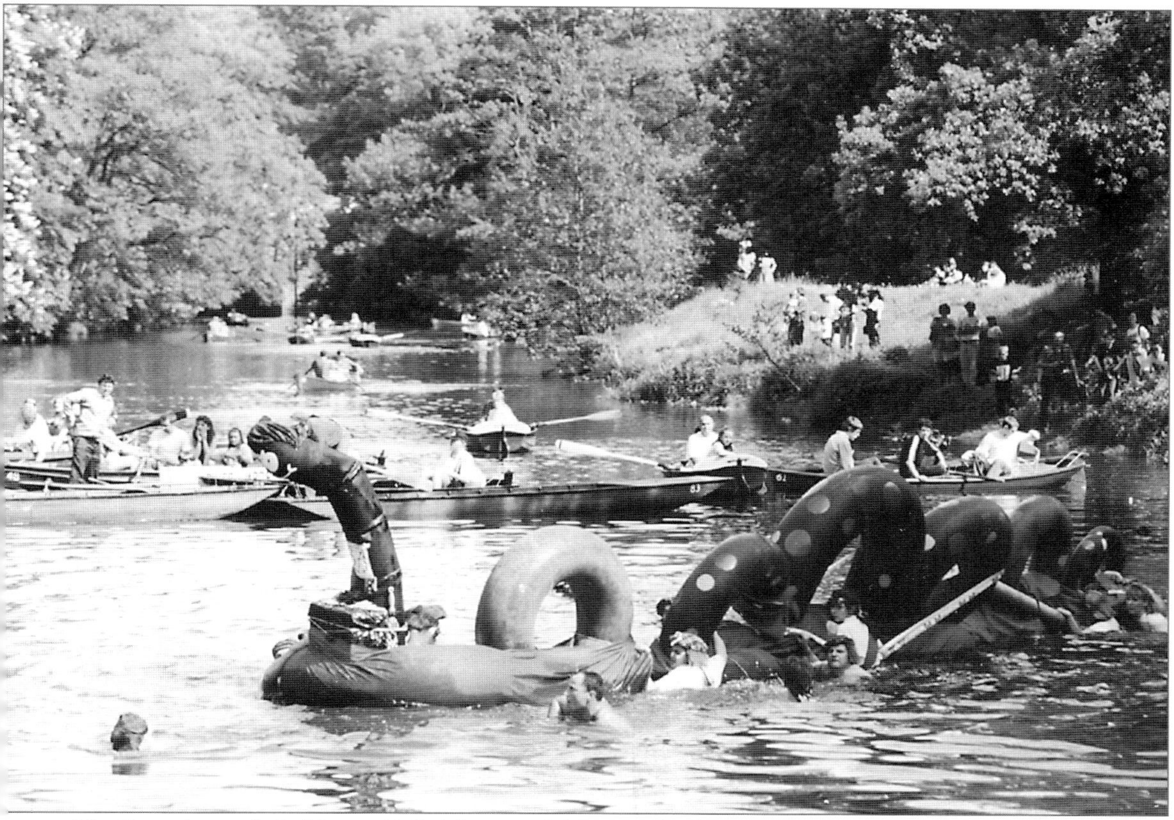

The Knaresborough Bed Race, 1969. This annual fun event has been organised by the local Round Table and Lions every June since 1966. The record time for the 2½ mile course crossing the River Nidd was established on 14 June 1975 – 14 minutes 9 seconds. The heroes were from the Harrogate Athletic Club. Skill and endurance together with a sense of humour are prerequisites. Today's *Guide to Harrogate* describes how 'a flurry of colourful contraptions' have to negotiate the perilous river crossing, egged on enthusiastically by their supporters.

Spitting would not appear to be the image aspired to by the lordly Harrogate inland resort but it was recorded in the *Guiness Book of Records* that in a test of cherry stone spitters 'John Crosby of Great Harrogate achieved a distance of 42 ft on 5 June 1976.' Competing spitters wear 12-in block-ended boots to measure distances without a tape measure.

Among old customs, Scarborough still rings the Pancake bell. Plough 'Stots' hark back to Plough Monday rites when 'Toms' dressed in fantastic costume accompanied the lads of the village leading a bullock and collecting money; any villager who would not contribute had his patch of land ploughed up. Linked with old customs were local characters. Historian J. Keighley Snowden, member of the Yorkshire Dialect Society, listed some: a one-legged clogger, a stonebreaker known as Tib, and Bob Green, roadmender, usually called 'Bob o' Bill's'.

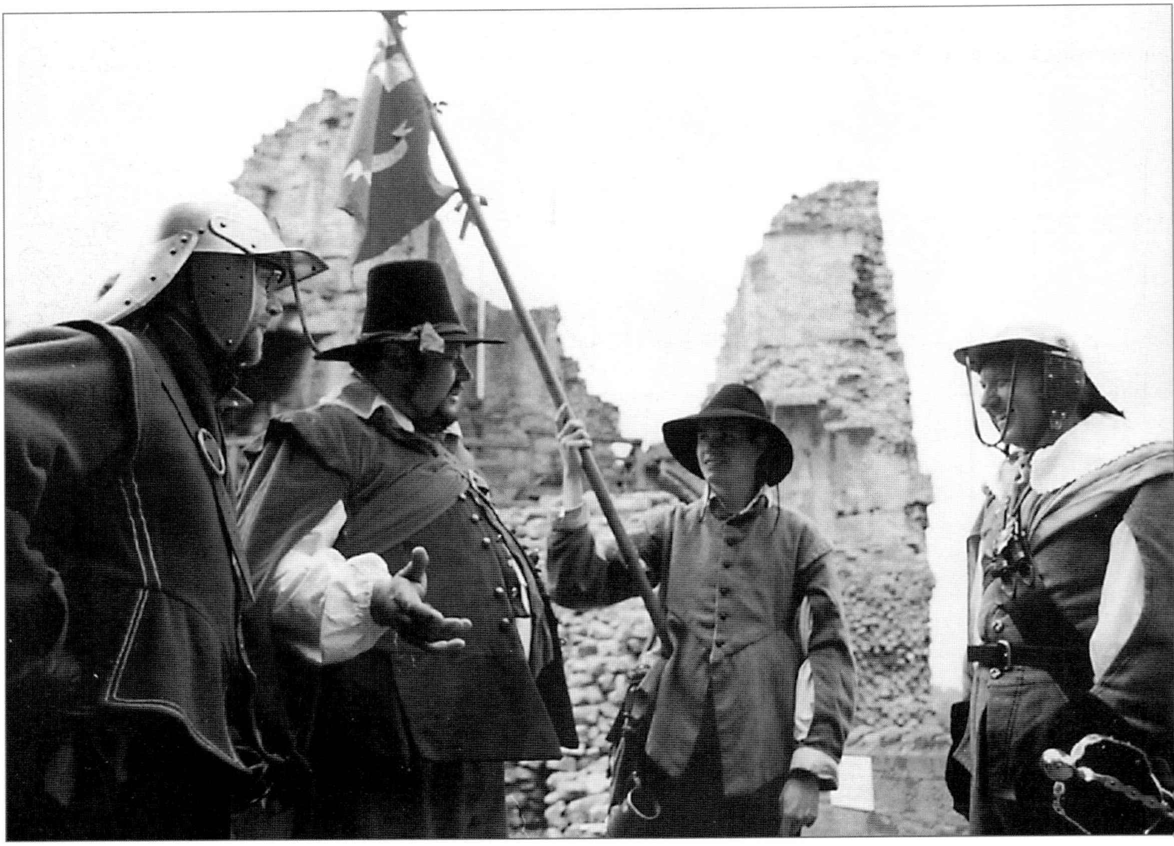

Knaresborough Festival, 1973. This ten-day festival in August includes folk music, blues, art, drama, street theatre, jazz, country and western music, morris dancing, photography, music and orchestral performances and buskers up and down the town. On 10 August, Charter Day, a highlight of the Festival, is celebrated because it reminds townspeople of the granting of the Royal Charter in 1311 which allowed a market to be held every Tuesday. Judging by the Cromwellian costume, this historic scene set against the remains of the castle 'knocked about' by Oliver Cromwell's men, is part of a Charter Day Pageant. During the early part of the Civil War the castle was an important post in the hands of the Cavaliers but General Fairfax besieged and took it after the Battle of Marston Moor. Four years later it was brought to ruinous state. The battlefield of Marston Moor could still be traced by visitors in the 1920s, the part adjoining the 'great ditch' being in its original state. This was where the Royalists were drawn up, facing the Moor, before battle commenced.

Not long after the Knaresborough Festival in Greater Harrogate's calendar comes Masham Sheep Fair, with morris dancing, tug of war competition, goat show, sheep races, handbell ringers and weaving demonstrations. The Masham Steam Engine and Fair Organ Rally has been held for nearly thirty-five years, and in its way is another colourful display of pageantry in the district.

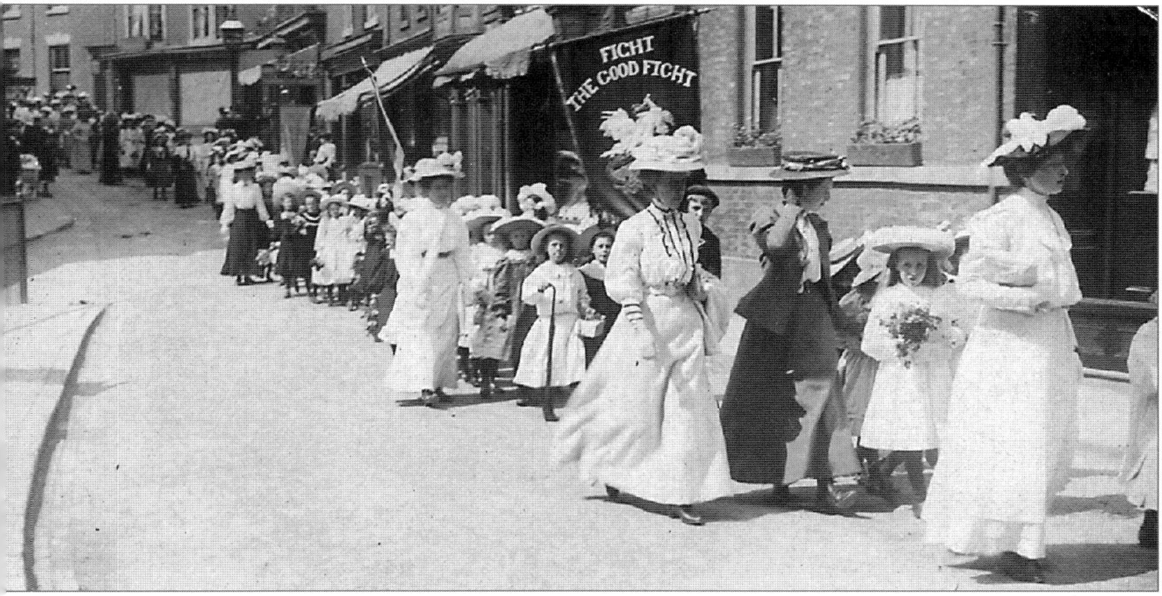

A Whitsuntide Walk in Ripon, 8 June 1908. Memories are of beautiful, sunny weather and this occasion appears to be no exception. All the churches took part, each having its own procession, followed by a 'field day', when races were held and baskets of sandwiches handed out. Most of the ladies and children wore white for 'White' Sunday.

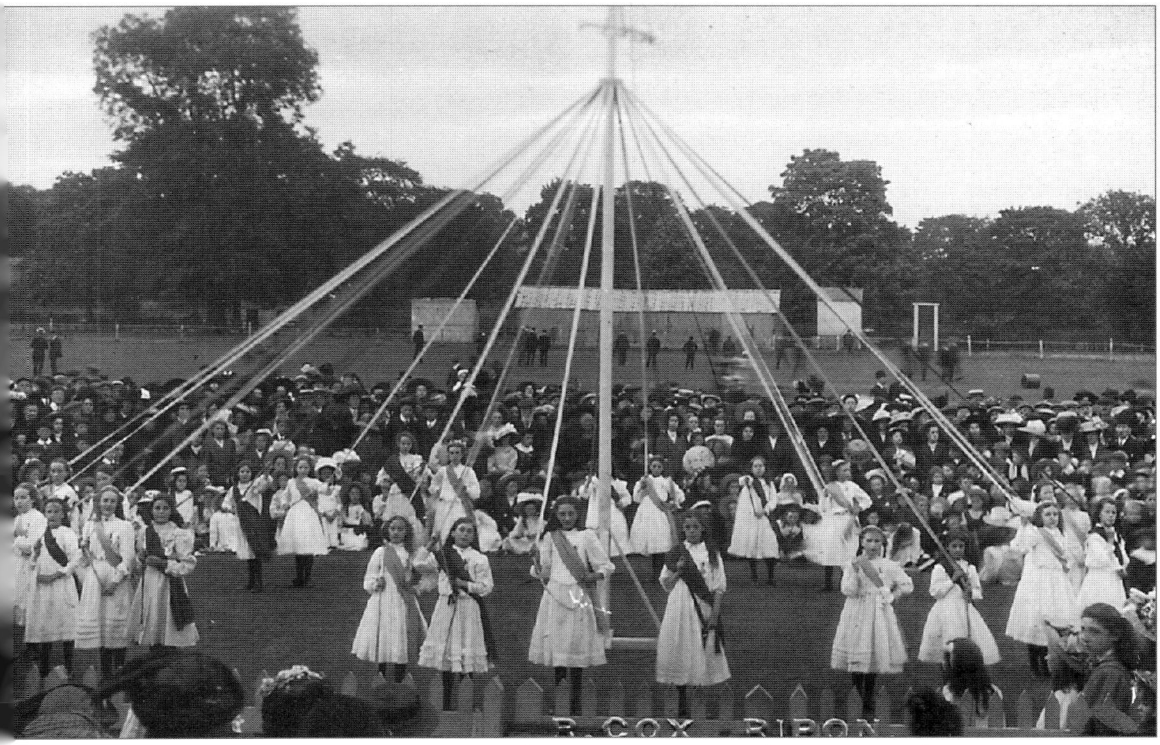

Dancing round the Maypole, *c.* 1900. Along with other May Day sports this was an annual event at Ripon. Many charming old customs were still observed and some are being revived. Morris dancers in traditional dress still perform in Grassington Square.

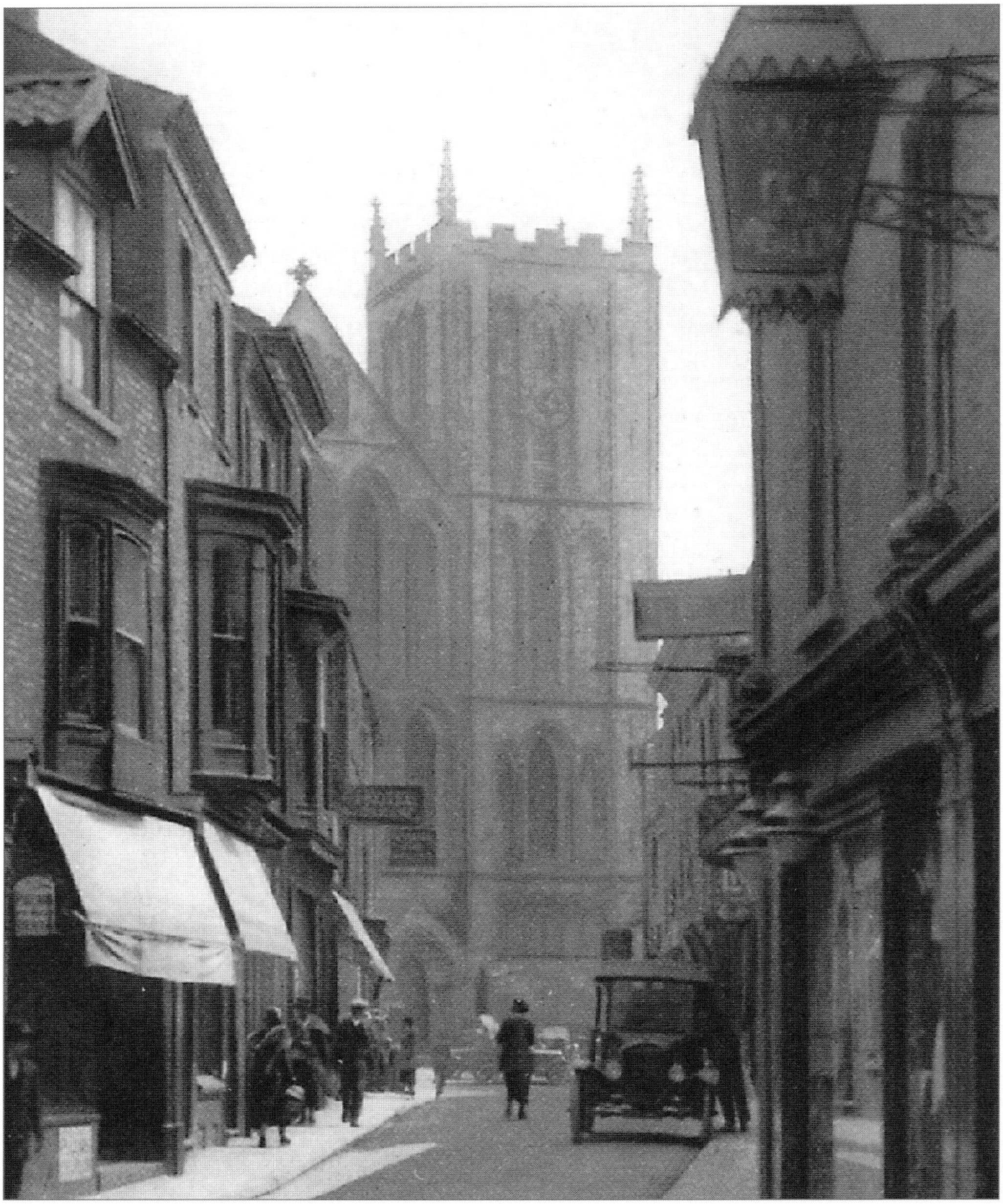

Kirkgate and cathedral, Ripon in the early 1930s when fox furs were fashionable. Across from the hotel the van would by now have achieved vintage status. Note also the large, fretted, wrought-iron lamp in the foreground advertising a long-established tea dealer in the city. Inside Ripon Minster, erected by Wilfrid, Bishop of Northumbria and dedicated in the presence of the King of Northumbria, an ancient Saxon crypt has survived. This rare crypt, built in 672, lies beneath the cathedral nave and is now a strong room where ancient church silver and other treasures are displayed. Annually in August a local man dressed as St Wilfrid, the founder, is led around the city on a white horse. Kirkgate (in this scene), Skellgate and Westgate are among ancient streets leading from Ripon's large market place. Simplicity combined with elegance is expressed in many of Ripon's buildings of note. In 1604 James I granted a Charter allowing the city to be governed by twelve aldermen, twenty-four assistants, two sergeants, a Clerk and a Court of Records. The first mayor and 'wakeman' was merchant Hugh Ripley.

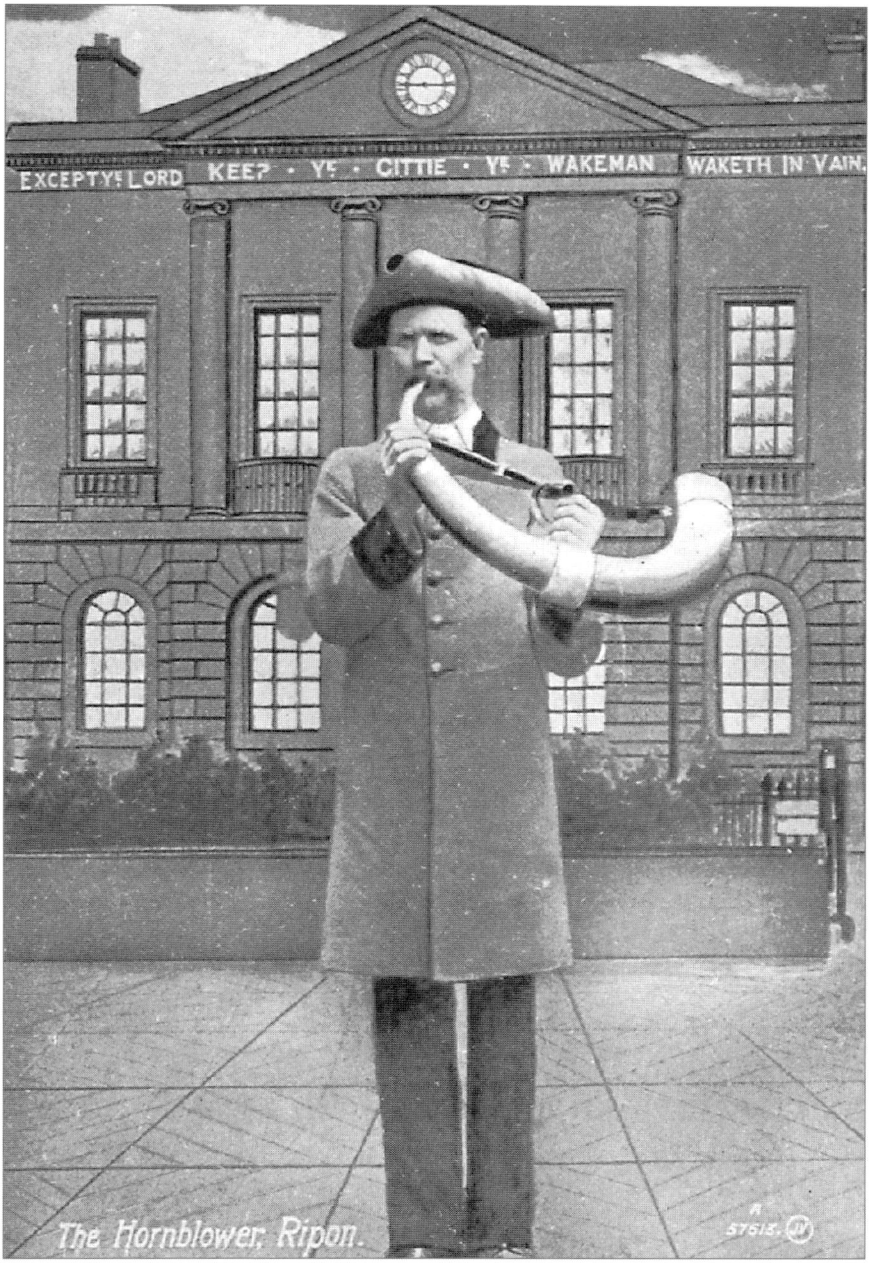

Harold Blackburn, the hornblower, Ripon, *c.* 1921, stands in front of an imposing building which bears the inscription 'Except ye lord keepe, ye cittie ye wakeman waketh in vain'; this is Ripon's motto. Nightly at 9 o'clock custom decrees that the hornblower or wakeman goes to the Mayor's house, blows the horn, then moves off into the market-place where he blows the horn four times. The custom originated in Saxon days over 1,100 years ago, when a wakeman or watchman responsible for keeping order had to blow the horn every evening at sunset, a custom followed in most towns and villages to mark the beginning of curfew period (from *couvre feu* or cover your fire). With so many wood-framed houses fire was a genuine hazard. The sixteenth-century Town Book details all his duties. His watch began at 9 p.m. and went on until 4 a.m. 'If it happen any house be broken into and any goods withdrawn out of the said house ye wakeman shall make good unto the partie so wronged.' The amount was to be decided by the other officers.

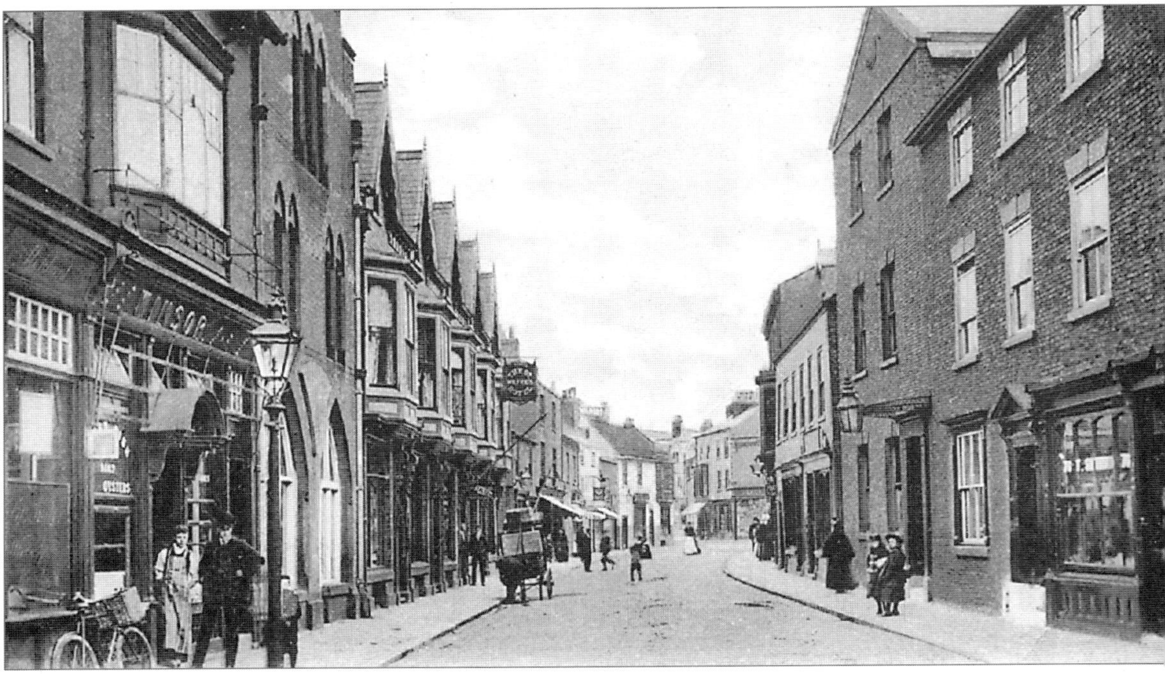

North Street, Ripon, 1904 reveals aspects of life at the turn of the century. On the far left by the cycle and lamp, oysters are being sold. Visitors are expected at St Wilfrid's Hotel further along the street. The main post office, situated on North Street, was open from 8 a.m. to 8 p.m.

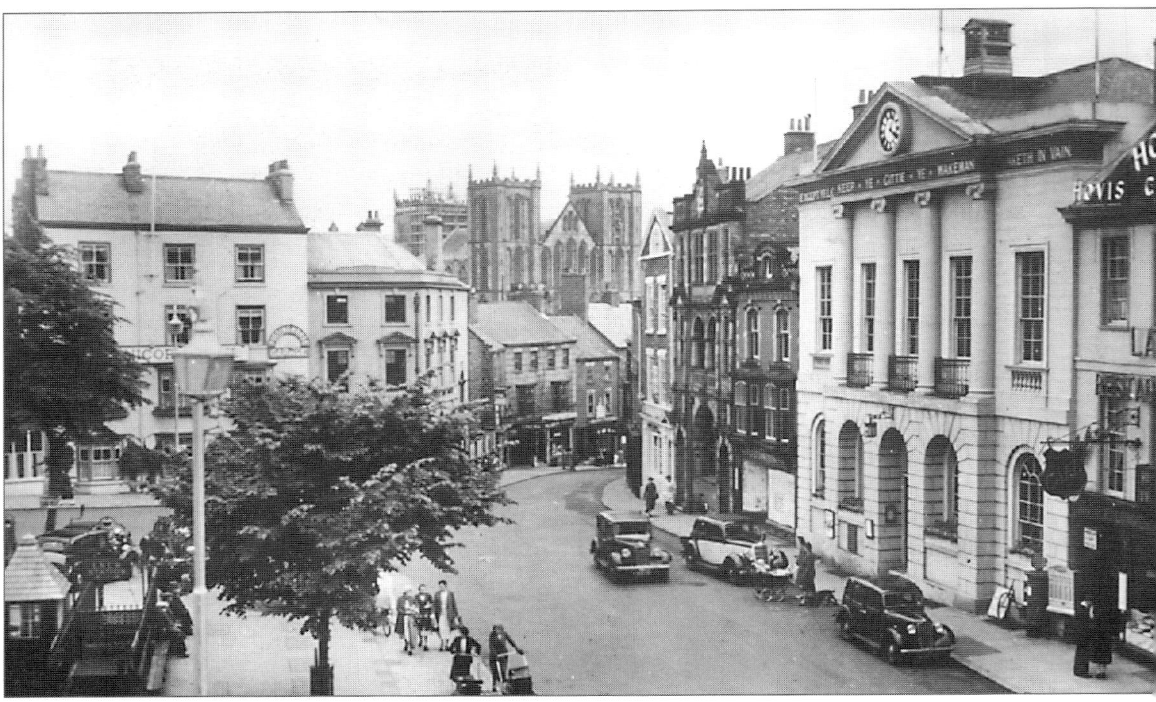

In this 1938 photograph the hotel and café on the right advertising Hovis bread stand next to the imposing Mayor's house, which proudly bears the city's motto beneath its pediment. A small vase and coins dating from Vespasian to Constantine were found within the city boundaries. Far left is the Unicorn Hotel.

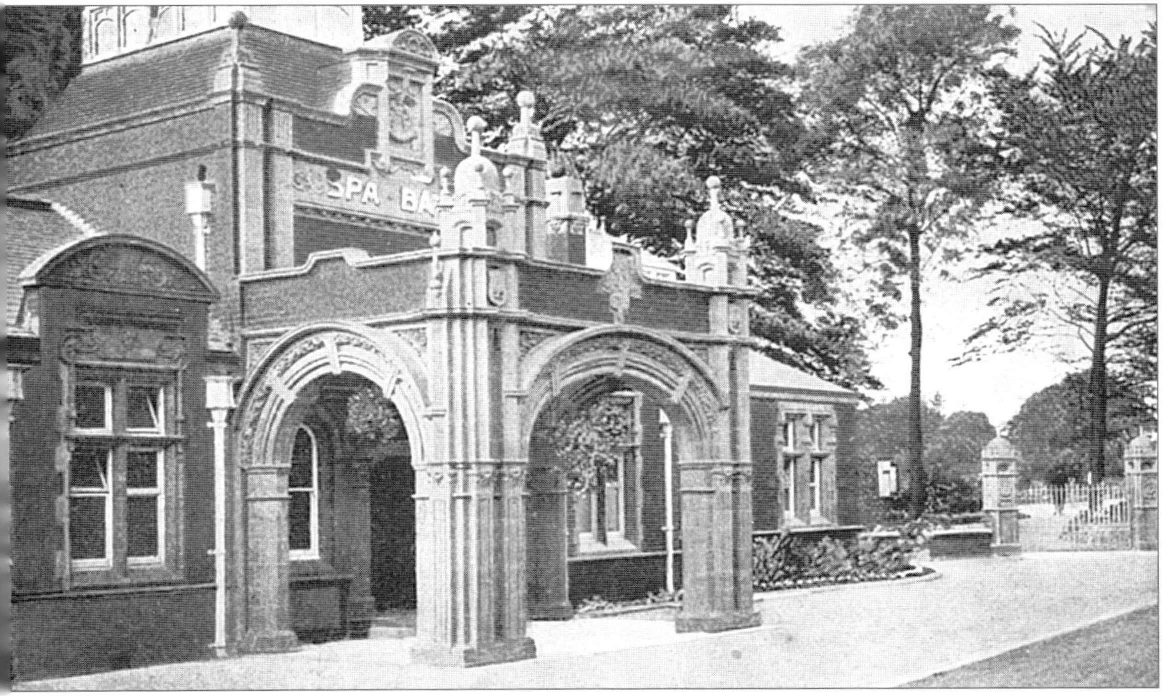

Ripon also had Spa Baths in Park Street, for which water was brought from a sulphur spring at Oldfield 4 miles away. This was described by a physician, Sir Thomas Stevenson, as 'water of an excellent mild aperient quality, of great organic purity . . . will prove highly beneficial to those taking it under medical advice'.

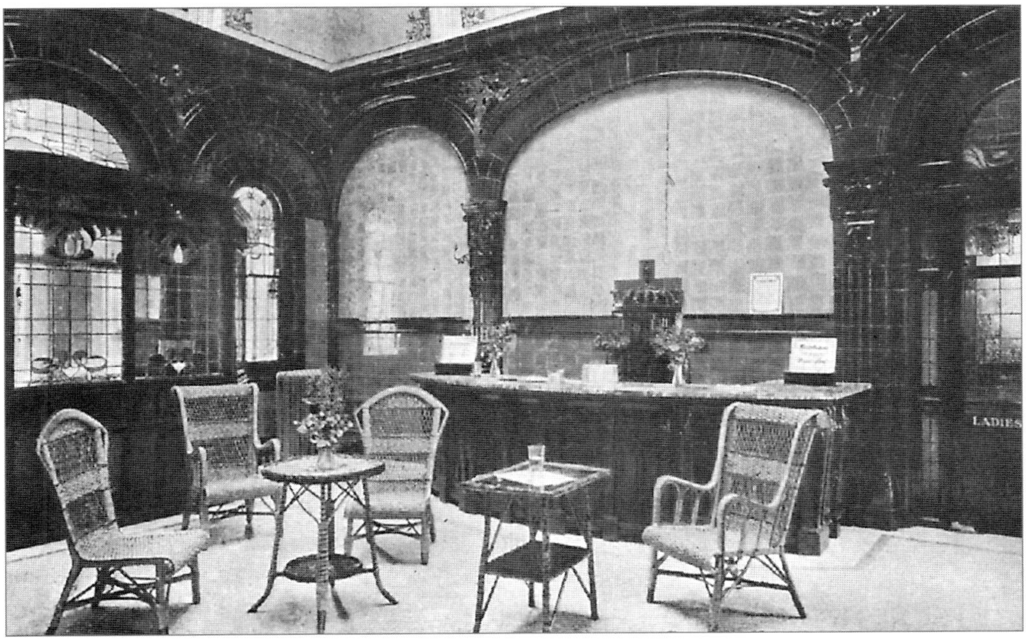

Spa Baths, Pump Room, Ripon, 1906. With its canework furniture, marble slabs, stained glass and heavy, carved woodwork it is a nostalgic reminder of the early years of the twentieth century. At the rear was a waiting room and a veranda overlooking the well-kept Spa Gardens.

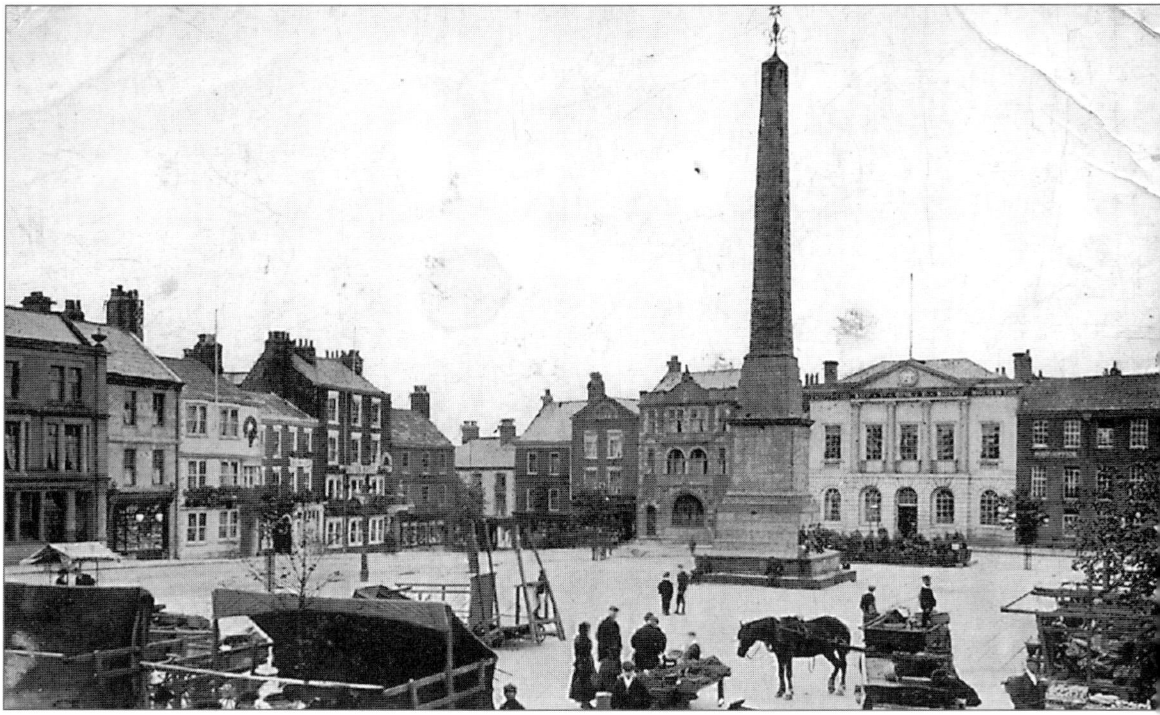

Market Place, Ripon, 1902, early in the morning before most of the traders have arrived to set up their stalls on this site, which measures 115 yds at its widest point. From early times the town was noted for horse fairs held in the market-place. The great obelisk was erected in 1781 by William Aislabie on the site of the old Market Cross. In the 1930s fairs were still held on the fourth Thursday in January, on 13 and 14 May, on the first Thursday and Friday in June, and the first Thursday in October and November. 23 November was the date of the general hiring fair for servants and the Mop fairs. Races are a feature of Ripon and take place on the Feast of St Wilfrid, there being fourteen racing days each year. In the thirteenth and fourteenth centuries Ripon was important for its woollen industry and the making of rowels or spurs, 'Sharp Rippon Spurs' being well known throughout the land up to the eighteenth century.

The oldest parts of the city are those facing Stammergate and All Hallowgate, these being close to the monastery around which the city grew up. In its long history Ripon was represented by two members of parliament from 1295 to 1346 and from the reign of Edward VI until 1897, when it lost a member. More power was lost in 1885 under the Redistribution of Seats Act.

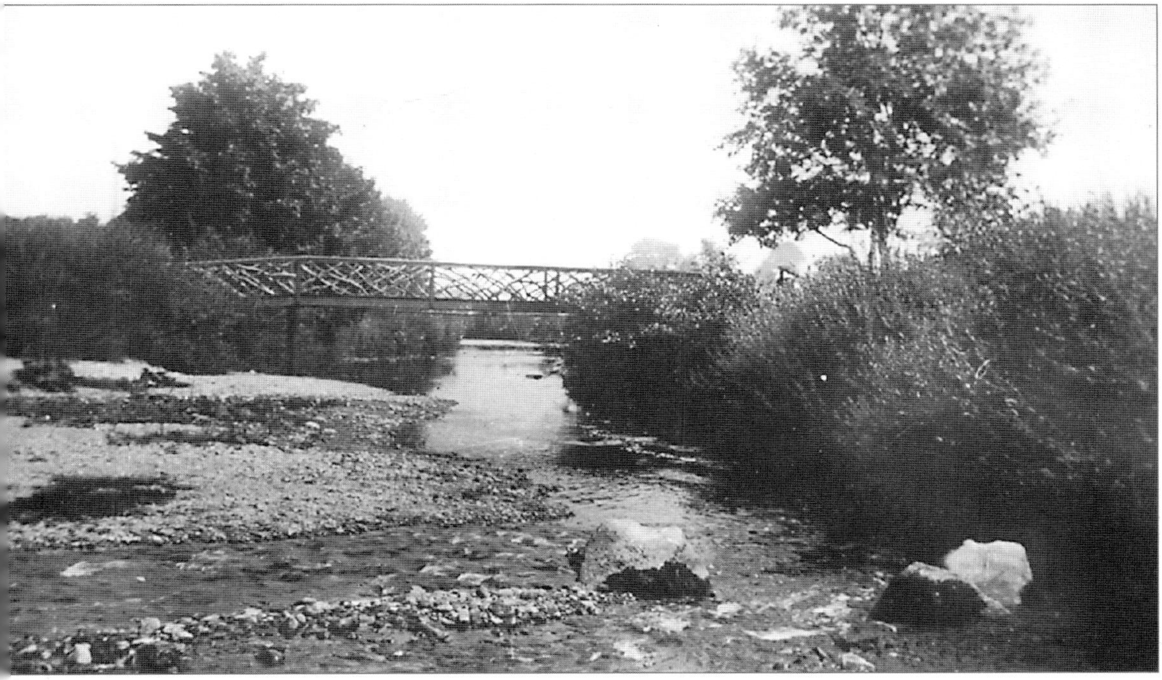

The River Skell at Ripon, *c.* 1932. Here three rivers, the Skell, the Laver and the Ure unite to form an important waterway. Edward Browne, who was a vicar at Ripon in 1550, was also schoolmaster at the Grammar School. With revenue from church lands plus his stipends he earned £18. The headmaster of Eton College at that time received only £10.

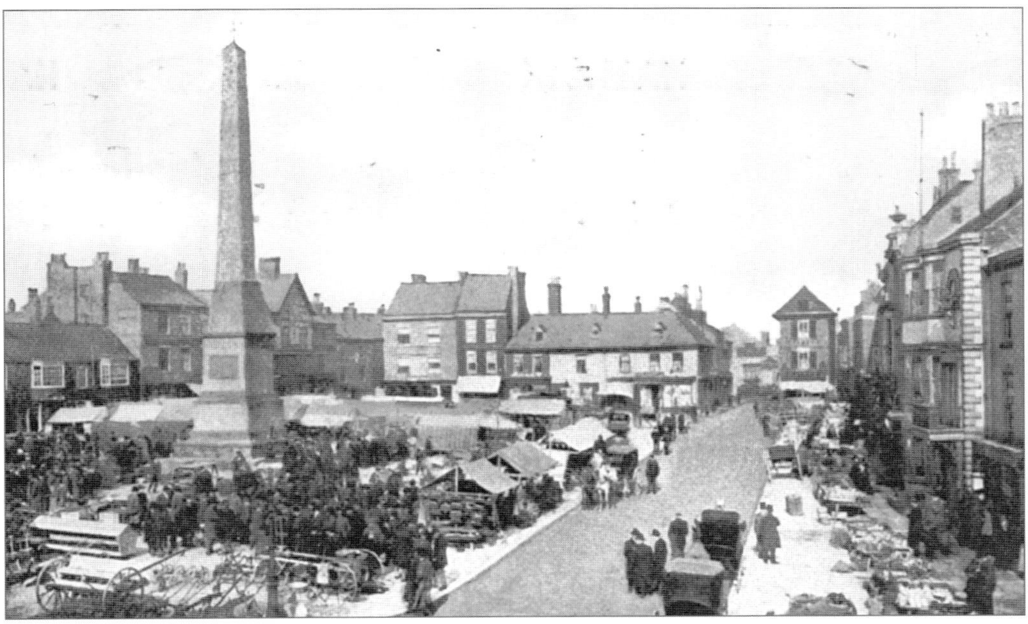

A view of the huge market-place, Ripon, in November 1924 shows on the right the area where clothes were sold and typical tarpaulin-covered market stalls of the day. In the distance is a parade of shops: Maypole, City Café, W. & E. Turner, shoe specialists.

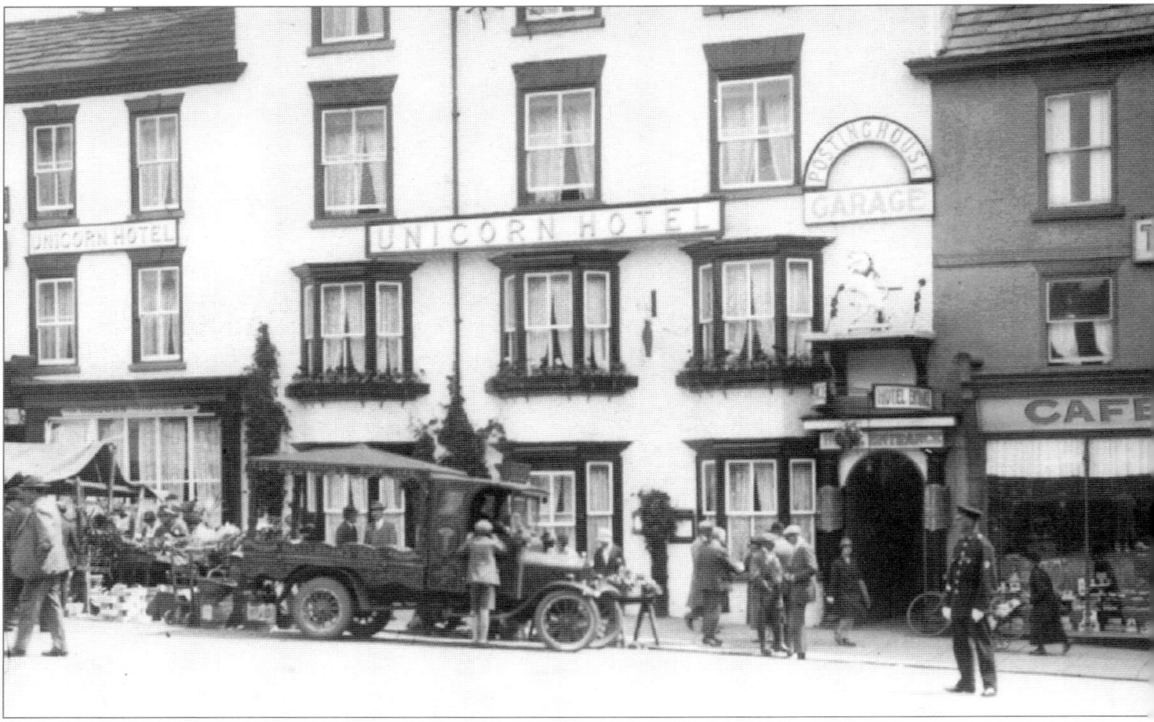

The Unicorn Hotel in Market Square, Ripon, 1930s, obviously Market Day. I am told that to commence trading the bellman made a great commotion at 11 a.m. although the market had been in full swing since 8.30 a.m! Boarding terms at the Unicorn were then 84*s* a week. There were two other hotels in the Square, but to stay at the Spa was the most expensive, costing from 105*s* a week.

In its day the Unicorn was an important posting house. In the eighteenth century its mews area would be constantly busy with coaches and horses. By the 1930s it had a garage. A character well known in the ancient city in the 1790s was 'Old Boots of Rippon' who was employed at the Unicorn where he remained until his death. Thomas Spence by name, he had a long, curved nose and a long, turned-up chin which almost touched. He was a source of great amusement to callers at the inn. Thomas's favourite trick was to hold a coin between his nose and chin. If he succeeded, most customers let him keep the money. With many passing travellers, Thomas probably did quite well from performing his party trick, and polishing boots.

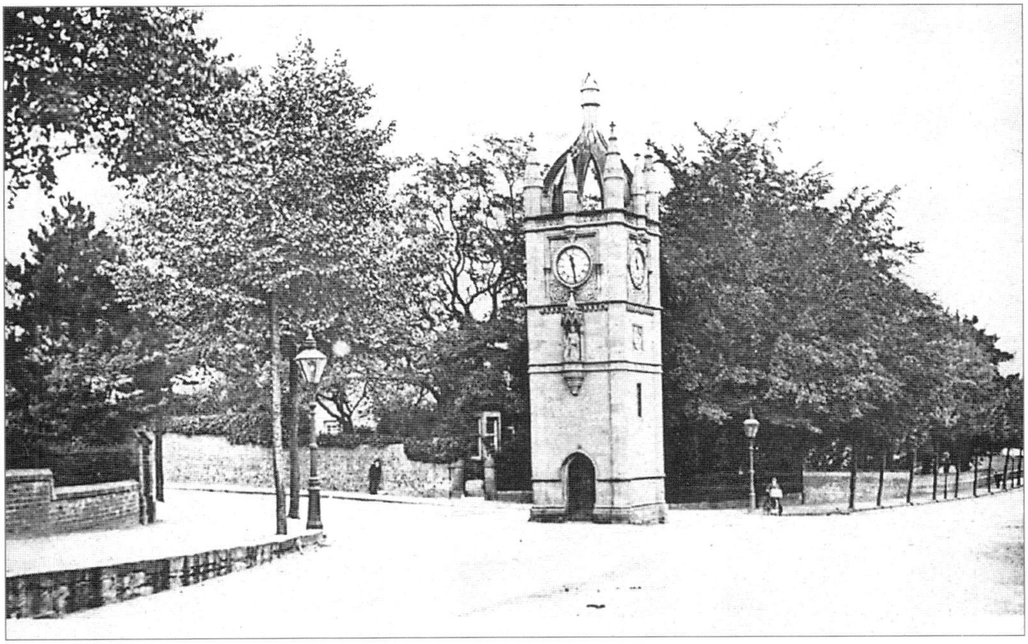

The Jubilee Clock Tower, Ripon, 1930. It was built in 1897 to commemorate sixty years of Queen Victoria's 'glorious' reign. The inscription around the Tower reads 'Length of days is in her right hand; in her left are riches and honour.' From the Market Square northwards down North Street was the start of a ramble by the River Ure, a favourite in the 1920s and '30s.

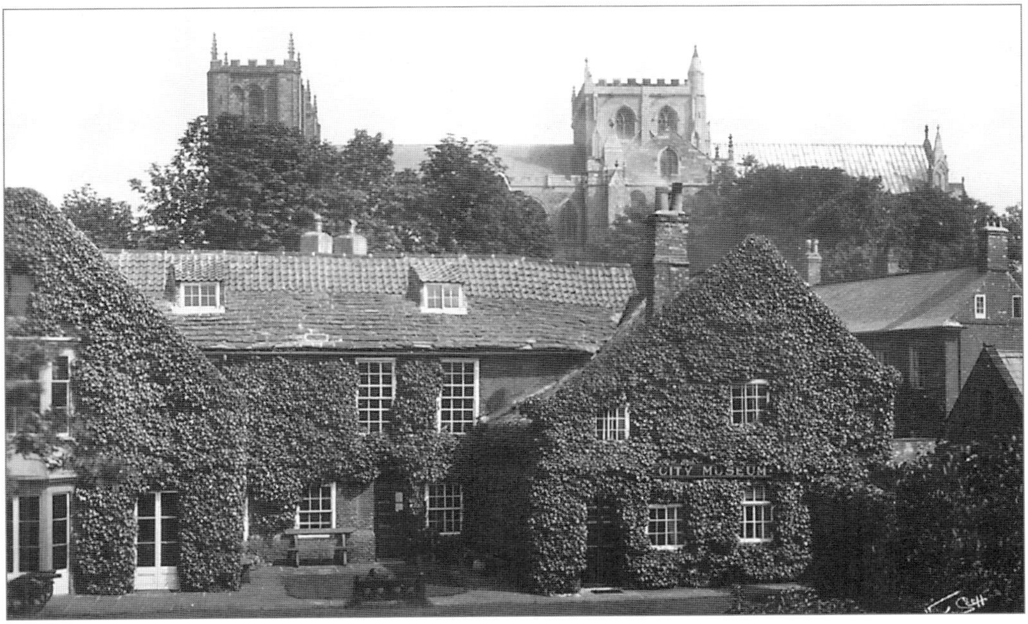

Thorpe Prebend House, Ripon, *c.* 1920. Situated between St Anne's Hospital and Bondgate Green Bridge, this had been used as separate dwellings until 1914 when it was restored to original condition. Inside is some fine panelling. It became a museum after presentation to the Corporation by the Darnbury family. Note the old stocks in front.

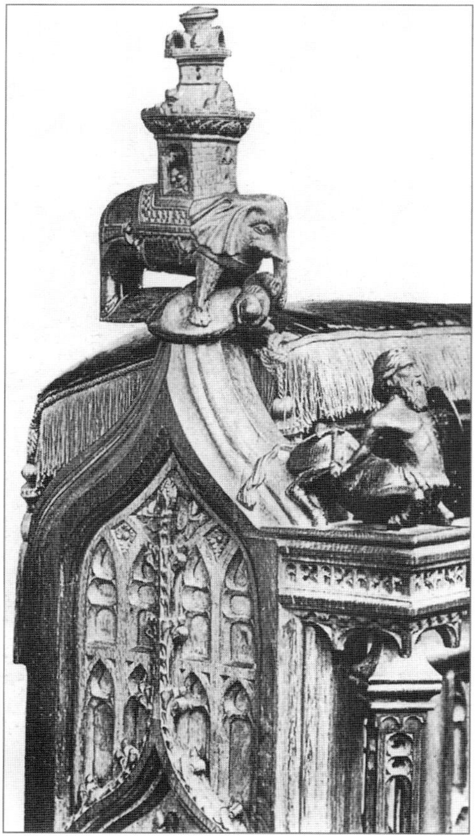

The Elephant and Castle finial on the bishop's throne in Ripon Cathedral, 1931. The finials of the stalls which were restored by Sir Giles Gilbert Scott according to a fifteenth-century design are also richly carved. These include such subjects as a lion attacked by dogs, a dragon attacked by dogs, dragon and birds, angel with shield, hart's tongue ferns, monkey and antelopes, birds pecking fruit, and a pelican feeding young. The wonderful skill and imagery drew many tourists from Harrogate and around.

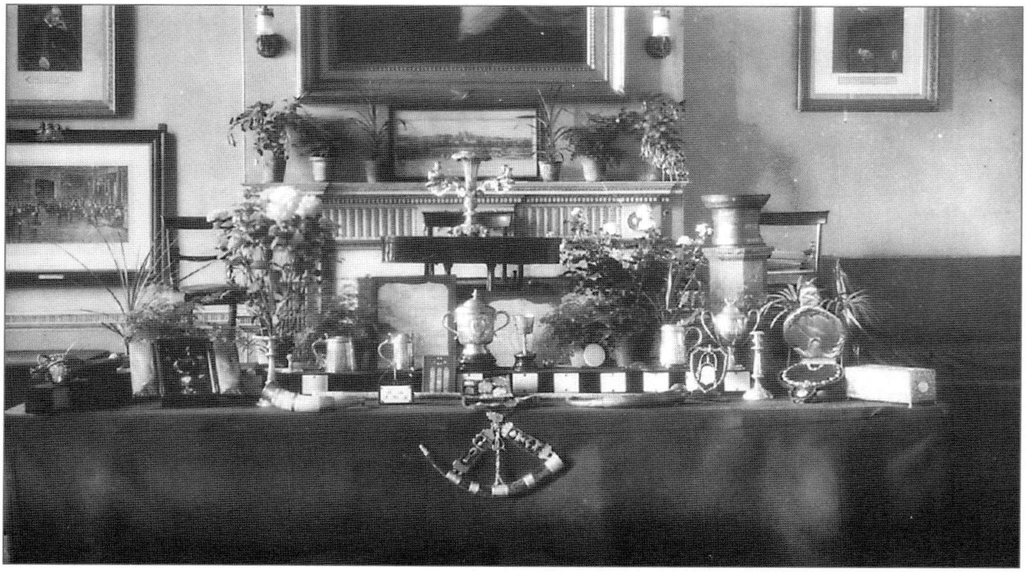

Ripon city regalia, *c.* 1940. Made by local man Walter Scott, among splendid candelabra and silverware is featured the horn blown by the wakeman. A 1928 report states: 'The city, the second oldest in England, was incorporated in the reign of Alfred the Great 866. The still existing Wakeman's horn was presented in token of the Charter.'

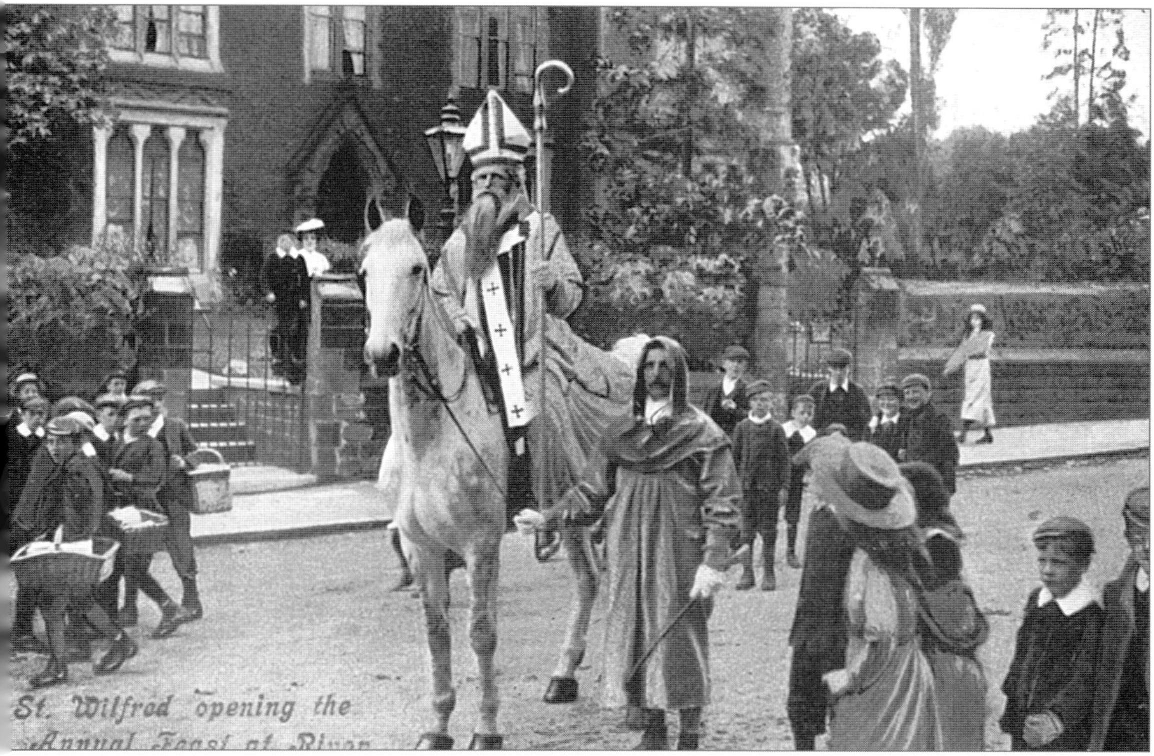

'St Wilfrid' opening the Annual Feast at Ripon, 1907. This ceremony is enacted annually by a local man who rides on a white horse and represents St Wilfrid, the missionary and bishop who was born in 634 and died in 709. A very important figure in church history, Wilfrid united the Celtic and Roman Churches. At the Synod of Whitby in 664 he complained about the many diverse practices in the Celtic and Latin Churches and desired their unification. He suffered much opposition, frequently being dismissed from office, but because of his strong personality he always gained re-instatement.

Ninety years after this scene, archaeologists believe they have found the original grave of St Wilfrid, one of the first compaigners for Christian unity in Britain. The Dean of Ripon, the Very Revd John Methuen, at the excavation site reported: 'When he came back from Rome he built the Church [at Ripon], the first stone building in the north of England since the Romans had gone. It was the wonder of the age, regarded as a marvel, with columns, passages and aisles. The crypt is the oldest in Europe north of the Alps.'

The almost complete skeleton found at the site is not that of Wilfrid because his body was removed in the tenth century, but it is most probable that it is the site of St Wilfrid's original tomb, for records place the position as the south side of the high altar. A piece of twelfth-century pottery was found near the skeleton, which may make the date of its burial contemporary with that of St Thomas à Becket.

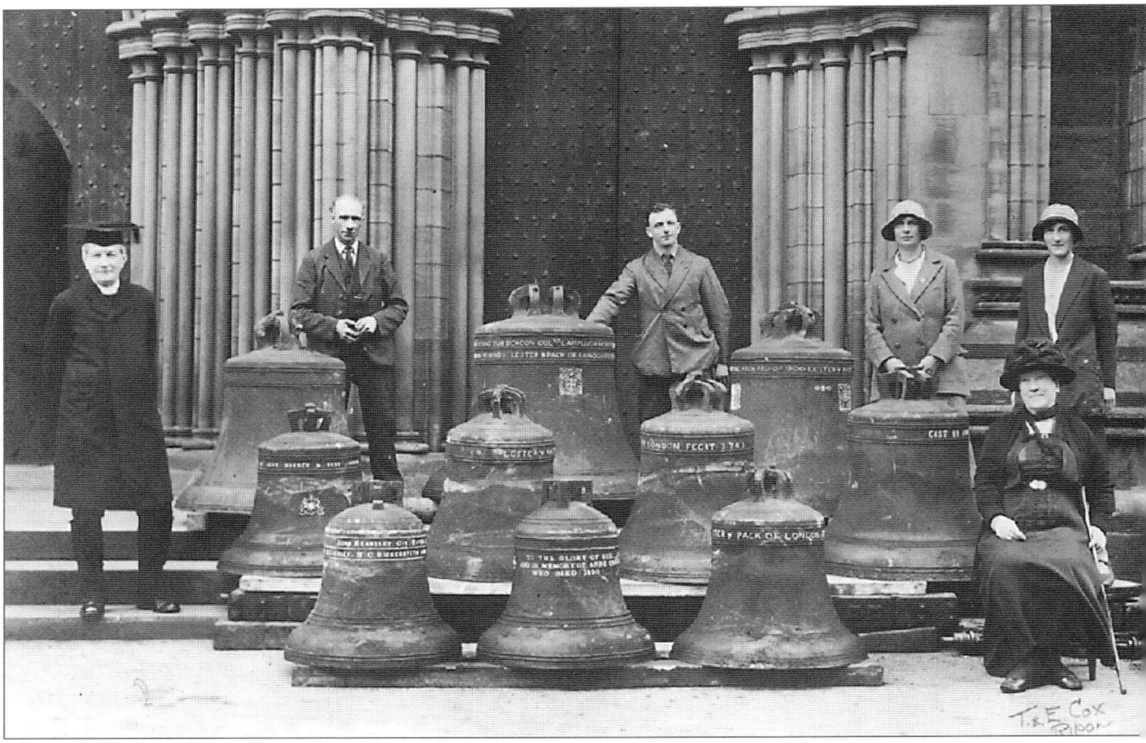

The bells about to go into Ripon Cathedral, *c.* 1900. Dean Owen stands on the left and the lady seated on the right is Miss J. White-Highfield, who gave the bells in memory of her family.

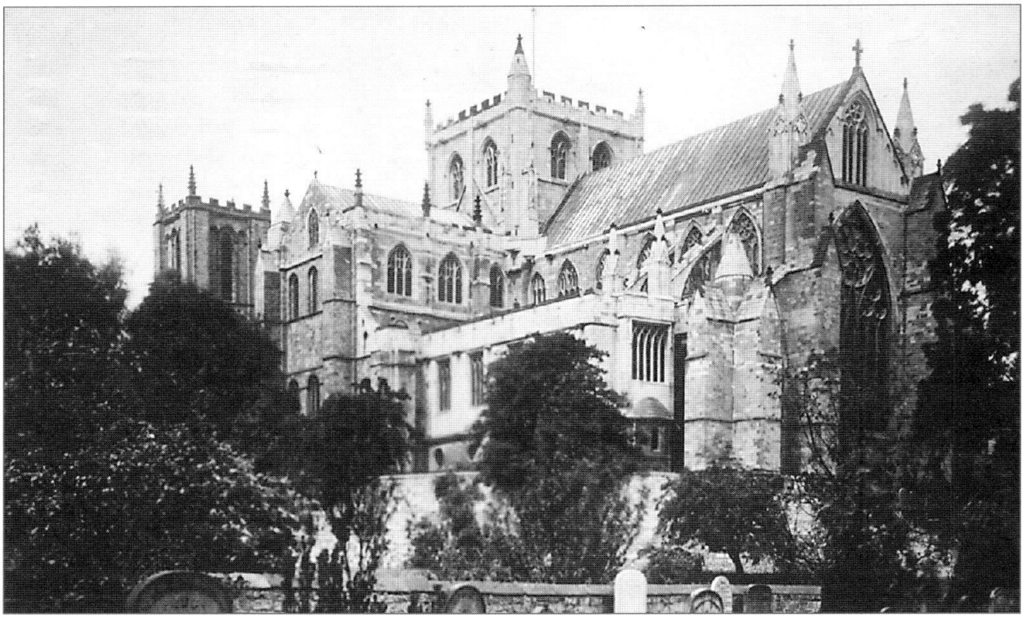

Ripon Cathedral, known locally as the Minster, has two crypts, one under the lantern (the square, central tower) and the other below the chapter house. The latter was for many years used as a charnel house but in 1865 it was thought more seemly to have the bones re-interred in the graveyard. Interesting monuments and fine stained glass are a feature of this cathedral.

Section Three

Around & About

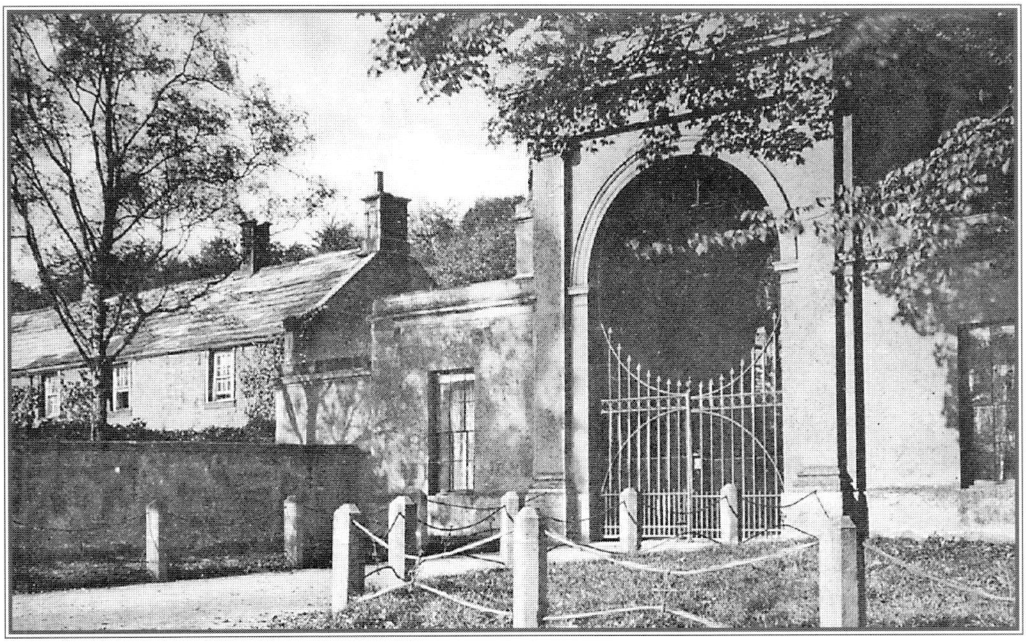

Rudding Park Gates, Follifoot, c. 1920. Rudding Park was the home of a prominent Roman Catholic family, the last member of which sold up in the 1960s. Rudding Park became a hotel with a golf club.

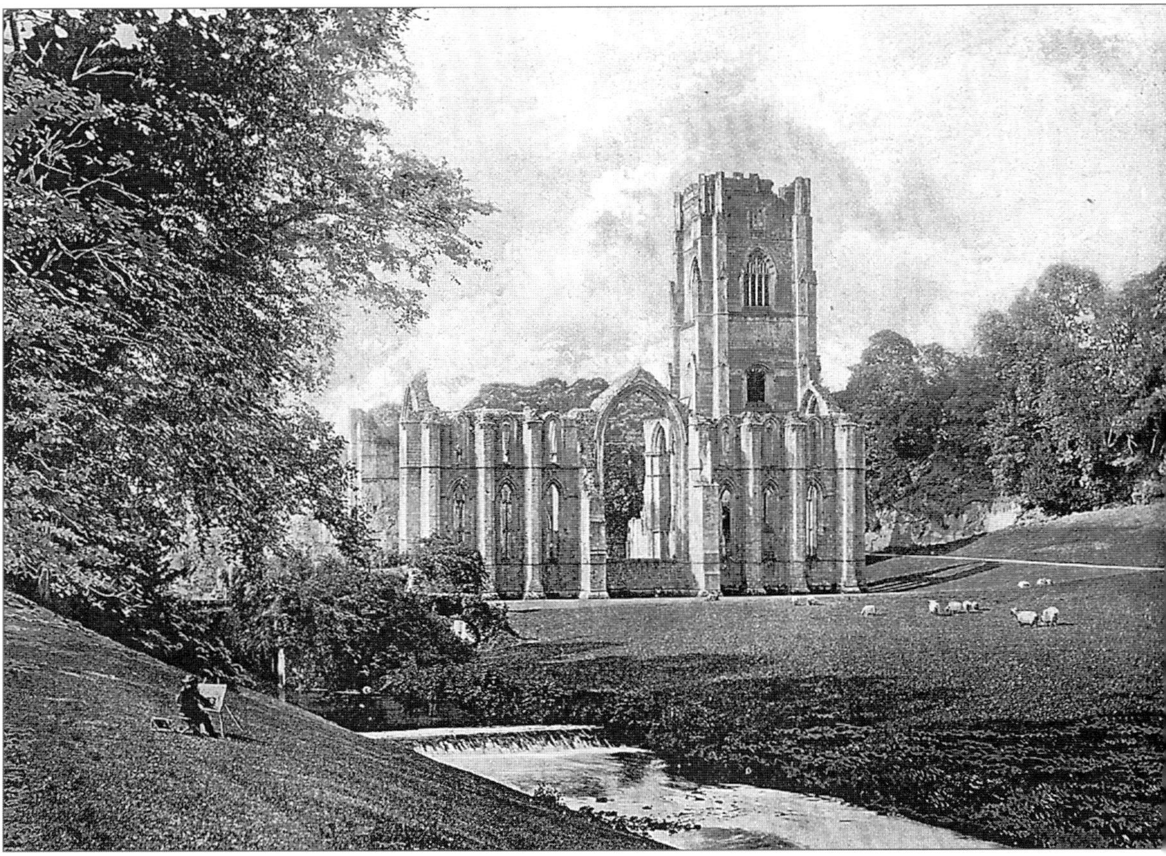

This photograph from 1902 includes an artist sketching the substantial and imposing ruins of Fountains Abbey. By the late 1930s the charge for admission was 1*s* for adults and for charabancs, which could wait in the 'Motor Parks', the abbey and grounds opening from 9 a.m. to 5 p.m., Christmas Day excepted. For centuries the River Skell silted and moved away from the abbey but in 1933 it was engineered into its original channel.

Among the magnificent abbey structure which visitors came to see are Nidderdale marble pillars in the chapel. As the number of Cistercian monks at Fountains increased in the thirteenth century, the Chapel of Nine Altars was constructed to give extra facilities for the saying of Mass. At the time of its suppression Fountains Abbey was one of the most powerful and important monasteries in the country. Chapter house, nave, cellarium, guest house for strangers, the infirmary of the lay brothers, the warming house, cloisters and so on all build pictures in the mind of what life in a religious house serving a wide area consisted of centuries ago.

A story attached to Fountains Abbey is that one of the monks renowned for strength challenged Robin Hood. The combatants wrestled long and hard but Robin won and the monk joined Robin's band. Yes, it was Friar Tuck!

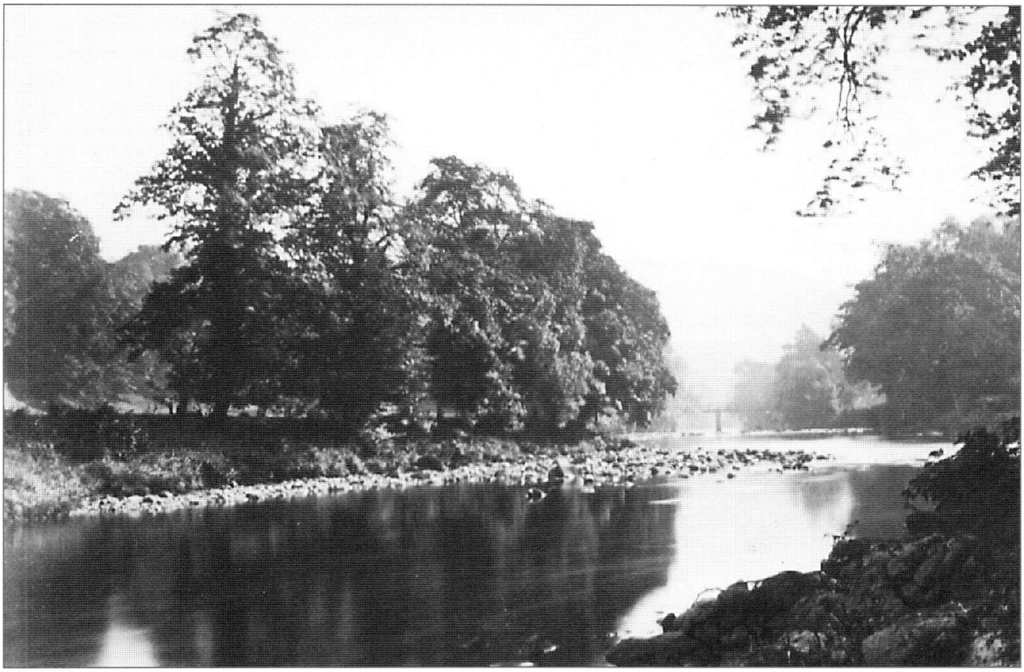

Bolton Woods, 1911. A diarist living 9 miles from Harrogate on 6 June wrote: 'Took the 1.49 train to Bolton Bridge and then on to the Strid. The woods are beautiful, the water clear as crystal.' The Strid was where lithe tourists made a daring leap across a narrow chasm. John, who bought a settle for £2 12*s* 0*d*, also recorded the River Wharfe freezing: 'February 16. Skating in full swing.'

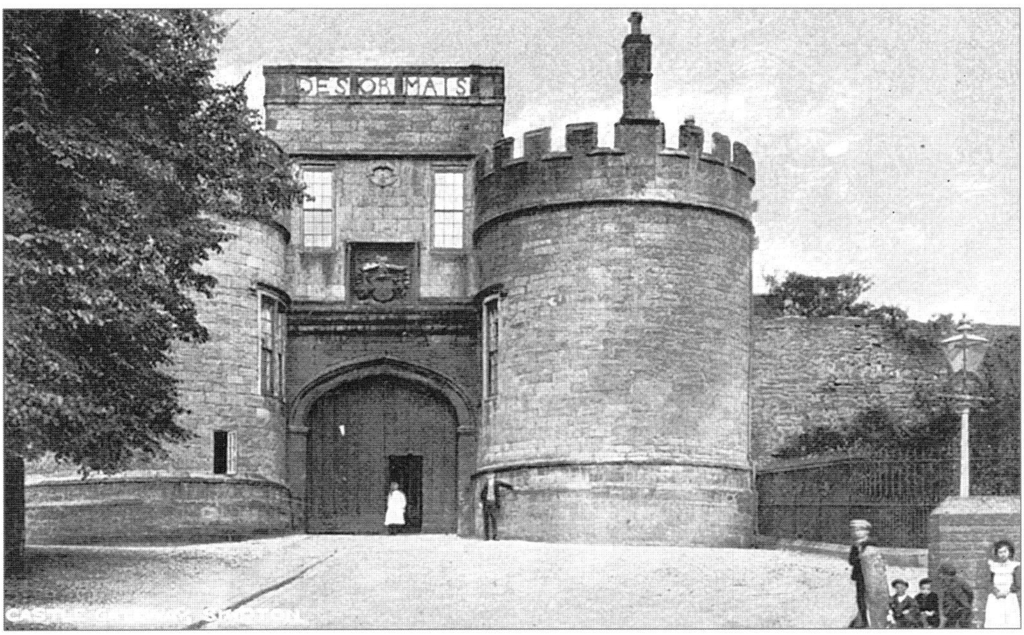

Skipton Castle, *c*. 1928. The gateway is the only remaining part of the first stone castle built by the Norman baron Robert de Romille, although the Saxon Earl Edwin, whose estates were centred on Bolton Abbey, was a previous overlord associated with the old market town. By 1309 Skipton Castle had passed to the powerful Clifford family of which Lady Anne was a prominent member.

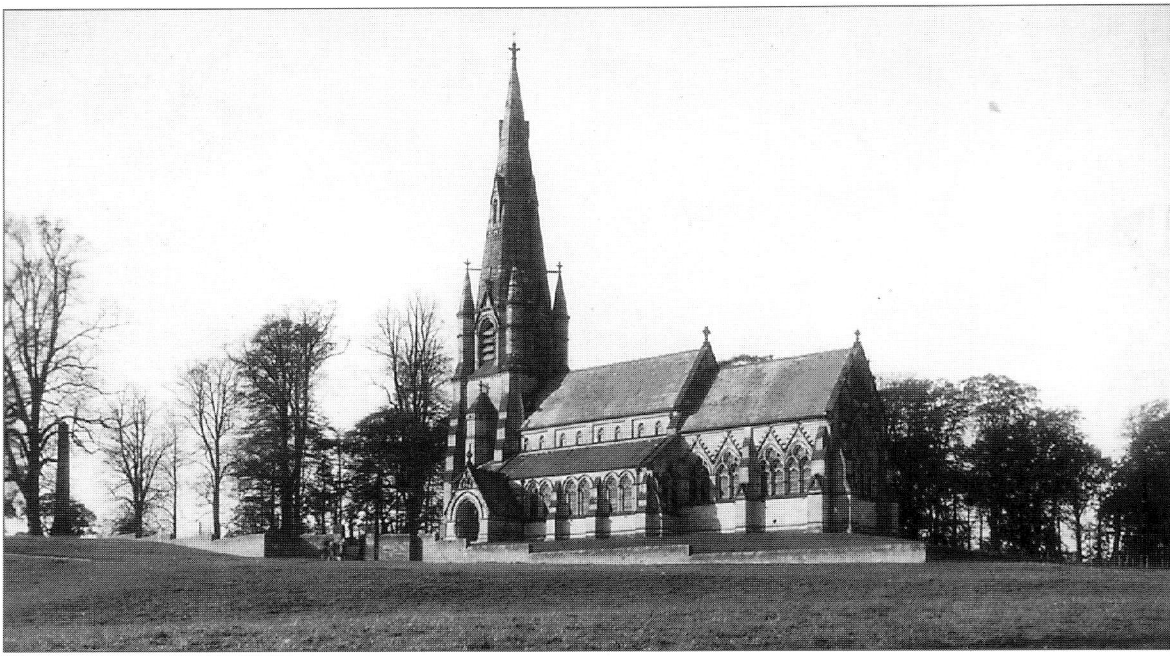

Studley church, photographed by Walter Scott of Bradford before the Second World War. Situated on the highest ground in Studley Royal Park, this church, dedicated to St Mary the Virgin, was built by the first Marchioness of Ripon in 1871. There is a tragic story of the Marchioness's brother in whose memory the church was built.

In 1870 he was murdered by Greek brigands. On capture, three friends were made to draw lots. One was to go to safety with details of ransom money. This fell to Mr Vyner, the marchioness's brother, but he gave up his chance to his young friend who was recently married. Before the ransom arrived Mr Vyner and his remaining companion were killed. This brave man's mother, Lady Mary Vyner, also erected a memorial, Skelton Church, on whose foundation stone the story is recorded.

Beautiful inside and out, Studley church has a wealth of marble: Purbeck, Sicilian, Tennessee and Belgian porphyry. The walls of the mosaic-bordered chancel are of alabaster. Visitors in the late 1920s were advised to set aside four hours to view the beauties of Fountains Abbey and Studley Park with its herd of deer. Studley Hall was rebuilt in the eighteenth century on the site of an old manor house. Before the Vyners lived there it was owned by the Marquis of Ripon. Leading to Studley church was a magnificent avenue of lime trees.

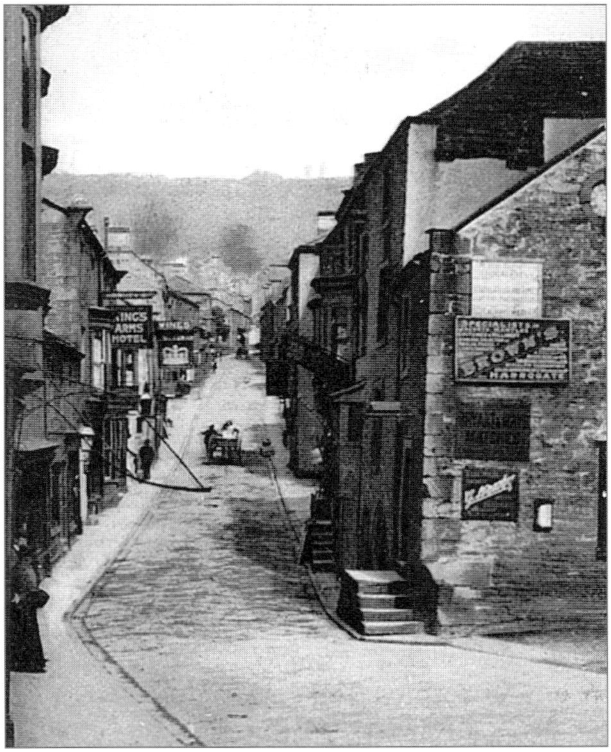

High Street, Pateley Bridge, early 1900s. On the limestone building on the right Brown's of Harrogate advertise as 'specialists in jackets, mantles, costumes, millinery'. Underneath is the advertisement for Bryant and May's matches, both discreet and restrained compared with their counterparts of the late twentieth century. Across the High Street the King's Arms Hotel displays a splendid inn sign depicting a royal crown. Two inns faced each other on this street, which was always busy on Show Day. With no motor traffic yet in evidence, a solitary cart wends its way in the direction of Nidderdale. Pateley Bridge received its Market Charter in the fourteenth century. The steep street used to be cobbled and was very busy in lead-mining days. Iron mining was carried on at Lofthouse 7 miles away and the monks of Fountains Abbey had a grange there where corn was stored.

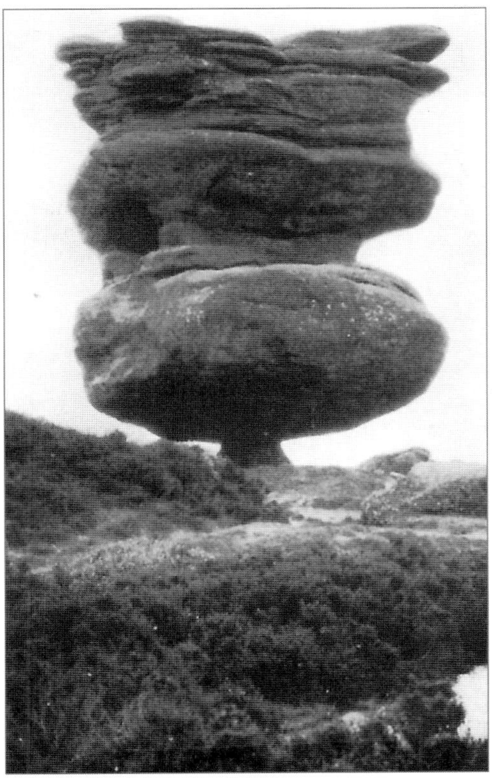

Idol Rock, Brimham Rocks, between Pateley Bridge and Ripon, 1928. These huge rock masses, set on heather-clad tableland almost 1,000 ft above sea level, each weighing up to 50 tons, were wrought into wonderful shapes by the action of wind, rain, snow and ice. Their fantastic shapes have led to descriptive and amusing names: Pulpit Rock, Parson's Head, Serpent's Head, Yoke of Oxen. Idol Rock, perhaps the most impressive, lies to the left of the last-named, with the Lamb nearby. There are references to druids (Druids Coffin, Druids Writing Desk) which may imply that some of the stones were used by druids, especially as there are grass-grown tumuli on Graffa Plain. The Devil's Arrows of Boroughbridge are thought to be druidical remains.

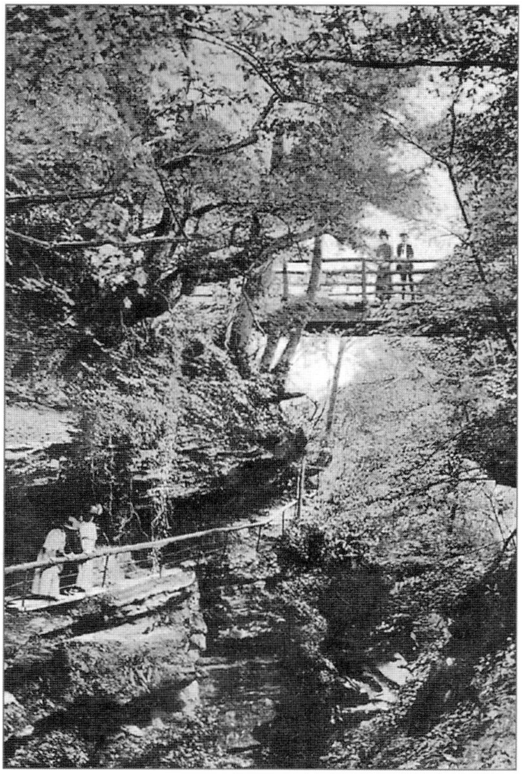

How Stean Gorge, near Harrogate, 1903. Stone Beck or How Stean separates the two parts of Nidderdale. A small charge was made to walk through in the 1920s and 1930s. One visitor wrote: 'We ascended a steep path, the ravine was very narrow, the cliffs on either side 70 ft high. Walking onwards for a mile, we crossed the chasm by one rustic bridge and presently re-crossed by a second. The waters crashing down Stean Gill Foot were impressive. There are interesting caverns in the cliffs called Tom Taylor's Chamber and Elgin's Hole. At High Riggs the stream flowed over Park Foss to fall 16 ft.' Tom Taylor's Cave was where thirty-two silver Roman coins were found in 1868. The cottage where tickets to view the gorge were obtainable was the home of Mr and Mrs Stevenson, who advertised this spectacular limestone scenery as 'Yorkshire's little Switzerland'. Eighty ft deep in places, it well deserves the name and remains as popular as ever.

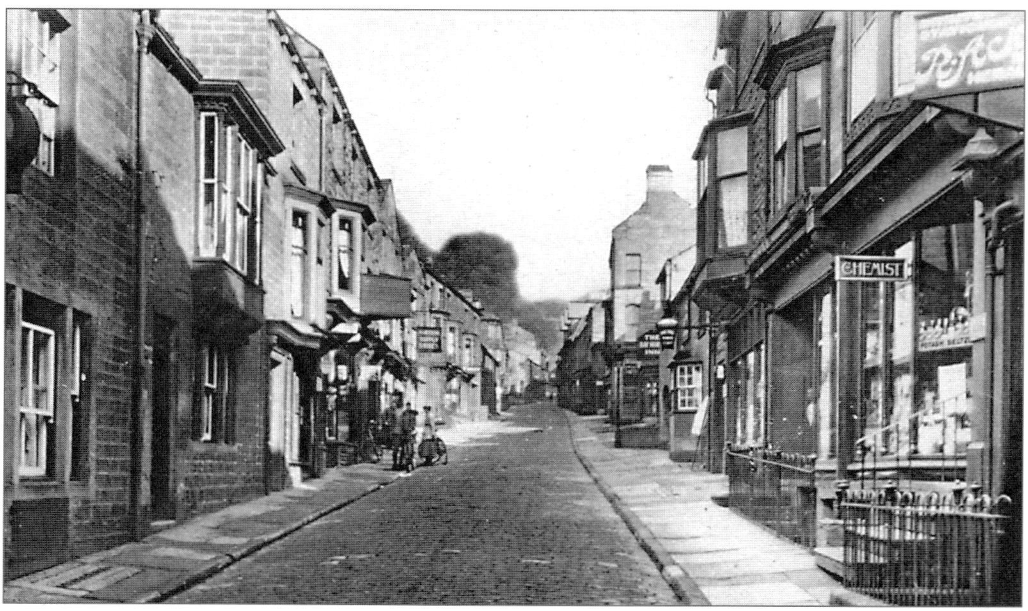

Further down the steep, narrow High Street at Pateley Bridge in the early 1920s, village shops with original frontage look delightful. R. Ackrill, stationer and printer, advertises above the chemist (right). Mr Ackrill also had premises overlooking the Stray, Harrogate, in the 1920s. For a while Rudyard Kipling lived at Pateley Bridge.

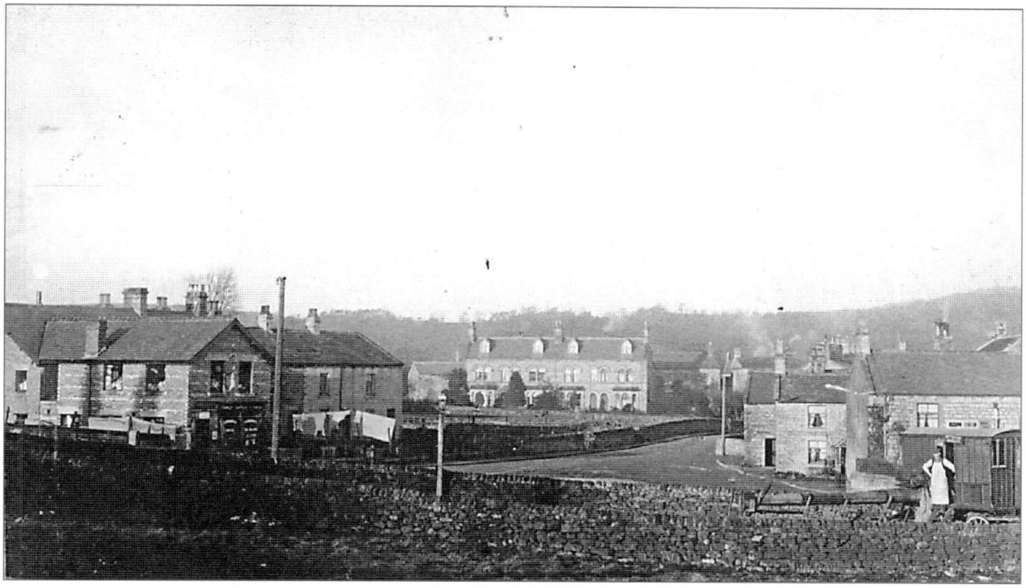

Dacre village, which had its own small station for Brimham Rocks, *c.* 1907. On the far right, in front of the 'family supply stores' and post office, stands a white-aproned tradesman, Mr Nettleton, saddler, with an early type of caravan.

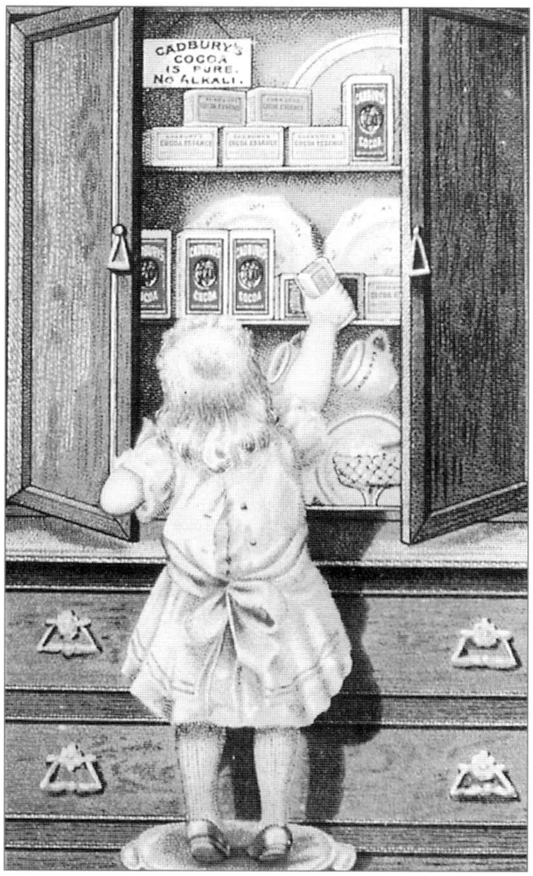

Around the turn of the century this poster was a familiar sight in village shops such as that on page 18. The little girl reaches for Cadbury's Cocoa ('is pure, no alkali') and Cream Crackers, which were a recent innovation. Purity was the watchword as in Victorian times some foods had been adulterated. In Harrogate and the villages Bumstead's Pure Salt ('known countrywide by Kangaroo trademark') was sold in stone jars as it had been for over a century. Old guides to Harrogate advertised bottles of Muscatol which 'kept mosquitoes and gnats at bay' – pocket size 2*s*.

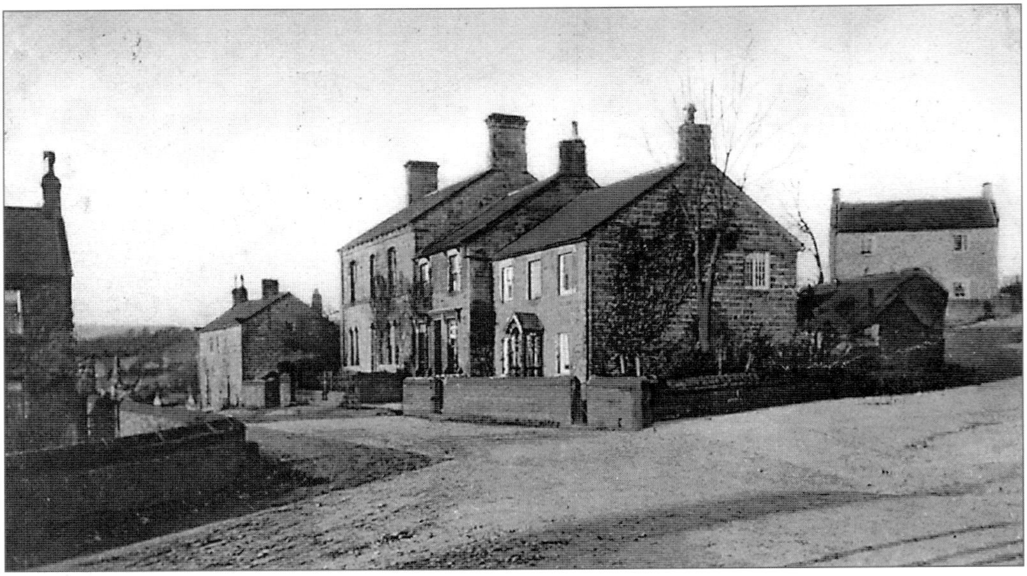

Summerbridge, 1907. This is a typical, quiet Dales village near Pateley Bridge, once part of the Royal Hunting Forest of Knaresborough where chasing red deer and wild boar became the sport of kings. The king gave forty oaks to make the bell cage in York Minster.

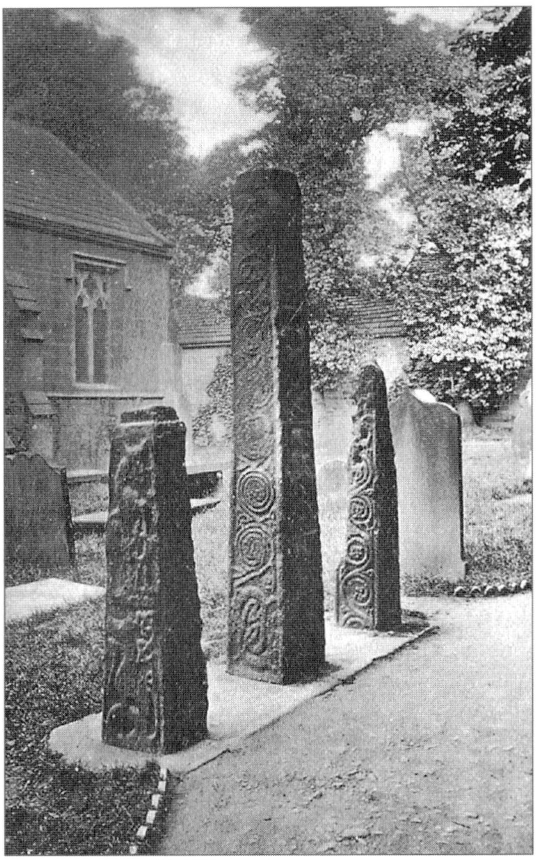

Anglian crosses at Ilkley at the parish church of All Saints, *c*. 1900. When the Saxons were converted from pagan practices to Christianity they erected many carved stone crosses which represent a mixture of religions. These are so numerous they may have marked actual graves. The top of the centre cross is carved with the four evangelists, Matthew, Mark, Luke and John, but elsewhere, intricately carved mystic symbols appear, perhaps remnants of the old Celtic faith. At Pancake Ridge, Ilkley, are found the ancient cup and ring markings of Early Man. The Romans left round gritstone mileposts scattered along their road systems. Sections of these are quite numerous in Yorkshire, for example Boroughbridge to Manchester via Ilkley. Two milestones were found in 1926 during ditching on the north side of the Roman road over Stainmore.

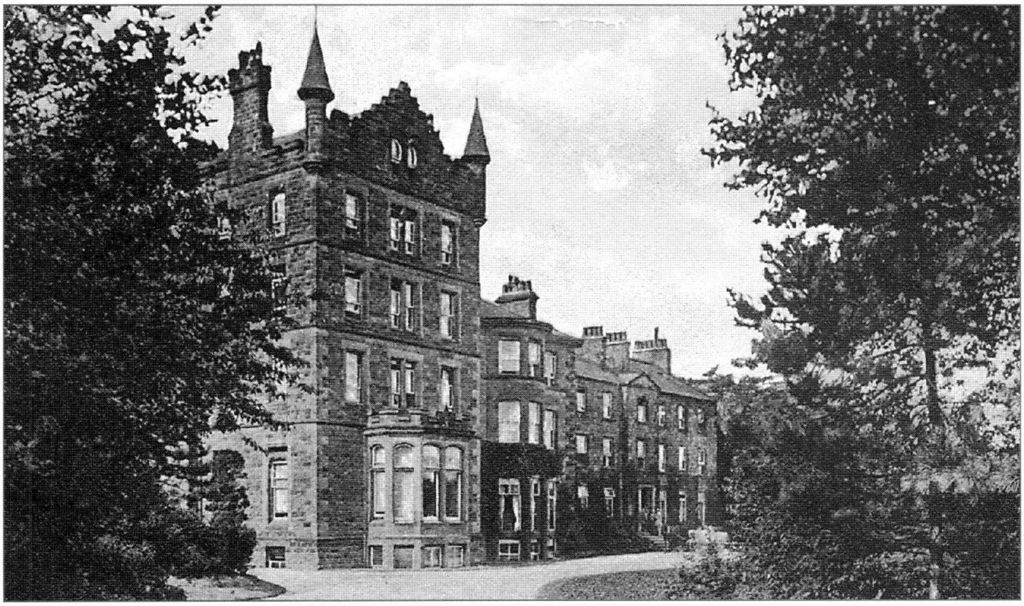

Craiglands Hydro, Ilkley, 1909. The early patients who came to the town for treatment were accommodated in lodging houses. The erection of the huge Ben Rhydding in 1844, the first of its kind in Great Britain, was followed by other hydros making special provision. Many thought it a sad day when this fine building was pulled down.

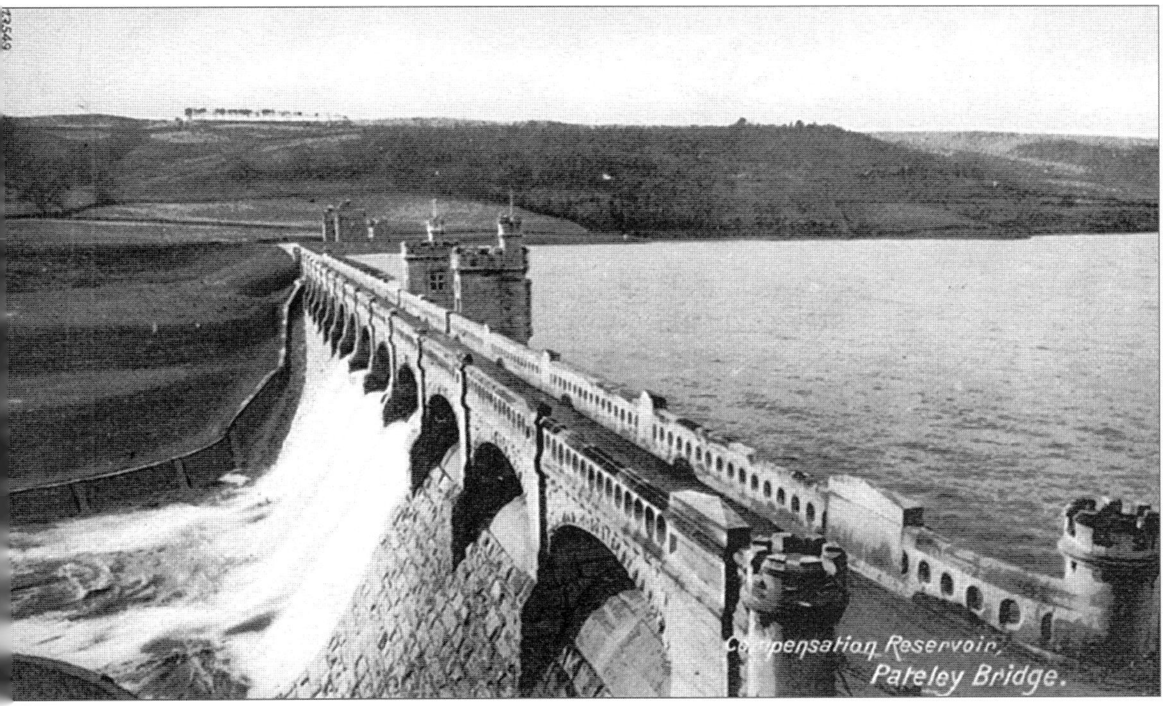

Compensation Reservoir, Gouthwaite, 1906. The dam is 1,800 ft long and 170 ft high. Before the valley was flooded Gouthwaite Hall stood at the head of Riddings Gill. The villages of Wath and Ramsgill are nearby. The Yorke family, lords of the manor, had to move to Bewerley Hall but built a new hall near the reservoir, and incorporated the mullioned windows from the ancestral building.

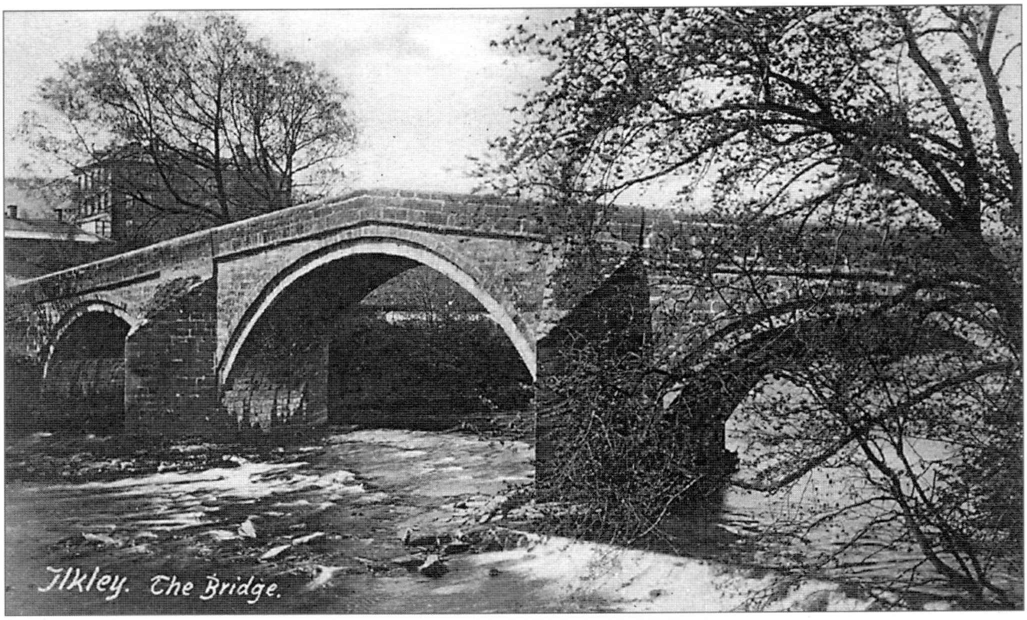

Ilkley Bridge, 1905. Off Church Street, this splendid stone structure some 250 years old leads to Middleton Park and Middleton Lodge, which was built in Queen Elizabeth I's reign. Mount Calvary, a Roman Catholic oratory containing religious statues, could be viewed by visitors last century for a small fee.

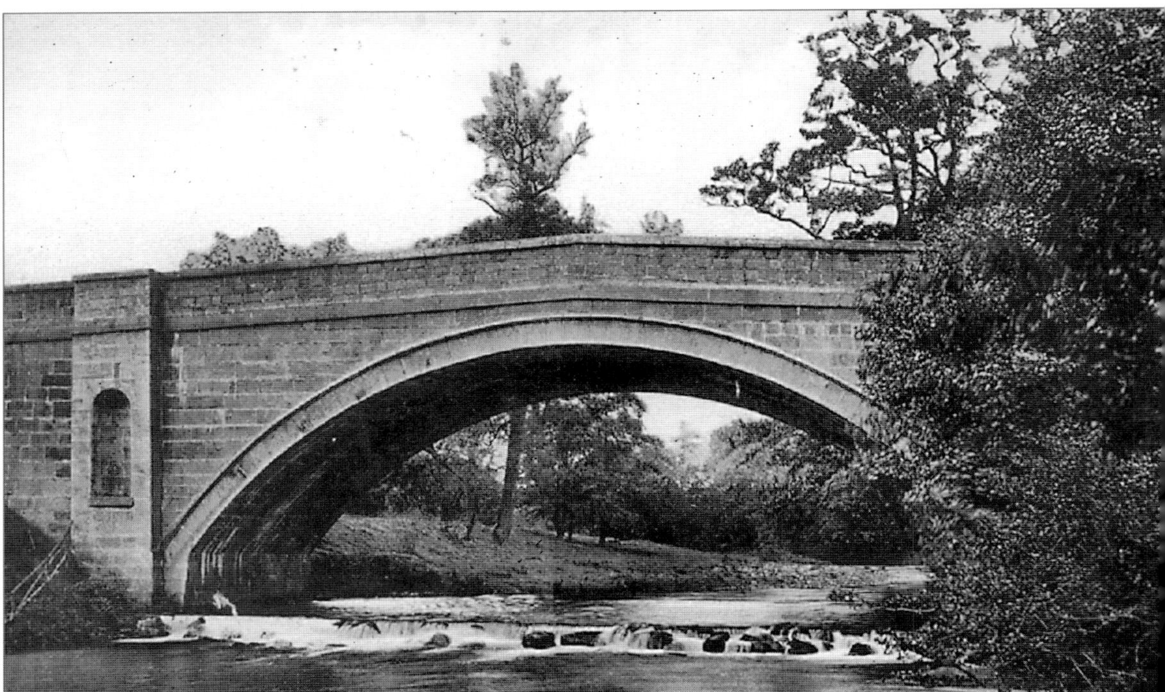

Burn Bridge, Masham, 1910. Harrogate and Ripon district offered excellent fishing. In the 1920s and 1930s it was necessary to procure the Yorkshire Fishery Board's trout licence at a cost of 2*s* 6*d*. For coarse fishing on the River Nidd, day tickets were obtainable for 6*d* from the Oak Inn at Vowthorpe. The Tanfield Club fished at Masham.

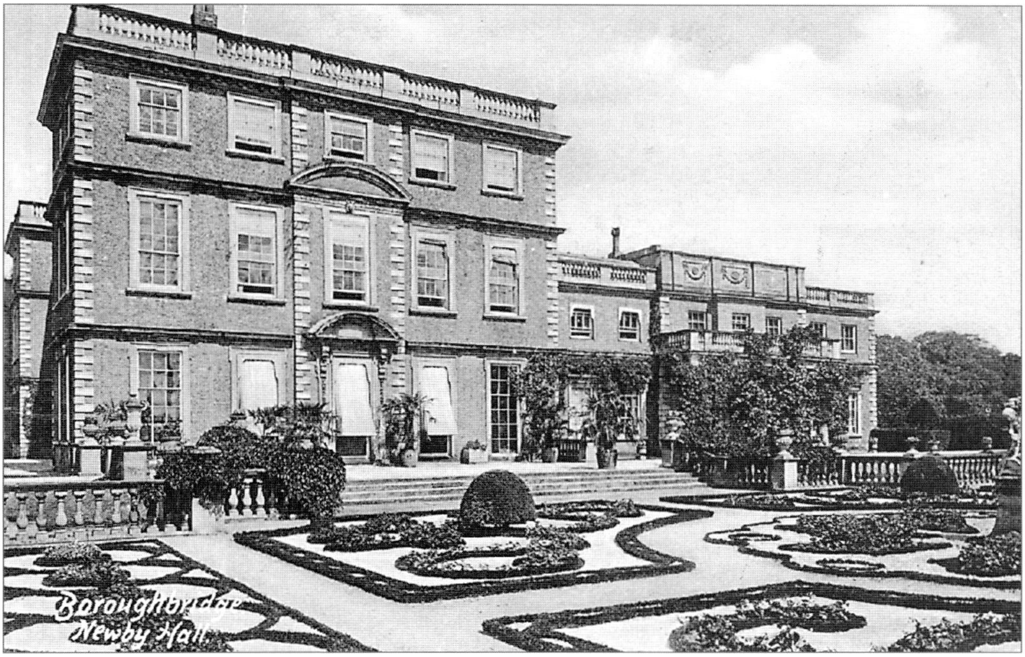

Newby Hall, near Boroughbridge, built from designs by Sir Christopher Wren, belonged to the Vyner family. In 1883 an unusual statue was brought to Newby Hall. Originally it depicted the King of Poland but was never delivered to him. Sir Robert Vyner, when Lord Mayor of London, replaced the statue's head with that of the King of England.

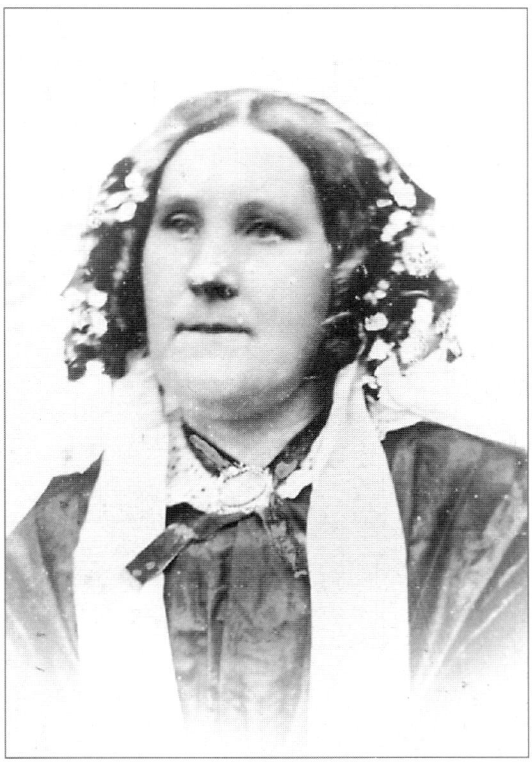

Photographed in a Shipley studio in about 1872, this lady came from Boroughbridge, one of the towns that grew up in the twelfth century on the Great North Road. When eventually bypassed in 1963, it was reported in the local press that it was 'the first time in 800 years that Great North Road traffic did not pass down Boroughbridge's High Street'. The Battle of Boroughbridge was fought against Scotland in 1322. Known as Devil's Arrows, three monoliths in a field near the town still puzzle historians, one of whom, the distinguished John Leland, reported that in his day there were four arrows, one having been pulled down by someone who hoped to find buried treasure. The pieces were built into Peggy Bridge over the River Tutt. The map of Yorkshire by the Dutchman Harmann Moll in 1724 has a quaint drawing of the Devil's Arrows at Boroughbridge. Nearby Aldborough was an important Anglian settlement.

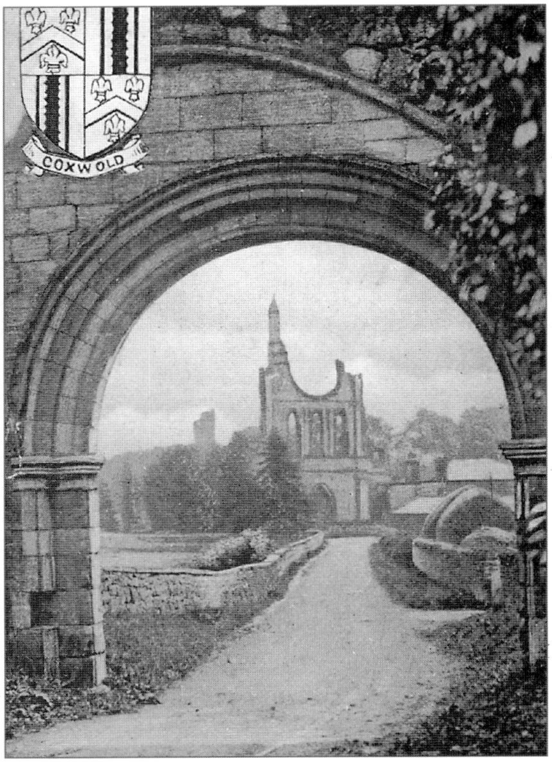

Byland Abbey, *c*. 1930. Founded in 1177, its remains are extensive but incomplete. As at Jervaulx, local farmers used parts that remained standing to build into barns and shippons or repair gaps in walls. Tourists usually travelled by United Autombile Services from Ripon, returning via Coxwold, the arms of which are to be seen on this view. Burrows Penny Guides were issued to cover most of the abbeys in the land. Written specially for tourists, they were wonderful value, giving historical and architectural details which made the visits vitally interesting and memorable.

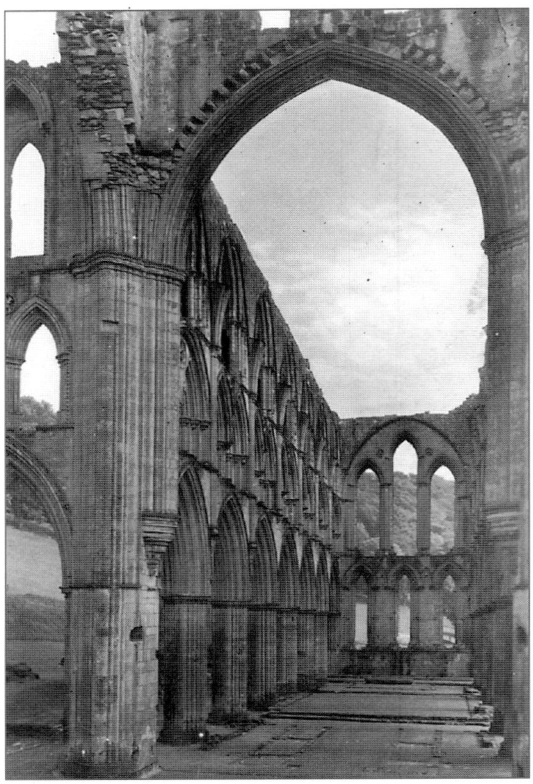

Rievaulx Abbey, the quire, looking east, 1946. The vale in which this abbey was built was once roamed by wolves. This first Cistercian house founded in Yorkshire stands on the banks of the River Rye and took more than a century to build. The nave was finished in about 1140, the monks living in rough wood and clay shelters while work went on. Stone came from two local quarries. Most Harrogate visitors did the tour of the great Yorkshire abbeys, Jervaulx, Fountains, Byland and Rievaulx. All these were in one county and belonged to the same order. Whereas the ruins of Fountains are the most complete, it was considered in the 1920s that those of Rievaulx were the more picturesque in architecture and situation. Rievaulx was the first of the Cistercian abbeys to be founded in the north and became the wealthiest in the country.

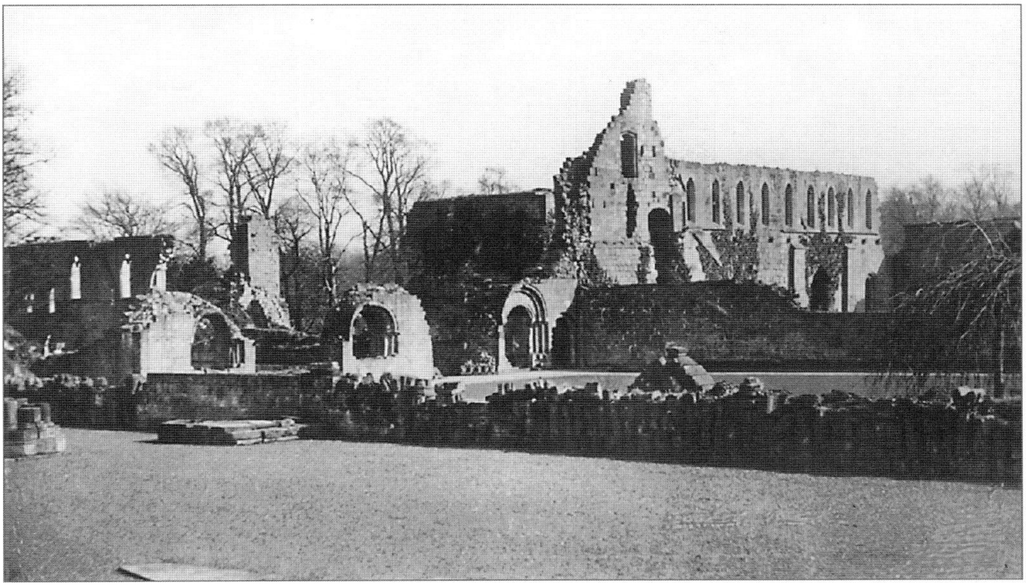

In the 1930s United Automobile Services from Harrogate and Ripon took visitors by motor bus to the beautiful Jervaulx Abbey (pronounced Jarvis), which rose shortly after Fountains. Monks from Askrigg, finding the site bleak, their flocks of sheep devoured by wolves, moved to Jervaulx, led by a monk named Peter de Quincey. At the Dissolution the abbey was utterly despoiled; even the church was untraced until revealed by excavations in 1805.

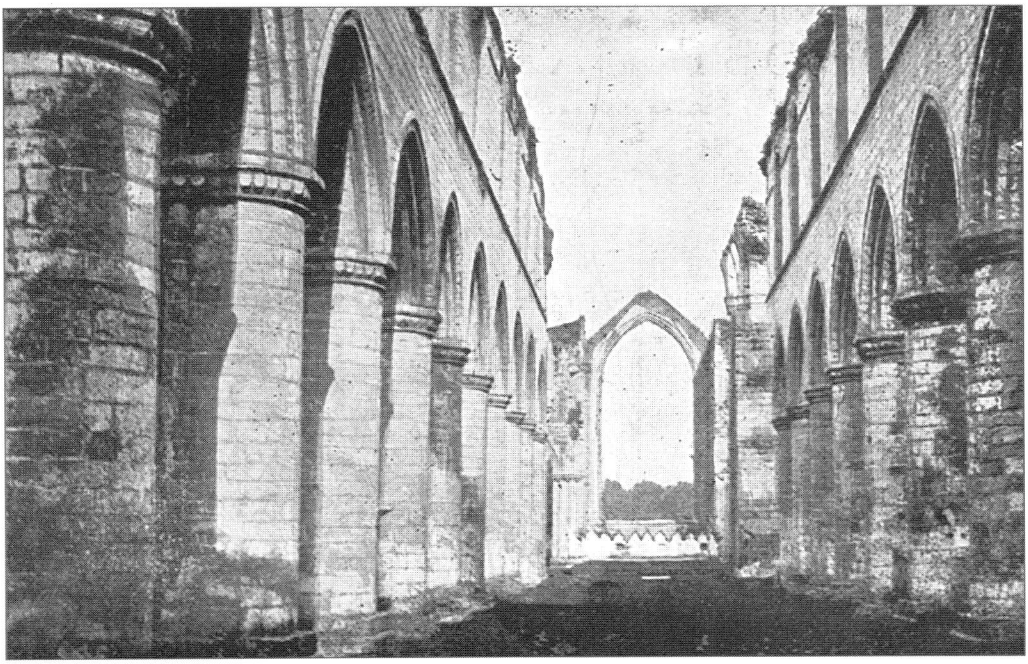

Fountains Abbey, the church, looking east, *c.* 1933. In 1132 a group of monks, feeling that rules had become slack, asked Archbishop Thurston of Ripon for land. The thirteen brothers were given a plot on the banks of the River Skell, a tributary of the Ure. Here they built Fountains and practised the strict Cistercian code of behaviour. Their industrious, useful lives brought wealth to their order.

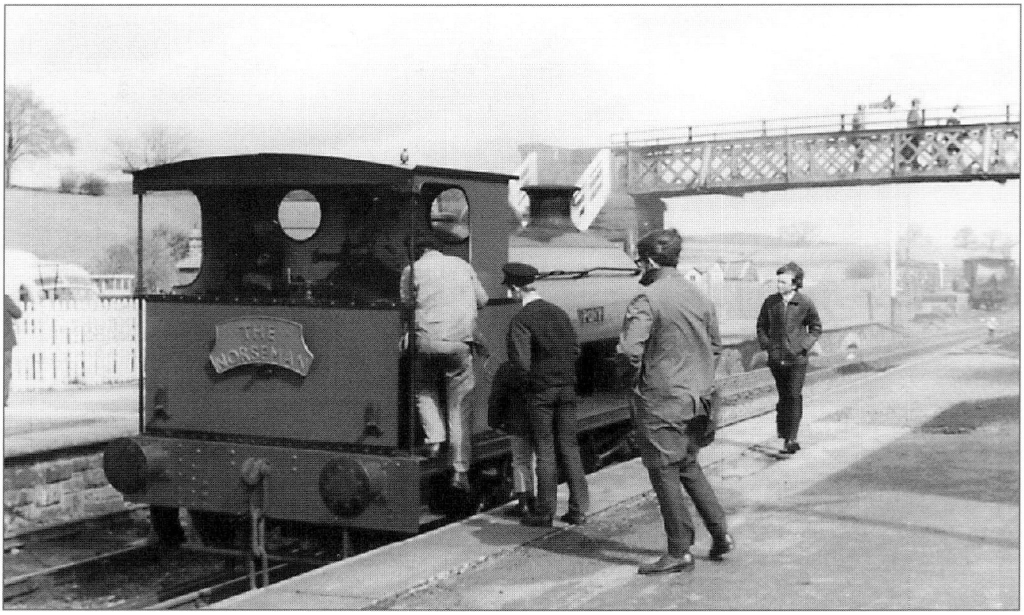

Embsay station on the Skipton to Ilkley line in the early 1970s shows the locomotive *Norseman* being eyed by 'gricers' (railway enthusiasts). Two miles of track and twenty locomotives thrill lovers of steam trains. Steam trains run every Sunday, and in 1997 the line will continue to Bolton Abbey.

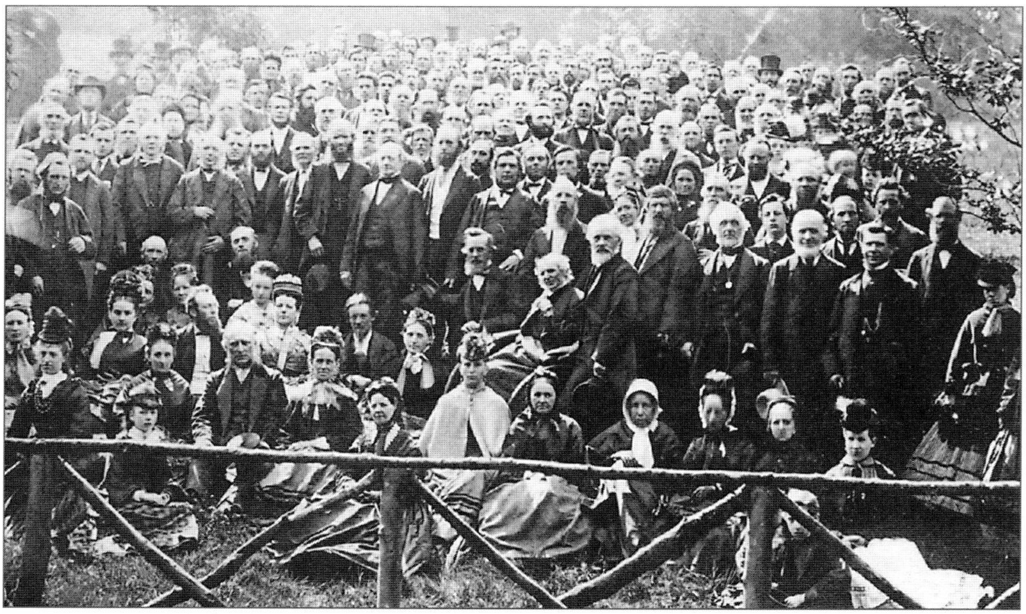

A Temperance Society outing to North Yorkshire, 1860s. Any householder with a 2 guinea licence could sell beer, so drunkenness was rife. The mainly non-conformist movement was based on strict teetotalism: 'signing the pledge', and processions and meetings aimed at controlling this evil. There was a temperance coffee house at Shipley Glen, and huts and small hotels serving non-alcoholic drinks were to be found everywhere.

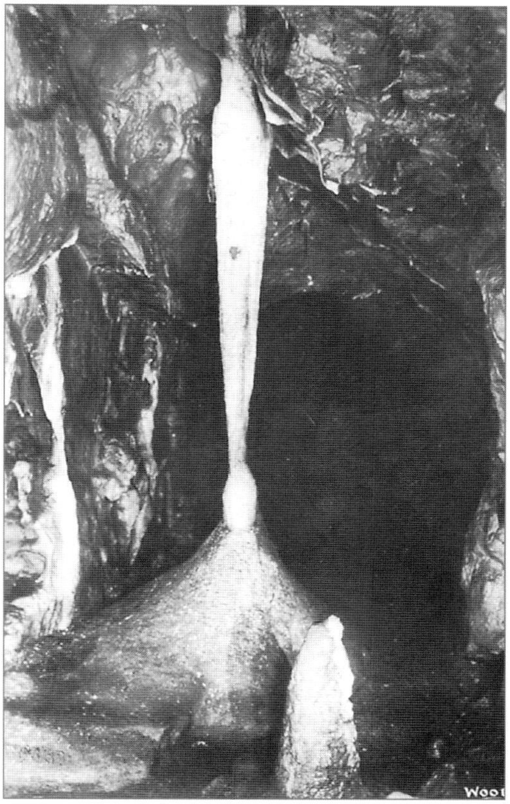

Curtain and Rod, or the Sentinel at the Stump Cross Caverns between Grassington and Pateley Bridge. These caverns were found by two miners in 1847. When detailed exploration was carried out in 1903 some interesting discoveries were made. The stalactite caverns vary in size and height. In some places they are lofty, in others so narrow that a stout person could not pass. In one cave snow-white columns rising from floor to roof led to the obvious name – the Pillars. The Parlour's floor resembles petrified sea waves and in the Church cave stalactites are arranged like organ pipes; when carefully struck they give out musical notes. In the 1940s Mr G. Cornes of Lancaster discovered caverns at Easegill, with beautiful calcite deposits resembling those at Yorkshire's White Scar Caverns.

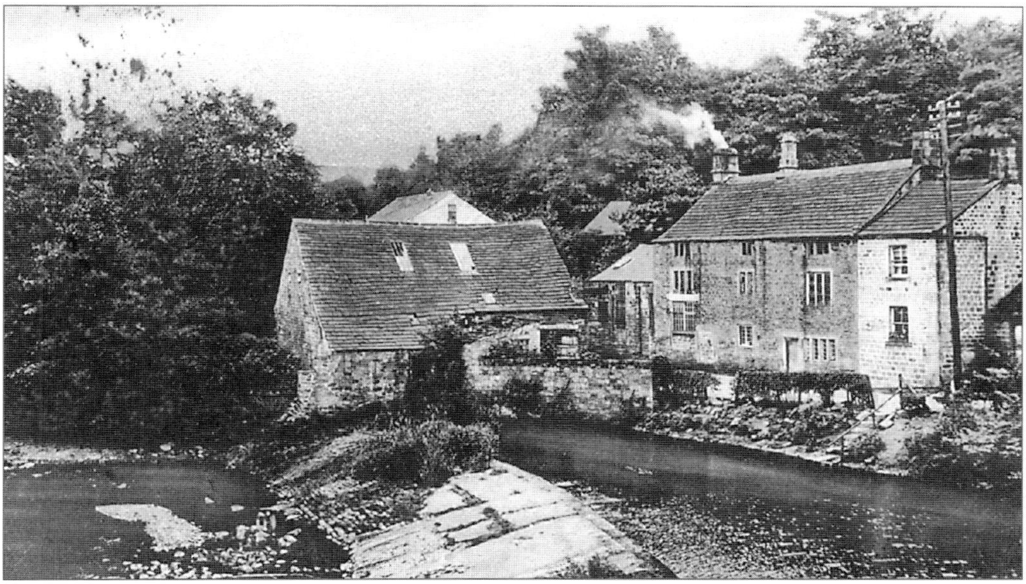

The Mill at Ripley, 1908, where corn was ground – part of a self-supporting tradition in the stone-built village in the Nidd Valley which rose from an ancient settlement. The forest timber for furniture, clay dug from the river for pottery, wool for clothing, bread, meat, milk and beer were all produced locally. Darley Mill Centre near Harrogate is based on a thirteenth-century corn mill. Foster Beck Mill near Pateley had a large water wheel used in rope making.

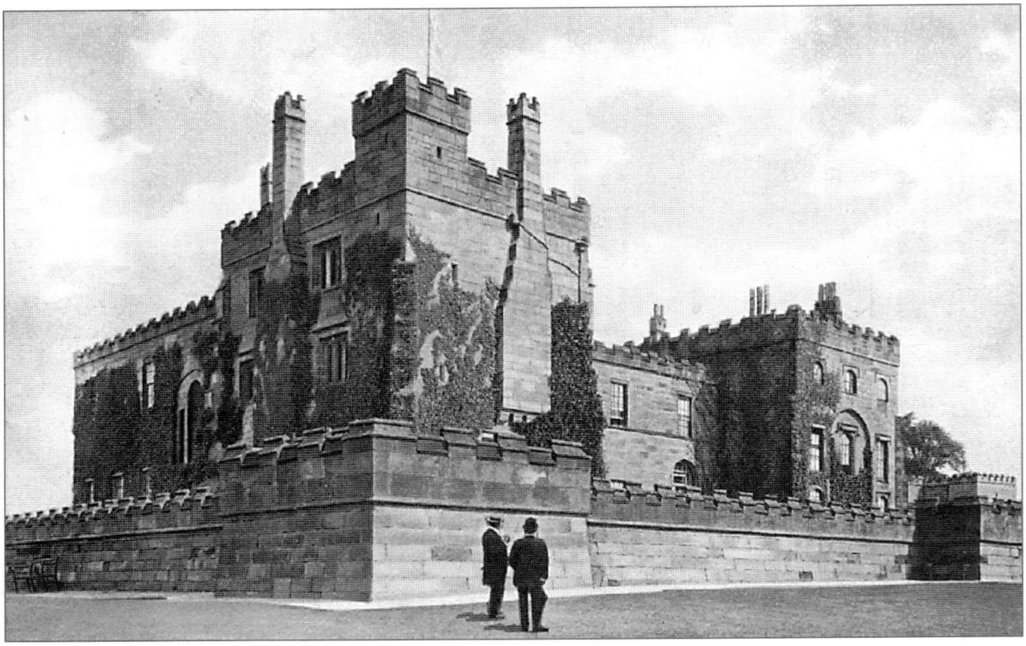

Ripley Castle, seen here in the early 1900s, was built by Sir William Ingilby in 1555. When the Royalists were beaten at the Battle of Marston Moor in July 1644 Cromwell sent one of his officers, a member of the Ingilby family, to the castle to announce his coming. The nineteenth-century account goes on to say: 'The master of the house was not at home but Lady Ingilby told the messenger to return to Cromwell and inform him that she could not receive such a man under her roof.'

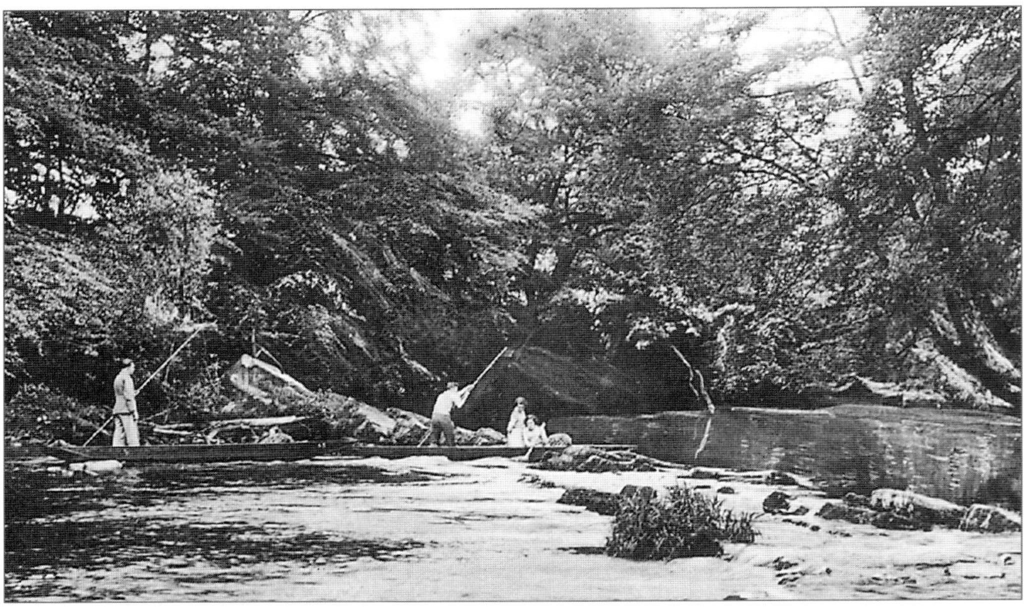

Rapids on the upper reaches of the Nidd, photographed in 1920, provided added excitement for punters on this beautiful river. With a pair of Kershaw's binoculars (they then cost £12 18*s* 6*d* complete with leather case, and had a magnification of eight times), bird-watching amid wooded scenery was enjoyable on calmer stretches.

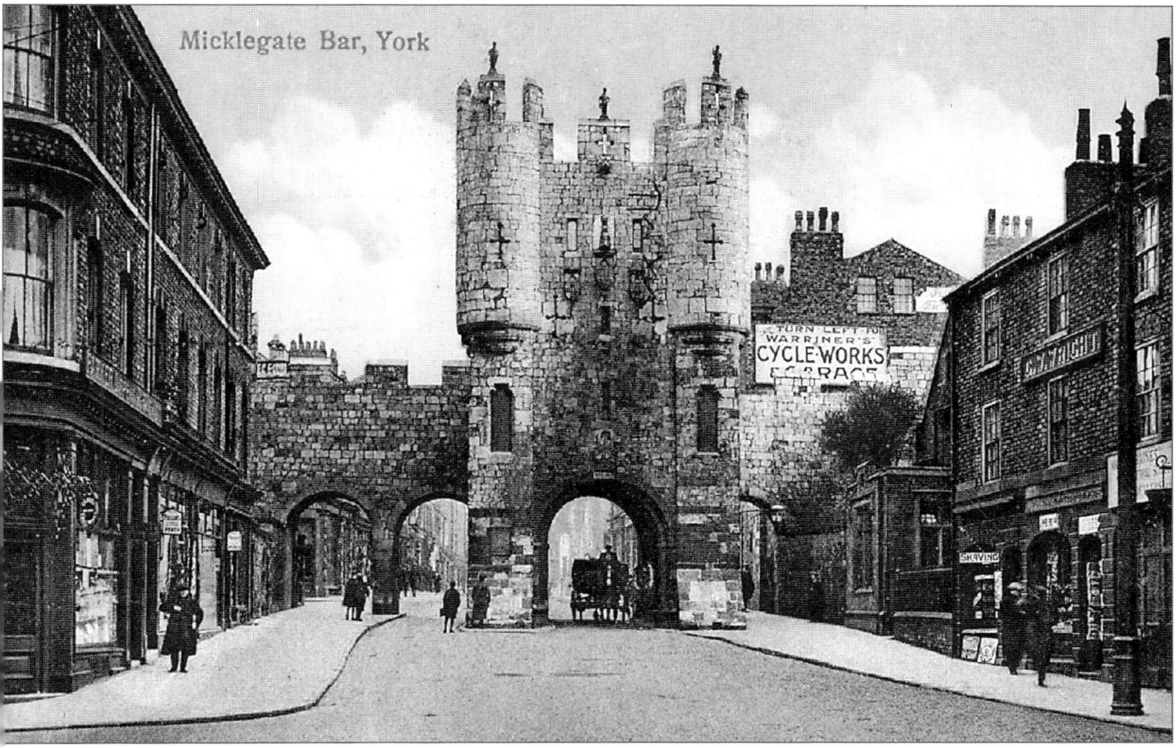

Micklegate Bar, York, *c.* 1909. On the left Parker's drapery shop advertises Pullar's of Perth cleaning services and across at C.W. Wright's you could buy a newspaper before turning left for Warriner's cycle works and garage. A day trip from Harrogate to nearby York was a 'must' because the city continued unique, possibly the oldest in Britain, no other having so many interesting buildings within so small an area. Two thousand years ago Roman soldiers marched its streets and after them the Vikings made a settlement, Jorvik in 867 AD. Arriving by motor bus or train, the visitor passing under the City Walls and crossing Lendal Bridge over the River Ouse, with views of the Water Tower and historic Guildhall, could appreciate York's further unique quality – a medieval walled city built on both sides of a river. Bootham Bar is one of the four Roman towered gates opening on to roads connecting with other Roman stations in the country. York (*Eboracum*) was the Headquarters of the 5th Legion. 'York Minster, York Races, electric trams, Roman Walls and Rowntree's Cocoa factories, the Ebor Handicap – York is various in activities and looks' quoted *The Times* sixty years ago. Among all York's treasures, perhaps the horn of Ulpha (1,000 years old and preserved at York Minster) is the most remarkable. It was carved from an elephant's tusk over 2 ft long and ornamented in the seventeenth century with silver gilt. Horns were a feature of medieval North Yorkshire, being sounded at dusk to guide any benighted traveller stranded in one or other of its thick forests.

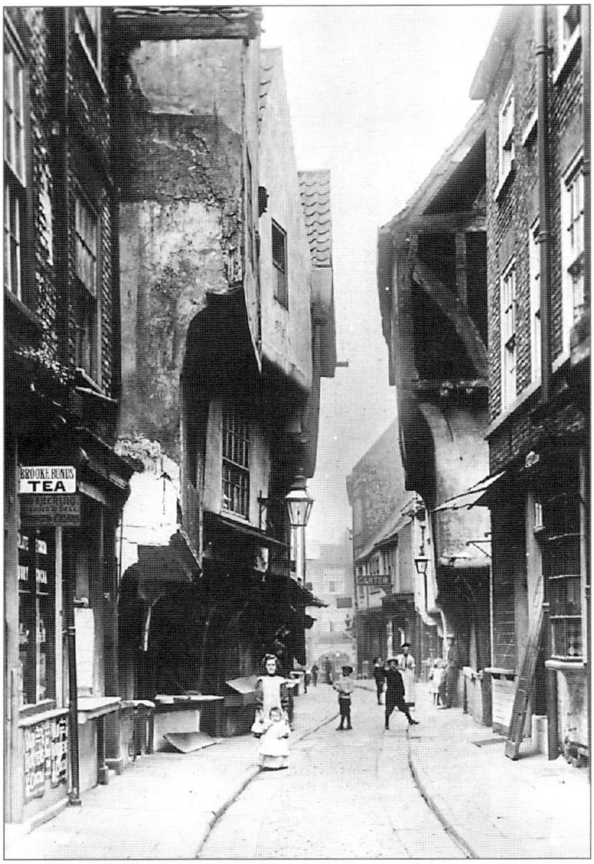

The Shambles, York, *c.* 1930, was reached from Pavement. This medieval street was the butchers' quarters where cattle were slaughtered. When this photograph was taken Roman remains of a wash-house of the Roman Imperial Barracks had just been found in the cellar of Mail Coach Inn. Visitors were allowed to view these and were given directions on how to find St Sampson's Square where the inn was situated. The walls and flues were reported 'still in excellent state of preservation' and the visitor was charged 6*d* to enter. Such finds are still frequent occurrences at York, where digs are organized especially if some building is to be razed.

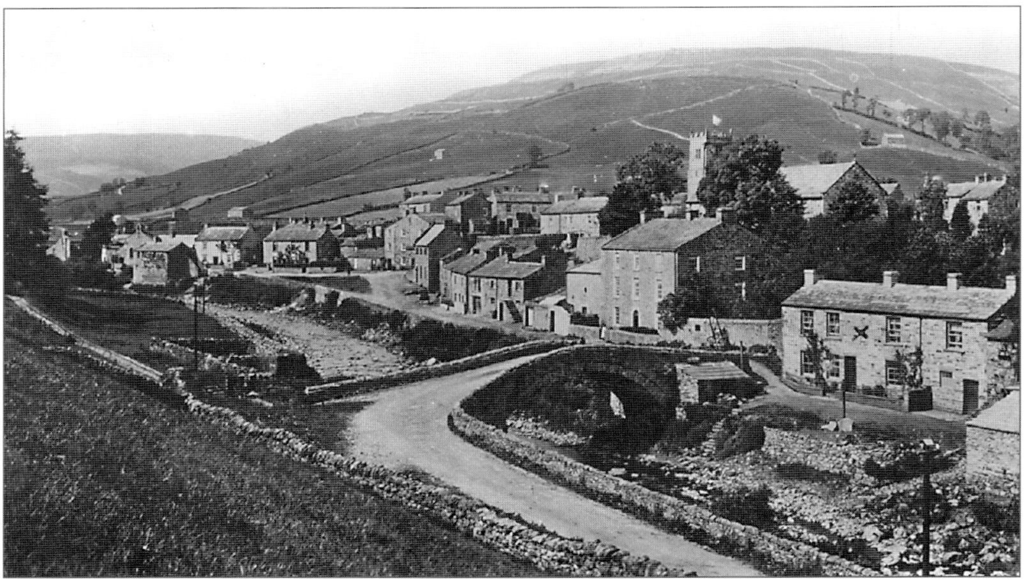

Muker from the east, *c.* 1920, a typical stone, North Yorkshire hamlet. From here visitors walked to Mill Gill Beck, the waterfalls on the River Ure and on over Buttertubs Pass, the 'tubs' being deep holes or pots in the moorland, characteristic of limestone country.

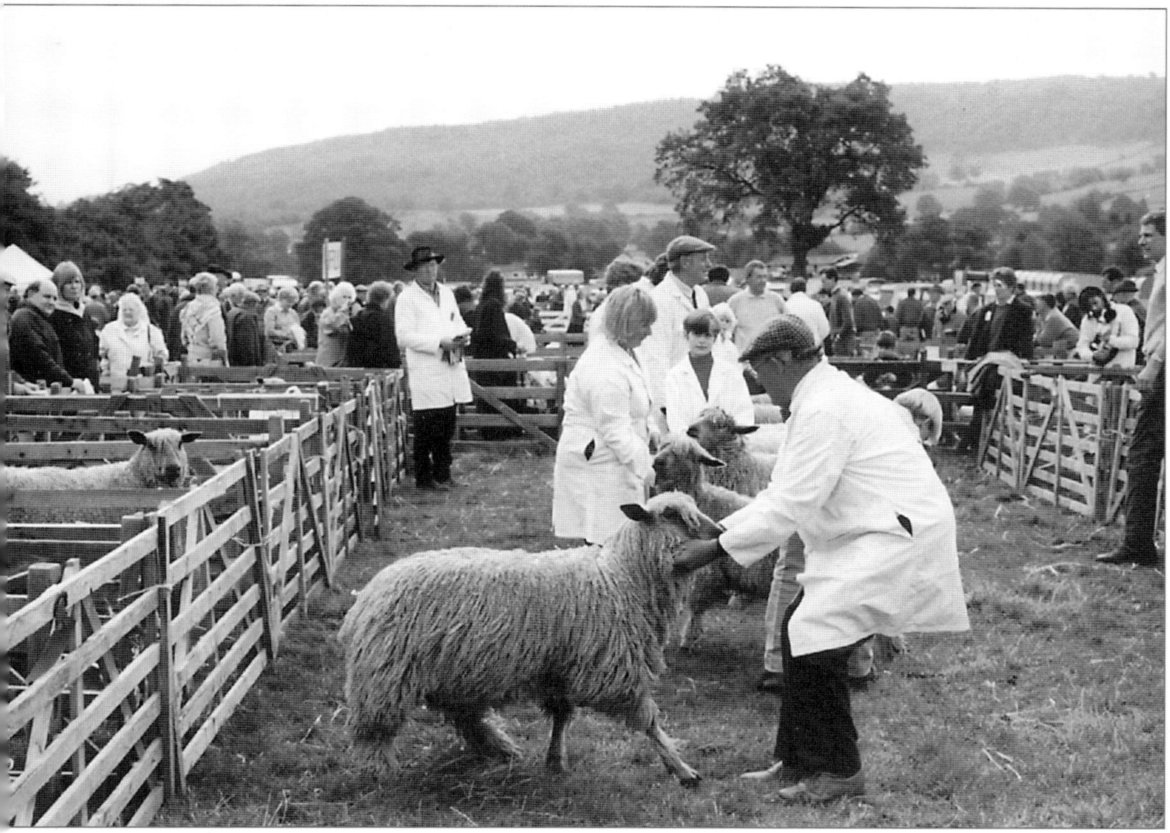

Nidderdale Agricultural Society's Annual Show, held at Bewerley Park, Pateley Bridge in the Borough of Harrogate on the last Monday in September. Now in its 102nd year, it is one of the most important. Visitors enjoy sheep dog trials, show jumping, dog show, dog scurry, tractor handling and a dry-stone walling competition. The park used to be part of the estate owned by the Yorke family, lords of the manor.

The Yorke Arms Inn was formerly a shooting lodge for the Yorke family. The steep road to Yorke's Folly climbs out of Bewerley to some unusual rocks and caves: Giant's Chair, Needle's Eye, Crocodile Rock. Nidderdale is unique among Yorkshire Dales as it can be entered from only one end, making it a wild cul-de-sac. Great Whernside and Little Whernside rise above the River Nidd which disappears underground at Manchester Hole.

A light railway used to run from Pateley Bridge to join the LNER line at Harrogate, but it was dismantled in 1936 when the Scar House Reservoir was completed. The Nidd Valley Light Railway served the series of reservoirs in Upper Nidderdale. A station was built at Lofthouse where iron mining was carried on.

ACKNOWLEDGEMENTS

In the preparation of this book, for supplying photographs and information I owe a special debt of gratitude to: The Revd Anthony Shepherd of St Peter's Church, Harrogate, Taylors of Harrogate, Wrays of Harrogate, the Ross Parry Picture Agency and Mr Martin Stray. I am also indebted to: Blackpool Stamp Shop, Peter Broadbelt, Ivan E. Broadhead, Stanley Butterworth, Richard Clegg, Jean and Gordon Dearden, Mrs J. Edwards, Colin Ford, H.D. Forton, Maggie Gell, Chris and Helen Gleave, Sue Harrison, Harrogate Borough Council Department of Leisure and Amenity Services, Harrogate District Tourist Information Services, Harrogate Library, Harrogate International Centre, *Knaresborough Post*, Eric Mills, North Yorkshire County Library, Don Potter, *Railway Magazine, Railway World*, Kevin and June Ramsdale, Red Rose Postcard Club, The Revd Dr E.J. Rothwell, Paula Ryder, Ron Severs, Spectrum Design Centre, Jack Stasiak, Albert Tunnington, Brenda Walmsley, Rosalind Watson, Yorkshire Film Archive, *Yorkshire Post* Newspapers, and also my family antecedents, the Briggs and the Lords, and the many Yorkshire-born people who have generously given their time to discuss the ever-rolling passage, the ever-changing pattern of the years.

BRITAIN IN OLD PHOTOGRAPHS

berystwyth & North Ceredigion
round Abingdon
cton
lderney: A Second Selection
long the Avon from Stratford to
Tewkesbury
ltrincham
mersham
round Amesbury
nglesey
rnold & Bestwood
rnold & Bestwood: A Second
Selection
rundel & the Arun Valley
shbourne
round Ashby-de-la-Zouch
vro Aircraft
ylesbury
alham & Tooting
anburyshire
arnes, Mortlake & Sheen
arnsley
ath
eaconsfield
edford
edfordshire at Work
edworth
everley
exley
deford
lston
rmingham Railways
shop's Stortford &
Sawbridgeworth
shopstone & Seaford
shopstone & Seaford: A Second
Selection
ack Country Aviation
ack Country Railways
ack Country Road Transport
ackburn
ackpool
ound Blandford Forum
etchley
lton
urnemouth
adford
aintree & Bocking at Work
econ
entwood
idgwater & the River Parrett
dlington
dport & the Bride Valley
erley Hill
ghton & Hove
ghton & Hove: A Second
election
stol
ound Bristol
xton & Norwood
ly Broadstairs & St Peters
mley, Keston & Hayes

Buckingham & District
Burford
Bury
Bushbury
Camberwell
Cambridge
Cannock Yesterday & Today
Canterbury: A Second Selection
Castle Combe to Malmesbury
Chadwell Heath
Chard & Ilminster
Chatham Dockyard
Chatham & Gillingham
Cheadle
Cheam & Belmont
Chelmsford
Cheltenham: A Second Selection
Cheltenham at War
Cheltenham in the 1950s
Chepstow & the River Wye
Chesham Yesterday & Today
Cheshire Railways
Chester
Chippenham & Lacock
Chiswick
Chorley & District
Cirencester
Around Cirencester
Clacton-on-Sea
Around Clitheroe
Clwyd Railways
Clydesdale
Colchester
Colchester 1940–70
Colyton & Seaton
The Cornish Coast
Corsham & Box
The North Cotswolds
Coventry: A Second Selection
Around Coventry
Cowes & East Cowes
Crawley New Town
Around Crawley
Crewkerne & the Ham Stone
Villages
Cromer
Croydon
Crystal Palace, Penge & Anerley
Darlington
Darlington: A Second Selection
Dawlish & Teignmouth
Deal
Derby
Around Devizes
Devon Aerodromes
East Devon at War
Around Didcot & the Hagbournes
Dorchester
Douglas
Dumfries
Dundee at Work
Durham People

Durham at Work
Ealing & Northfields
East Grinstead
East Ham
Eastbourne
Elgin
Eltham
Ely
Enfield
Around Epsom
Esher
Evesham to Bredon
Exeter
Exmouth & Budleigh Salterton
Fairey Aircraft
Falmouth
Farnborough
Farnham: A Second Selection
Fleetwood
Folkestone: A Second Selection
Folkestone: A Third Selection
The Forest of Dean
Frome
Fulham
Galashiels
Garsington
Around Garstang
Around Gillingham
Gloucester
Gloucester: from the Walwin
Collection
North Gloucestershire at War
South Gloucestershire at War
Gosport
Goudhurst to Tenterden
Grantham
Gravesend
Around Gravesham
Around Grays
Great Yarmouth
Great Yarmouth: A Second
Selection
Greenwich & Woolwich
Grimsby
Around Grimsby
Grimsby Docks
Gwynedd Railways
Hackney: A Second Selection
Hackney: A Third Selection
From Haldon to Mid-Dartmoor
Hammersmith & Shepherds Bush
Hampstead to Primrose Hill
Harrow & Pinner
Hastings
Hastings: A Second Selection
Haverfordwest
Hayes & West Drayton
Around Haywards Heath
Around Heathfield
Around Heathfield: A Second
Selection
Around Helston

Around Henley-on-Thames
Herefordshire
Herne Bay
Heywood
The High Weald
The High Weald: A Second
Selection
Around Highworth
Around Highworth & Faringdon
Hitchin
Holderness
Honiton & the Otter Valley
Horsham & District
Houghton-le-Spring &
Hetton-le-Hole
Houghton-le-Spring & Hetton-le-
Hole: A Second Selection
Huddersfield: A Second Selection
Huddersfield: A Third Selection
Ilford
Ilfracombe
Ipswich: A Second Selection
Islington
Jersey: A Third Selection
Kendal
Kensington & Chelsea
East Kent at War
Keswick & the Central Lakes
Around Keynsham & Saltford
The Changing Face of Keynsham
Kingsbridge
Kingston
Kinver
Kirkby & District
Kirkby Lonsdale
Around Kirkham
Knowle & Dorridge
The Lake Counties at Work
Lancashire
The Lancashire Coast
Lancashire North of the Sands
Lancashire Railways
East Lancashire at War
Around Lancaster
Lancing & Sompting
Around Leamington Spa
Around Leamington Spa:
A Second Selection
Leeds in the News
Leeds Road & Rail
Around Leek
Leicester
The Changing Face of Leicester
Leicester at Work
Leicestershire People
Around Leighton Buzzard &
Linslade
Letchworth
Lewes
Lewisham & Deptford:
A Second Selection
Lichfield